AF554008

Effective Manners of Teaching Environment

Effective Manners of Teaching Environment

Dr. Ahmad Husain

Mahaveer & Sons
(Publishers & Distributors)
New Delhi-110002

First Published 2007

ISBN 978-81-8377-164-1
Rs. 550/-

Published by :
MAHAVEER & SONS
(Publishers & Distributors)
3072/28, First Floor, Gola Market, Darya Ganj,
(Near Golcha Parking) New Delhi-110002
E-mail : mahaveersons_publishers@yahoo.com
mpspubdist@rediffmail.com
Ph. 23287638, 23272330, Mob. 9811008339

PRINTED IN INDIA

Published by Sh. Mukul Sharma for Mahaveer & Sons, 3072/28, First Floor, Gola Market (Near Golcha Parking) Darya Ganj, New Delhi-110002, Printed at Himanshu Printers, Delhi.

Preface

This book is a study of effective manners to increase of the environmental education in our society. In this scientific age with the development of science and technologies and new discoveries, the environmental condition of this world has been completely changed. It has become a challenge before the whole world to project the environment. A number of schemes and plans are launched by national and international bodies. Environmental education is one of them to face such challenge. In may 1988 the Resolution of council and ministers of education of the council of the European community stated that: "The objective of environmental education is to increase the public awareness of the problems in this field, as well as possible solutions, and to lay the foundations for a fully informed and active participation of the individuals in the protection of the environment and the product and relational use of natural resources."

This book has focused on the methods by which people could be aware. To make this education interested so many manners and suggestions have been mentioned in the presented articles of this book. Present scenario of India and the world has been examined and this possible solutions have been mentioned is subsequent chapters.

So many schools, colleges and universities have applied Environmental Education in their syllabii. This book stresses that the environmental education problems as post-graduate level must be interrelated with various disciplines like physics, chemistry, biology, mathematics and managements. The articles presented in this book offer a rich source of ideas, examples and discussions. They will be aid to educationists who wish to begin to explore the issues more thoroughly. The conditions are contemporary one which should enables pupils educational experience to be relevant to the real world.

Contents

	Preface	*iii*
1.	Environmental Education	1
2.	Environmental Education in India	9
3.	Managing of Natural Environment	25
4.	Legislation and Pollution in Calcutta	38
5.	The Role of Forests	42
6.	Educational Impact of Projects for Improvement of Rural Housing	46
7.	Environmental Education and other Cross-Curricular Themes	52
8.	Integration of Ecosystem and Urban Systems	65
9.	The Citizenship and Environmental Education	78
10.	The Environmental Education and Core and Foundation Subjects	96
11.	The Science Education	102
12.	The Geography	114
13.	The Global Environmental Trends	138
14.	The Environmental Education and Other Relationships	163
15.	The Social Sciences	183
16.	Key-Issues of Human Settlements in Indian Perspective	201
	Bibliography	*207*
	Index	*209*

1

Environmental Education

The articles in this book reflect the controversy and range of opinions and responses which environmental issues seem to elicit from commentators and teachers. Despite the lack of consensus regarding causes and remedial action, however, it seems clear that certain issues are now established which need consideration. Despite the lack of guidance about cross-curricular themes, and Environmental Education in particular, in the most recent reports on the National Curriculum, schools whould do well to recognise the importance of such issues to their pupils. Progmatically, teachers will be reluctant to abandon all their curriculum design efforts and investment in resources. They would be hard-pressed to do better than regard consideration of environmental education as evidence of 'added-on value' which would have practical benefit to both pupils' long-term prospects and a school faced with OFSTED inspection.

There has been a huge increase in the range and amount of human activity since the turn of the century which makes increasingly large demands upon raw materials, energy sources and human resources. By compounding population numbers with average per capita consumption, one is able to obtain a rough indication of the totality of human activity. King and Schneider estimate a forty-fold increase over the century to date. (King and Schneider, 1991b) Human lifestyles which threaten the ozone layer are being curtailed as public awareness rises and demands action by producers.

Although the issue is complex, the 'greenhouse effect' appears to contrain the extension of an economic approach to social organisation. The exact consequences of the heating of the earth's surface are still open to debate but there to be general agreement as to what the general trend is. The estimated rises in temperature caused by a doubling in carbon dioxide equilibrium concentrations is much greater than any alterations which have arises through historical cyclic fluctuations. The effects are thought to be smaller at the equator and much greater at higher latitudes, altering thermal gradients, changing precipitation patterns, modifying climatic zones and thus changing agricultural viability.

Human activity which alters agricultural potential and removes fertile land for other purposes, such as mineral extraction or transport, may be linked in its effect with a rising world population. Technically, one may be able to grow sufficient food to support a population of twenty billion, but this is to discount the huge demands on energy which would be needed to suppy sufficient fresh water to support the enterprise. Morever, the agricultural revolution, which has produced food surpluses, has not let to the elimination of hunger. Even in countries such as India, where the food is being produced in reasonable proximity to the hungry, problems of malnutrition and famine persist. Transport difficulties, from surplus-producing regions such as North America, to deficit areas, and the reliance of modern agriculture upon energy-expensive methods of producing fertiliser and weedkillers question the future of a surplus in food supply. There has also been a recent and dramatic fall in food reserves following the droughts since 1989 in North America. Harvests fell by 31% in the USA and 27% in Canada.

Large demographic changes are to be expected in the industrialized countries caused by their ageing populations and falling birthrates. Automation and increasing productivity may generate sufficient national product to maintain living standards with a reduced workforce, but a substantial burden will be placed upon pension and health care systems. Additionally, adjustments will have to be made to educational systems as the success of family-planning attitudes works its way through the population. Differences between countries in the opportunities for individuals to succeed could cause population movements. Conditions of tyranny and oppression and population pressures may well cause irreversible migratory waves North and West. The populations of rich countries will have to prepare themselves to accept the reality of the need for the cooperation to reduce, significantly, economic disparity.

The development of an information or post-industrial society is a major result of, and cause of, global changers. It is possible to communicate wise, constructive developments which could benefit the whose of humankind. It is equally possible to communicate, recism, greed, envy and tyranny. Technological innovation has always influenced society's beheviour patterns. A society after the Industrial Revolution had significantly different organisational and beheavioural beliefs than its agricultural predecessor. An increase in information technology and automation may produce new products, industries and markets but one has yet to see whether it will produce jobs to match the level of employment of the industrial society it overtakes.

These issues are interlinked and it makes little sense to tackle them individually. Although this linkage makes any study complex, it does highlight the need for educationalists to begin to think on an international scale rather than just in localised contexts.

Environmental education has close links with the other four cross-curricular themes, sharing many of the same features of investigative skills and bodies of knowledge. Pupils may research original and secondary sources, set up simulations, reach conclusions and discuss the validity of their ideas. The five themes share the possibilities for promoting the discussion of values and beliefs, extending knowledge and understanding, encouraging practical activities and decision-making and providing opportunities for pupils to make positive contributions to their community's way of life.

Yet the human race is faced with the actualities of increasing air and water pollution, the 'greenhouse effect' and global warming, the increasing destruction of rain forests and its consequences for weather patterns. On all continents the deserts advance steadily and daily the extinction of species occurs whose role in world ecology has never been assessed. The importance of the environment has been forecefully set out by Bellamy:

- a need for a diverse genetic bank, especially to ensure continued food production;
- all life depends ultimately upon food production by plants which use the sun's energy;
- diverse habitats are little studied and may contain unknown sources of medicine;
- clear air and water are finite resources;
- energy sources are finite;
- humans seem to need wild places for their spiritual and physical well-being.

The finite nature of the world's resources and fine balance between the existence and collapse of delicate ecologies has never been more clearly brought to our attention.

Obvious as these environmental issues may appear to be, this is still an area of considerable debate and contention, especially among those practising scientists and philosophers of scientific methodology who adhere to Karl Popper's belief that Science is a discipline which continually tries to prove its ideas to be wrong. His methodology is one of conjecture and refutation. But Popper is concerned with how scientists ought to behave and not so much with how they do behave. (Castri, 1990) Whilst in Physics a number of hypotheses have withstood the rigorous testing of time and intellect to attain the status of theories, in Biology many hypotheses have not yet attained the same status through the rigorous accumulation of data. For example, while Newton's Theory of Gravity is now accepted (though the Graviton, the particle responsible for carrying the force of gravity remains a theoretical notion), Darwin's Theory of Evolution still evokes rather greater debate in scientific circles.

There is the opportunity for educationalists to concentrate upon fundamentally important issues for the human race. One must recognise that only the most impartial and regorous of approaches to questions about the survival of the human race allows for useful conclusions to be reached. It is not satisfactory for challenges to current ideas to be met by the introduction of auxiliary hypotheses which are designed to meet the criticism. This methodology merely allows a hypothesis to survive a little longer despite mounting evidence that it is inadequate or even wrong. It is not a methodology of which Popper would approve.

'Global warming' is likely to involve a number of complex, interconnected factors. One may hypothesise that one recognises a particular product by its logo. However, no amount of empirical observation will overcome the 'Problem of Induction' which always prevents one from saying that the product will always be recognised by that symbol. One observation of a product without that trademark is enough to falsify the hypothesis. With an issue like 'global warming an observation that thousands of hectares of rain forest can be seen buring everyday from space satellites may be an indicator that such production of carbon dioxide causes 'global warming'. The discovery of high levels of carbon dioxide in factory or traffic emissions does not disqualify forest burning as a factor. We may be dealing with a multi-faceted network of human activities which have to be unravelled. The National Curriculum Council advice:

> ...environmental education is the subject of considerable debate, and that there is no clear consensus about many of the issues. (NCC, 1990a).

is corrrect in its caution and echoes similar difficulties to be found in issues connected with Citizenship.

In May, 1988 the Resolution of the Council and the Ministers of Education of the Council of the European Community stated that:

> The objective of environmental education is to increase the public awareness of the problems in this field, as well as possible solutions, and to lay the foundations for a fully informed and active participation of the individual in the protection of the environment and the product and rational use of natural resources.
>
> (NCC, 1990b)

The Resolution suggested some principles which might inform

environmental education:

— the inironment as the common heritage of mankind;

— the common duty of maintaining, protecting and improving the quality of the environment, as a contribution to the protection of human health and the safeguarding of the ecological balance;

— the need for a prudent and rational utilisation of resources;

— the way in which each individual can, by his own behaviour, particularly as a consumer, contribute to the protection of the environment.

(NCC, 1990b)

Even here a subjective vocabulary is used: e.g. 'possible solutions', the 'quality' of the environment, and 'rational' utilisation of resources. These are, and have to be, political decisions which carry difficult, moral and value-ridden meanings. Effective environmental education accepts these problems and recognises the richness of them as sources of moral debate and development. The knowledge content of Environmental Education as suggested by the National Curriculum Council is reasonably straightforward provided teachers are able to use contemporary findings and developments. The skills of communication, numeracy, study, problem-solving, information technology, and personal and social interaction are broadly shared with the other cross-curricular themes. The possitive attitudes to be encouraged include:

— appreciation of, and care and concern for the environment and for other living things;

— independence of thought on environmental issues;

— a respect for the beliefs and opinions of others;

— a respect for evidence and rational argument;

— tolerance and open-mindedness.

(NCC, 1990d)

It is important to note that there is a degree of selfishness here as each individual tries to survive or avoid censure by community norms or national laws of equality. Education about the environment, its climate, geology, water, resources, living systems and human activities can only provide a common framework within which the moral and values debate takes place. One cannot teach about the environment without ascribing values to the existence and desirability of certain kinds of environment. Pupils may debate how to ensure the best immediate and future use of the environment.

They may consider possible solutions to environmental problems taking into account conflicting interest and making informed choices. In doing so, they are taking part in a moral and political debate.

One effective way of ensuring that the issues are fully, identified is through practical, firsthand enquiry, research and investigation. In this respect one is fortunate that local environmental issues are so often a small-scale echo of much larger, global issues. Primary school conservation projects reflect major conservation programmes across the globle. Suggestions by pupils about traffic control around their school relate to national issues of road building, pollution and the use of finite resources such as land and fuel. Initiatives within schools to deal with vandalism, graffiti and the design of and access to buildings touch directly upon wider questions of how society might be governed, respect for the law and community relationships.

These connections reflect questions and assumptions back upon the possible solutions to environmental problems. However, these solutions are likely to depend upon how pupils see themselves in term of their citizenship. Their responsibilities for the environment may be defined by whether they consider themselves as citizens of a community, country or international group like Europe. As pupils search for answers and develop their perspectives and wider understanding so their own solutions to environmental problems may also change. Pupils' ideas may challenge a school's or their parents' assumptions. These aspects need sensitive consideration for there are no right answers and teachers must be prepared to be challenged by pupils' reactions and suggestions.

The complex and transient nature of environmental issues precludes any definite statement of how those problems might be solved. Teachers should encourage pupils to seek their own logical solutions and to examine, impartially and critically, the solutions currently offered. We have to do this against the background of two, interrelated phenomena. Moral awareness has been lessened by the questioning of ethical structures and role models as an increasingly heterogeneous society gains access to more information. There may be a tendency to retreat from the daunting scale of global change. For example, there has been a resurgence of political instability in various countries which has moved towards nationalism or individualism.

At the same time, the information society has enabled a progressively more complete awareness of environmental issues and problems to take hold of the public imagination. While expections for solutions and reseach into possibilities are encourage, the mass of information, uncritically presented can be overwhelming. Issues may be clouded, leading to repetition of compounding of errors. Spiritual, ethical and moral dimensions which redefine the quality of the environment and of human life should not be a matter of indifference, irrelevance or scorm but a vital ingredient in the search for a new humanity.

Schools could try to make sure that the learning opportunities they offer are a part of that essential process whereby solutions to environmental, problems are found and implemented. Ideally every pupil ought to participate in seeking and defining the 'right' or best solutions among the many possibilities. This must mean appreciating the complexity of the network of issues to be considered. Further, pupils might be enabled to recognise that positive improvements to the environment can only be rooted in the motives and value systems that govern behaviour. Indeed the behaviour of nations, their alliances and society structures, in general reflects the behaviour patterns exhibited by their individual members. It is unlikely that any single action at government level will alter the environment for the better. It is more likely that it will require many individual acts, at the local level, in order to bring about significant change. If every individual were to buy ozone-friendly products, burn less fuel and join recycling schemes then producers would have to change. As consumers each individual does not have to accept what is on offer but can make demands upon the providers of goods and services. With the priviledge of belonging to relatively advantaged society comes the responsibility of seeking solutions to environmental and social problems.

In 1989, some forty decision-makers in Colorado came to realise the importance of global-local interaction. In cooperation between the United National Conference on Environment and Development and the Club of Rome, further national initiatives have continued in order to foster the message of local action. These initiatives in some thirty countries on five continents advocate local individual interactions with a view to transforming citizens from being inactive and isolated persons into becoming aware human beings ready to take cohesive action.

As empowered citizens we could know a lot about the environmental issues we face by using the information systems technology has provided. This does not make it easier to understand the issues or make decisions about proposed solutions. One has therefore to learn how to proceed in the face of uncertainty. Political decisions often have to be taken when the possible outcomes of contributory factors are not completely identified. As individuals or as members of institutions, one is incresingly asked to adopt attitudes and approaches of greater flexibility and adaptability. One real challenge is to make links of common understanding between the language and concepts, of economics, morality and environmental issues. One might adopt environmental and moral considerations in the assessment of economic analysis; or take account of economic viewpoints in approaching environmental problems. Careful definition of the environmental issues and their causes and the kind of economics being used is needed. More effective ways of integrating environmental issues with macro-and micro-economic perspectives have to be found.

Citizens involved in local initiatives who are concerned about future generations and their well-being would have to balance and reconcile present and future problems and values with needs. The creation of a sustainble world system suggests that profligate lifestyles need to be diminished by decelerating consumption of finite resources. As ethical imperative also requires one to alleviate poverty wherever possible. Current ethical decisions are largely undefined, diffuse reactions against environmental ills such as pollution or selfish exploitation of resources. In some countries, a business-based system of regulation offers some protection against various forms of malpratice, but local action based upon ethical consideration deserves to strengthen systems of regulation. Practitioners in the business of industry, commerce, service or conservation would then have to accept a higher degree of social and environmental responsibility in their own and consumer's long-term interests.

The articles presented in this book offer a rich source of ideas, examples and discussions. They will be an aid to educationalists who wish to begin to explore the issues more thoroughly. The considerations are contemporary ones which should enable pupils' educational experience to be relevant to the real world. Otherwise one may take refuge in having a curriculum which is sentimentalized or cliche-ridden. Quite rightly, HMI have already pointed out the biased nature of some curricula, which simply label all industrial and technological activity as environmentally, 'bad'.

An ethical perspective of international relations cannot evolve unless it has a positive effect at a national, community and individual level. Schools could help foster positive attitudes on the part of pupils towards being involved in sound local initiatives which promote care for the environment at a local level while echoing global issues. The development of effective strategies to deal with environmental issues requires research into, and an understanding of, the real causes of the problems. This would be more easily done if pupils were encouraged to consider local problems and become involved in local initiatives to solve them. Schools would thus play an essential formative role in the development of aware citizens who would be equipped to tackle the complex environmental issues they will face in the future.

2

Environmental Education in India

Concern for the environment has been a part of India's social and cultural heritage. This land of ours is the birthplace of sages and of religions preaching love for every living thing, a concern for life and conservation of nature. India, of the bygone eras, was in a way the land of milk and honey, whose vast resources were exploited by many maurauders, and lastly she was colonized by the British. Post Independence India has seen great achievements: on the one hand we have to Green Revolution ushering in an era of self-sufficiency in food, and on the other we have made giant strides in the utilization of resources, particularly petroleum, and in the development of industries. India today is a leader amongest developing countries. There is however a gloomier side to this picture.

- Our population is rising at a very high rate and is predicted to reach 1250 million by 2000 A.D.
- Total area under the threat of periodic floods has more than doubled in the last decade.
- The National Forest Policy Act, 1952 prescribed a minimum of 33% of the country's land area under forest cover, today there is only 12% and that too is fast depleting
- More than 6000 million tonnes of the fertile topsoil are lost every year due to erosion.
- According to National Environmental Engineering Research Institute, Nagpur (NEERI), industries of Greater Bombay add about 1000 tonnes of pollutants to the atmosphere every day of which 38.4% is corbon monoxide and 34.4% is sulphur dioxide, rest particulates, ammonia and oxides of nitrogen.
- and of course, there is Bhopal-a tragedy which will linger in the minds of every conscious citizen of the world.

Our concern in this country is but a reflection of what is happening the world over. This concern found expression when UN convened the Conference on the Human Environment it Stockholm in 1972. Addressing the Plenary Session of the Conference, our late Prime Minister, Indira Gandhi said:

> "...one cannot be truly human and civilized unless one looks upon not only all fellowmen, but all nations with eyes of a friend... Even though our industrial development is in its infancy and at its most difficult stage, we are taking various steps to deal with the incipient environmental imbalances, more so because of our concern for the human species which is also imperilled. In poverty he is threatened by malnutrition and disease, in weakness by war, in richness by pollution brought about by his own prosperity.. Environmental problems of the developing country are not a side effect of excessive industrialization but reflect the inadequacy of development. Life is one and the world is one and all these questions are interlinked. Population explosion, poverty, ignorance and disease, pollution of our surroundings, stockpiling of nuclear weapons and biological and chemical agents of destruction, are all parts of a vicious circle. Each is important and urgent... The modern man must re-establish the unbroken link with nature and with life. He must again learn to invoke the energy of the growing things and to recognise as did the ancients in India, centuries ago, that one can take from the earth and atmosphere only so much as one puts back into them. In their hymn to earth, sages of the Atharva Veda chanted: I quote,
>
> "What of thee I dig out let that quickly grow over, let me not hit thy vital organs or thy heart."

It led the conference to proclaim "to defend and improve the environment for present and future generations." Subsequent developments such as the formation of UNEP, the Belgrade Charter (1975) and the Inter-Governmental Conference on Environmental Education, Tbilisi (1977) highlighted the role of education in the halting of destruction of the enviroment. If man is to survive he can only do so in harmony with nature. His superior brain has given him to power to mould the environment to his needs, to draw from the mother earth all he needs to sustain himself and his vagaries and luxuries. He has forgotten that he is but a very small part of this delicately balanced system, nature. Realization has come to him, hopefully, not too late. The lessons he has learnt the hard way must be passed on to the future generations.

Society expects the education system to build up environment-concious citizens. The necessity of environmental education, was voiced by the International Union of Conservation of Nature way back in the sixties and reiterated over the years in many conferences. We in India, may justly feel proud that our national documents, like the Report of the Education Commission (1964-66) and Curriculum for the Ten-year School: An Approach Paper (1975), all emphasize the need for environmental education. The present curricula of general education that is classes I-X, has in it, ample materials on the environment, its problems and conservation. But environmental education, to mind is not just awareness and knowledge, it is far more. It is development of proper attitudes, the awakening of the urge to make the world a better place to live in, to be aware of what is happening around and above all, to act without fear.

The formal education system has no doubt created awareness, but how far can a rigid examination-based system lead to the development of proper attitudes is a question that remains to the answered. If we could rid the formal education system out of the fetters of examination, take education out of the classroom and let the children indulge in activities suitable for the conservation of the environment, we would probably be building better citizens for the future.

We aim at universalization of education. To my mind literacy should not only be the three R's but also include environmental education. This need not be taught as separate subject but could be interwoven into the fabric of the three R's, thus enriching the design of the curricula. This sort of interweaving should be possible both for the formal and non-formal systems. A beginning has been made under the various UNICEF projects currently being conducted by NCERT. There are varied approaches which will be presented in another paper highligting the NCERT activities in the field of environmental education. I hope that this will be discussued in this august body and that its deliberations will help us in imbibing more life into the primary curricula.

The general education upto class X should also be appraised in terms of making environment conscious citizens. While the curricula developed by NCERT have many environment-based concepts, the State syllabi lack much of it. Besides an environment-based, child-centered approach which is based on activities and projects is necessary for the inculcation of proper attitudes and values. However, one again the examination system has defeated the purpose of such curriculm designs. More stress is laid on the congnitive domain than on the pschyomotor or affective domains and hence learning becomes a drudgery. To my mind the only way out of this dilemma is the proper organisation of extra-curricular activities. Science clubs, drama, debates, painting competitions, all could highlight environmental issues, thus not only creating an awareness amongst peer groups but also amongst the parents. It is hoped that projects carried out under the aegis of science clubs would ultimately lead to the development of proper attitudes.

Such extra-curricular activities cannot be only the responsibility of the schools. Agencies, both voluntary and government, must come forward to help in this matter, through organising activities, giving expert advice and providing suitable information. It is rather sad that in this country where we have so much expertise, so many questions that arise in the minds of children remain unanswered for lack of communication between the young and the old. Is it not the time for the experts to step down from their ivory towers and to lead the future generation to better understanding of his natural, social and cultural environment?

The NCERT is going to set up a National Science Centre at New Delhi as part of its Silver Jubille Celebrations, 1986. This centre with its broad scope of envisaged activities. exhibitions lectures, science clubs, teacher programmes, and innovations in terms of classroom experiments and kits will further the cause of environmental education by filling the lacunae between scientists, teachers and the younger generation. It will be, I hope, a centre for dissemination of information for not only the educational community within India but also those from abroad and thus help improvement of science education in general and environmental education in particular.

I would like to tell you at this stage about another exciting programme which has been launched last year. It is called "Reading to Learn." Our children are starved of proper and attractive reading materials, and thus to not develop the habit of reading. Inculcation of such good reading habits lends to continuing education through life. We are proposing to bring out low priced reading kits, which will highlight current issues like deforestation, pollution, conservation of wild life, equality of sexes. For the elementary level these will be read aloud by the teachers. We hope these kits will lay the foundation for environment consciousness and the urge to improve the quality of life.

This brings us to the key-question of the training of teachers. Teachers play the pivotal role in conveying the underlying message of the curricula, and in the development of proper attitudes. However, if the teachers do not have proper understanding about the topics they teach or the attitudes that require to be included in their pupils, they will fail to realize its educational objectives. Our teachers, therefore, need to be informed about the goals of environmental education, and how to achieve them. They must also be made aware of the environmental problems that exists within this country and their solution so that they may face their classes with confidence. This is no mean task considering we have 13 lakhs primary teachers, 8 lakhs middle school teachers, 5.5 lakhs secondary teachers and 2.9 lakhs higher secondary teachers, and most of them without an adequate background of the natural environment its problem and conservation. This massive task can only be attempted if all types of organisations come forward to lend hand. NCERT has carried out much innovation in this area through its intergrated B.Sc., B.Ed courses, and M.Sc. Ed (Life Science) course. The curricula of both have recently been revitalized the emphasize environmental aspects. Several in-service courses are being organised for various levels. However, much more needs to be done. The governmental and voluntary agencies could also play a key role in teacher training and teacher updating.

The 'communication setellite and ETV are also going to be a boon' for the environmental educationist. Mass media has an appeal to both old and young. Usually children pick up much more from the media than from their teacher. To make ETV a real instrument of change, the programmes need to be specific as well as attractive, so that they draw the attention to local problems and also advise what actions are possible to overcome these drawbacks. It can thus not only enlighten the community but also point the way towards action. NCERT has started preparing ETV programmes, however such programmes need a lot of back-up support from other agencies both during their development and during their use. The follow-up action needs the cooperation of all types organi-zation, so that the programme can have a real massive impact.

This gathering, where representation from many and different types of organisations from India and abroad, will, I Hope, deliberate at length on the strategies of implementation of environmental education programmes so that we prepare action-oriented citizens who will work for the conservation of the environment.

NON-CONVENTIONAL ENERGY SOURCES FOR ENVIRONMENT PROTECTION

Environment and Human Development

Man lives on earth. A deep relationship exists between the environment on earth and his life. The main factors of environment are Biological and Physical. The physical environment consists of land, water and air, bio-sphere provides the food and other requirements of man. Environment creates favourable conditions for the existence and development of different creatures. As a noted author has said:

> "The great numbers of living species on earth, hundreds of thousands of kinds of animals and plants, are arranged over the planet, not at random, but in organised and structured communities of living things... Each community is distinct. The species within each are tied together, in intricate net works of energy-flow or

pathways of chemical raw materials from soil, air, and water; through various plants to various animals... Distrurbance of any part of a community affects all parts."

The ecosystems are essentially self-regenerating and self-sustainable in which different components are interconnected, interrelated and interdependent. "There is no waste in a natural scheme of things, as the waste of one species becomes food for another. The only external input is the sunlight." But the considerable waste generated by the human species caused environmental degradation; this throws the life support system out of gear. Our planet is a vast civilization reserve which needs to be conserved as a whole at all cost.

The level of economic development and distribution of population of any region depends on the relationship between man and the environment around him, different elements of which are used for different requirements. Land is used for meeting the food and raw material supplies. Water is used for irrigation and power generation. The use of all these elements should be made while keeping the ecological balance.

Present Scenarco

The Indian environment has been viciously affected and destroyed in the last century due to unrestricted felling of the forests. The consequences of excessive deforestation are increasing floods, soil erosion, heavy siltation of dams built at an enormous expense, and changes in micro-climates; in other words, a progressive depletion of the country's ecological bank, driving it incessantly towards bankruptcy. Flood damages alone, it is estimated, now average about Rs. 1000 crores every year. What is worse in human terms is the increasing denial to a large section of the country's population of forest products like firewood, which are vital for human survival.

River water pollution in India has reached a point of crisis The Ganga river system has been converted into a network of cesspools and drains due to the effluents of industries and municipalities in the region. The water of many other rivers in India has been polluted by sewerage, industrial wastes and industrial effluents which have led to mass fish kills. The Ganga, despite its high self-purification capacity, is among India's most polluted rivers. Shockingly high levels of pollution exist along vast stretches of the Yamuna river. Everyday, its 48 km portion through Delhi picks up nearly 200 million litres of untreated sewage. Twenty million litres of industrial effluents including about half a million litres of DDT wastes enter the Yamuna in this stretch. From Delhi to Agra, the Yamuna water is unfit for drinking and bathing.

Air is a precious natural resources without which life cannot be sustained for more than a few minutes, yet the concern for clean air and protection of the atmosphere from damage by human activities is only a recent phenomenon. Human activities like industrial production, motor transport and domestic burning of fuels are adding large amount of harmful pollutants to the atmosphere, triggering off a host of global and regional environmental problems.

Air pollution reminds most people of high chimneys at factories belching out thick clouds of black smoke. The fact that old people, women and children face far more serious risks due to pollution from smoke inside their homes, is not even generally known.

There are nearly a million motor vehicles on the roads of India. The exhaust fumes they emit contain carbon monoxide, nitrogen oxides, hydrocarbons, aldehydes and lead-oxide. The black smoke emitted by diesel engines contains more particulates than the exhaust of petrol engines though other pollutants stated above are less. Carbon monoxide decreases the capacity of the blood to carry oxygen from the lungs to the tissues.

Destruction of forest-cover and tress for whatever purpose and reason, have serious repercussion and deep-rooted effect on the environment. The population explosion, poverty and resultant need for clearance of large extent of forests endangered irreplaceable life forms (plants and animals), and drive them to the threashold level of extinction. Our late Prime Minister, Smt. Indira Gandhi, had rightly observed:

> "The environment in which animals and plants become extinct is not safe for the human beings either."

According to the National Fuelwood Study Committee 1982, more than 4.5 million ha of forests are lost upto 1980 due to agricultural and other development activities. The fuelwood requirements which are well in excess of rate of reforestation and causing additional losses of forest cover at the rapid rate.

India adopted the National Air (Preventation and Control of Pollution) Act only in 1981. This act vests the authority in the Central and State Boards for Prevention and Control of Water Pollution set up under an Act of 1974. These Boards are preparing to lay down and enforce standards. The Indian Standards Institution (ISI) has proposed standards for ambient air quality in respect of sulphur dioxide and particulate matters. Sulphur dioxide concentration in ambient air shall not exceed 60 µg/m (0.023 ppm) as annual 24-hour arithmetic mean with 200 µg/m (0.080 ppm) not to exceed more than 2 per cent of the time and not on two consecutive days in a year. The particulate matter in ambient air shall not exceed as 24 hours annual arithmetic mean, 200 µg/Nm in coastal areas; 300 µg/Nm in inland areas, and 500 µg/Nm in northern areas.

Normal particulate concentrations vary from 150 to 100 µg/m, that observed in coastal areas being up to 150 μg/m, ranging upto 250 μg/m in inland areas and upto 500 μg/m in the northern areas (except during dust storms).

For emissions from thermal power plants, ISI has recommended for particulate matter limits ranging from 250 mg/Nm for new pulverized coal-fired boilers in urban areas to 1,000 mg/Nm for old stocker firing boilers. For sulphur dioxide, the recommended emission limits in 600 mg/J of energy produced.

One can see, even without these figures how much needs to be done. Smoking chimneys are the general order, both in our urban and rural areas. Furthermore, emissions from automobiles, buses and trucks are visibly polluting urban areas in particular, and, in growing measure, the rural areas. This kind of pollution can and must be curbed. Reasonable air quality can be achieved with relatively modest addition or improvement to equipment and by better maintenance of equipment. In fact, air pollution often results from imcomplete combustion, and reducing emission will improve fuel efficiency. Thus, energy cost reduction and environmental quality can be had by the same action.

Conventional Energy Sources and Environmental Degradation

All forms of conventional energy sources viz. Coal, oil, hydro and nuclear have environmental ramifications. In coal-based energy plants (power and industrial boilers) the environment has to be taken into account at the extraction, transport and generation stages. In the open-cast mining of coal, rehabilitation of the land is feasible and its cost low relative to the value of the coal mined. A proper understanding of the need for such rehabilitation can ensure that it is invariably done and pre-planned.

A major problem with thermal power generation is that of air pollution by stock exhausts. It is necessary to lay down and enforce air quality standards. Setting of standards is difficult since scientific information about the effects of air pollution on human health is not adequate. In some countries standards have been relaxed. For example, the nitrogen oxide standard in Japan has been raised from 0.02 ppm to a range of 0.04 to 0.06 ppm because of a feeling that the latter levels may not be harmful to health whereas the cost of attaining the lower level would be extremely high. Similarly, in the USA, analysis of dose response data and costs of achieving more stringent standards has led to the raising of the standards from 0.08 ppm (8 hour's average) to 0.12 ppm.

This brings us to the need for proper evaluation of benefits and costs, even through rough approximations may be possible. In some cases damage or loss of benefits may greatly exeed pollution control cost and also be large by themselves. In other cases the cost of pollution control may be substantial and yet achieve little additional benefits. However, such analysis can at least provide a basis for the choice of technology.

Electrical energy generation by hydro-electric power plants is non-polluting, and uses a renewable source of energy. However, there are several problems associated with the construction of giant dams on natural waterways. The construction of such dams alters the downstream ecology as well as that in the lake area behind the dam. Huge areas get submerged, flore, fauna or any agricultural produce of this land get affected. People and towns in this area have to be removed and re-allocated, causing disturbance and sometimes hardships. Again the time, taken for such large schemes to fructify is usually quite long. For these reasons, increasing thought is now being given to supplement such large projects with more small size hydroprojects called mini-hydel or micro-hydel, which can be built on steams and even on canals, without large dams.

Nuclear energy can be obtained both through fusion and the fission processes. Enormous amounts of energy is released from small quantities of fuel in both these processes e.g., one ton of Uranium can theoretically yield energy equivalent to about three million tonnes of coal. The problem of disposal of the radioactive wastes which create environmental problems and possibilities of accident leading to release of radio-activity have, however, caused concern and opposition is some quarters. Scientific work is continuing on both these aspects.

Non-Conventional Energy Sources

The non-conventional sources of energy like solar, wind, biomass, etc., are of vital importance for the present situation of energy crisis in third world and for protection of environment. The non-conventional energy sources are non-polluting and non-exhausting in nature. The Department of Non-Conventional Energy Sources (DNES) programmes stress the creation and strengthening of indigenous scientific and technological efforts in this area, and also the need for creation of proper delivery systems and extension services and removal of non-technical constraints and institutional or cultural barriers that hamper the wide diffusion of mature non-polluting technologies. Besides a proper infrastructure there is the need for appropriate economic policies and fiscal incentives to encourage and provide back-up to scientific and technological advances in this area.

Non-Conventional energy technologies are ideally suited for decentralized or small-scale energy supply systems which are particularly relevant for India's rural agricultural economy. The Government has embarked upon a major well co-ordinated effort to harness and develop non-conventional energy sources. Although certain technologies were known, recent developments have broadened their applicability, reduced costs and improved efficiencies. Many technologies have reached the stage of maturity, that is, they can be applied economically in a commercial manner, and on a large scale, particularly in rural and remote areas. The approach paper to the Seventh Plan approved at the highest level, has included the development of non-conventional energy sources as one of the priority areas.

Biogas

Biogas is one of the most important components of renewable energy supplies today. A by-product of biogas is a very valuable enriched fertilizer. Its other benefits include reduction in demand for fuelwood, improvement in sanitation, reduction in the incidence of eye diseases among village women and easy and efficient cooking and thereby reducing the drudgery in women's life thus making their time available for creative and developmental activities. Versatility is one of the greatest merits of biogas. It can be used for cooking, lighting, or for generation of power. It can be produced from a large variety of materials ranging from cattle, human and agricultural wastes and water hyacinth to industrials effluents.

At present, there are already more than 276,000 family type biogas plants working in the Country. Computing an average size 4 cu. m gas per plant, these are producing 8 lakhs cu.m gas per day which is equivalent to 240 million cu.m gas per annum or 44 million litres of kerosene oil valued at about Rs. 26.5 crores per year. In this financial year alone 150,000 plants are being installed which will save about 600, 000 t/yr of fuelwood equivalent and provide clean cooking conditions in villages throughout the country.

There are 14 crore households in this country. Nearly 80% of them use wood and/or cow dung for generating cooking energy. The Chulhas (stoves) which are used for this purpose are inefficient. It has been calculated that if the efficiency of traditional chulhas is raised by just 1% from the present level, it will result in annual saving of 4 million tonns of wood. The Department has recently launched a programme for the demonstration and installation of improved chulhas which aims at setting up 5 lakh chulhas during the current plan period. These chulhas will have an efficiency of 15-25% as against the 2-10% efficiency of traditional chulhas. The potential impact of these chulhas can be easily imagined. The improved models are both portable and fixed and have been chosen with a view to acceptability in the user community as well as efficiency. It is proposed to launch a much more massive programme in this area in the Seventh Plan.

Solar Energy

That sun in the source of practically all energy on the earth need not be emphasised. It is however surprising how of ten we tend to forget this basic fact of life on this earth.

While biogas derives specific energy from the sun in an indirect complicated manner; involving many principles of microbiology, solar thermal, and solar photovoltaic devices and system make use of the sun in a more direct manner. At present in this country, solar thermal systems are available for large scale use in the following areas: water heating, air heating, air drying, water desalination and solar cooking. Temperatures upto 100°C are easily obtainable in these devices, depending on the system.

The Government has supported, financially and otherwise, a large number of solar heating systems in the country. For example, a solar water heating system of a capacity 60,000 litres has been completed recently at Lodhi Hotelin Delhi. A 30 tonnes multipurpose solar driver was commissioned recently in Kerala. A tea drying plant using solar energy and waste heat was installed recently at Tocklai in Assam. Similar plants for coffee and tobacco are under construction. Solar water heating systems have been installed in public and private industries all over the country. It is proposed to give a major thrust to all the solar energy systems during the current year, and spread them far and wide in the country during the seventh plan.

One of the most successful application of solar water heating is found in the textile industry. Lead was taken by a textile mill in Ahmedabad to be followed by number of other heating and drying systems to be installed in a big way in the next 2-3 years in hospitals, hotels, textile industries, tea industry, distilleries etc. Contrary to general feeling the solar heat/drying systems are cheap as compared to conventional systems. They are also easy to maintain.

Solar Photo-Voltaic Systems

Solar photovoltaic systems can convert the energy of the sun directly into electricity. This is a high technology area. There are some problems relating to the materials to be used as medium for such conversions and the percentage output of electricity as a function of the total solar radiation received. High level R&D efforts are going on in the country to solve these problems in a more effective manner. At present technologies are available to enable 9-11% output in terms of electricity as a function of the solar radiation received by the system. This may not sound very high, but it should be remembered that an ordinary incandescent bulb uses only about 3% of the energy it consumes. An internal combustion engine does not use more than 30% of the energy it consumes. Solar photovaltaic devices are at present expensive but the costs are expected to come down in the next 5-6 years. Even now these are quite competitive for remote areas and special locations. Solar photovoltaic systems are being used in the country for a variety of purposes including water pumping, street lighting, communication, powering television, radio sets etc.

The Department of non-conventional energy sources is running presently a National Solar Photovoltaic Energy Demonstration Programme achieve a production capacity of one MW (obtained) per year by Sept. 1985. By that time BHEL, Bangalore, would also attain a capacity of 250 kW (electricity) per year. It is proposed to give a major boost to the solar photovoltaic programme in the current year and make it a substantive contributor to rural electrification of remote villages in the 7th Plan. R&D in this area is proposed to be particularly emphasized including work on amorphous silicon cells and modules, ribbon silicon cells and modules, etc., so as to reduce the present high costs.

Wind Energy

Indian potential for harnessing wind energy is not as great as the size of the country would lead us to imagine. However, there are large coastal and other areas where wind energy can be usefully exploited for pumping water and electricity generation. 900 wind pumps have been installed under Demonstration Programme in the country by the department so far. It is expected that by the end of the current year more than 1,000 wind pumps installed. The Government provides handsome support to the wind pump user by bearing entire cost of the mechanical system, leaving the cost of civil work to be borne by the beneficiary. Extention programme for water pumping wind is proposed to be taken up shortly. In the seventh plan, the extension programme will be enlarged greatly.

Small capacity generators of Wind Energy Conversion System (WECS as they called) have been developed in the country and are being field tested.

Indigenous manufacture of some low capacity systems may also start in the near future. Wind farms of upto 5 MW capacity are planned for the known windly locations in India. Wind monitoring stations and developments of prototypes of medium sized wind generators will be taken up at a wind energy centre, being established by the Department and the CSIR.

Certain Government Department like Railways and Posts and Telegraphs have made small but definite steps forward in the use of wind energy and solar energy in their installations.

Energy From Urban Wastes

A major thrust has been given to various programme for generation of energy from urban wastes. These programme include power generation through incineration, pyrolysis, landfills and generation of gas from sewage. The Prime Minister recently announced the setting up of a Central Ganga Authority, which will oversee the implementation of a plan aiming at providing the basic facilities of sewage treatment coupled with recovery systems for fuels and fertilizers, for major cities and towns like Calcutta, Allahabad, Varanasi, Kanpur, Patna, on the Ganga river system, Large-scale generation of biogas for production of power and or domestic fuel from sewage are proposed to taken up in these cities, other cities in different parts of the country will also be provided with this facility depending on financial allocation. Work on an experimental project for incineration of 300 milion tonnes of solid wastes per day and generation of 3.74 MW power has already been started in Delhi.

Energy Plantation, Power Generation and Environment

One of the important methods of insulating their country against impending disaster is to be take to the Photosynthetic Model of development through large-scale use of biomass, particularly firewood. Such as option, apart from meeting energy needs would help to restore the relationship between man and his environment. Therefore, a very massive tree plantation programme is necessary both for energy needs and overall eco-development. Prime Minister Shri Rajiv Gandhi in his first address to the nation declared the constitution of Wasteland Development Board to cover at least 5 milion ha of wasteland annually. In our country, the shortfall in firewood production by 2000 Ad has been estimated at 137 mill, tonnes, which would require 34 mill. ha of land, at about four oven-dry tonnes wood per ha\year, and a minimum annual outlay of Rs 500 crores for 17 years to be made good. Once such a programme is successful, dung and plant-based residue would be available as organic fertilizer and as industrial feed stock, respectively.

Among the renewable alternatives, solar energy, captured by the plants through the process of photosynthesis, is the most important, especially because photosynthesis is the key process in the life-support system of this planet. Furthermore, the plant-pased energy systems are not only renewable but they remove carbon dioxide from the atmosphere before turning it back with no overall quantitative increase, as also help to contain environmental pollution. Photosynthesis is at the base of all biomass production and food chains. It converts physical energy into chemical energy and generates oxygen, the life sustaining gas. Whereas net photosynthesis uses only 0.1% of sunlight it produces organic matter of which only 10% accounts for the total energy used by mankind and only 0.5% accounts for the entire food requirement of the human race. Increase in photosynthetic efficiency automatically increases production of organic matter. Various types of biomass and/or bio-fuels available area: firewood, agricultural alcohol, vegetable oil, hydrocarbon plants, particularly those yielding rubber and petroleum like materials; fresh weeds, sewage-grown algae, algal hydrocarbons and biologically produced hydrogen using halobacteria, algae, Azolla and even higher plants. Every feedstock or bioconversion process has its own merits and demarits, and the different routes available to generate solid, liquid and gasous fuels are: anaerobic and enzymatic digesting and thermochemical conversion.

Biomass may not be panacea for all our energy problems but it will, no doubt, help to reduce substantially our dependence on fossil fuels. Being socially and environmentally relevant, biomass enables us to keeep our air, water and land clean, and manage our life support system in a sustained manner. Two things are needed: first, in view of our country being predominantly agricultural, a perceptible tilt in favour of plants and plant sciences in our planning process by adoption of the Photosynthetic Model of Development, and secondly, India has to be made increasingly greener. Among other things, such a model envisages revegetating the uncultivated half of India to make the country fresh and verdant. This would have distinct environmental, social and economic benefits and will help in many ways.

The Department of Non-Conventional Energy Sources (DNES) has planned to set up a chain of Biomass Research Centres in the country. Integradation of production, conversion, utilisation and conservation of woody biomass is an important feature of this programme. It has been proposed to cover 1.5 million ha of sub-standard soils under energy plantation during Seventh Five Year Plan (1985-90).

It has been estimated that about 1000 ha can generate about 3 MW of power, besides providing fuelwood or charcoal which can support the energy needs of a population of 125 to 150 families. In India, even if one-fifth of the estimated 80 million ha of barren and waste land can be covered by such a programme, a generation capacity of about 48,000 MW can be created, which is considerably more than the entire installed power capacity in the country today from all thermal, hydro and nuclear sources. Moreover, power from energy plantations could be made available from a number of decentralised installations to minimise transmission and distribution costs. This would also provide fuelwood and charcoal to meet cooking needs of the rural poor, provide green biomass cover in area zones and raise rural incomes. The investment cost for such projects could be only about Rs. 12, 000 per KW.

According to a calculation, the cost of electricity produced in such a programme woud be about Rs. 0. 87 per kw hr. assuming capital costs of local generation of Rs. 12,000 per kw. fuelwood is priced at Rs. 50 per quintal, O&M costs as Rs. 0.10, an annual capacity factor of 0.60 and a rate of return of 0.12. If the fuel wood is priced at Rs. 25 per quintal (since it is available next to the power unit), the cost of electricity comes down to Rs. 0. 62 per kw hr. This can be favourably compared to a cost of Rs. 0. 96 per kw hr for electricity from a central power station, to a village having a load of 20 kw, and at a distance of 10 km from the grid; these costs increase to Rs 1.11 per kw hr at a distance of 20 km, and Rs. 1.26 per at a distance of 30 km from the grid. Thus power from energy plantation is a very promising option for substantial power needs.

Biomass Gasifier

Partial combustion of wood with air yields gasous mixture capable of producing gas which can be burnt in boilers designed for liquid for gaseous combustion, and engines after purification. There are a veriety of applications were this technology has far-reaching impact particularly for irrigation, crop drying, dairies and chilling centres, rural electrification and sawmills. Adequate supply of water is one of the major limitations, to boost up food production of afforestation programmes. During 6th plan, it is envisaged to energies 25 lakhs irrigation wells. The energy for lift irrigation can be obtained only from firewood which implies emphasis on energy plantation. With fast-growing tree species irrigation can triple production to that obtained under rainfed conditions. The approach of combining biomass production and gasification will result in many benefits, viz. wasteland utilisation, energy supply and generation of employment potential. This would help the farmer to be energy-independent and free from shortage of diesel and electricity. Supply of water from tubewells will help in increasing yield even in non-irrigated areas with poor and unreliable rainfall. There are many potential areas for its application but the success depends upon the development of small-scale gasifiers (5-20 hp) based on wood and agricultural residues available in the country.

Other Sources of Energy

Water can be used for power generation even from the low and ultra-low heads available in canals, flowing streams in hills, river slopes, small irrigation dams, etc. Research and Development and pilot programmes have been taken up by the Department in these areas. Work is also being carried out on improving the designs of hydrams and water mills. Ocean thermal gradient energy, wave and tidal energy are yet another potential sources for coming years. A feasibility report is being prepared for setting up a one megawatt ocean thermal energy conversions pilot plant in Lakshdeep island, which envisages production of power and aquaculture based on nutrient rich cold water, from the deep sea. Research and

Development Projects on production, storage and utilization of hydrogen energy geothermal based cold storage systems and fuel cells are also taken up. Proto-types of 3-and 4-wheeler battery powered vehicle have been developed and are undergoing field performance tests.

Role of Environmental Education

The World Environment Day is observed every year on June 5 with a view to arusing the masses and bringing the environmental issues to the forefronts of thinking and planning and also to remember this mother earth; the only environment we have to take stock of its great capacity to assume all, of the lasting prosperity. The citizens role in environmental protection needs no special emphasis. The fight against environmental degradation is not the only concern of the scientists, engineers or government agencies: but to be readily effective; it has to be an issue of everybody's concern. Much of the success in environmental preservation in advanced nations, is due to intevention and involvement of enlightened citizen-action groups debating on public forums, environmental issues like felling trees, construction of dams and location of nuclear power plants. The recent controversy over the Silent Valley project and the 'CHIPCO-MOVEMENT' in Himalayas in India (Almora Hills) is a welcome sign of people's awareness. The role of students and rural women folk in the 'CHIPCO-MOVEMENT' is heartening. Environmental education to understand the intimate relationship between the quality of the environment and human well-being has an important role to play in the direction of presserving the environment and ensuring the quality of life.

During early eighties, environmental studies were introduced into school curricula in the country with tremendous enthusiasm with an objective of new approach to education. It was hoped that children would grow up with a keener awareness of their environment. NCERT published number of documents in 1975 on environmental education. It was also recommended that the child should also develop habits of cleanliness and healthful living and understanding of the proper sanitation and hygience of its neighbourhood.

To promote the environmental education both formal and non-formal, there should be involvement of each and every human being on the continent. Children's literature should be produced bringing out various aspects of environmental problems. State-level symposia should be conducted in collaboration with the State Education Department. Departments like Environment and Energy should form a small unit monitoring progress. A term of experts should be charged with the responsibility of developing and producing creative Environmental Educational material for countrywide use.

3

Managing of Natural Environment

Background to Environmental Concern

Few would quarrel with Caldwell's views but perhaps we need to pause more often to enquire how it was that human society surrounded itself with invironmental problems of its own making or to ask, 'Under what practical, spiritual or ethical principles will we bring about improvements and survival?' To attempt to answer these questions we of course need to know more about the human condition than about natural environments; there is no better way in these circumstances than to examine the lessons of history. Becuase our species has intelligence it has the power both to think in the abstract and in advance of observations and to learn and react to observations. We therefore need to examine the roles of both the abstract and the concreate in shaping our modern environmental concern.

The groundswell: culture, ethics and environment

Our hominid ancestors are said to have evolved under conditions of environmental stress: the savannah plains of Africa, habitat for our early evolution, exhibit highly irregular climate cycles and market seasonal shortages of good, together with a need for shelter. Thus, it has been argued, the very origins of our communal behaviour, communication and technology occurred in what editors might now headline as 'environmental crisis'. We may therefore take a measure of optimism about the innate ability of our species to manage out of trouble, but only if certain lessons are learned about the basic dimensions and limits of human society; these lessons have been central to the 'deep green' movement (e.g., Naess and Rothenburge, 1989) and the 'small is beautiful' attitude to technology and settlement.

It is also clear from archaeological and anthropological studies, as well as from contemporary investigations of the behaviour of indigenous peoples, that some form of environmental spirituality–a reverence for the individual elements and totality of the natural environment–steered the sustainable lifestyles of early humans. The widespread occurrence of artefacts symbolizing an earth mother female fertility deity in evidence of this spirituality.

However, the guiding spiritual element for that contemporary civilization putting most pressure on environmental systems, i.e. Western, Christian society, is less unanimously associated with sustainable use of the earth. The form of the 'right' relationship between 'Mankind and Mother Earth' has been the subject of many deep philosophical reviews. Toynbee (p. 38) charts the progress of human impacts from prehistoric times, stressing that

> when a hominid chipped a stone with the intention of making it into a more serviceable tool, this historic act, performed perhaps two million years ago, made it certain that, one day, some species or genus of the hominid family of primate mammals would not merely affect and modify the biosphere, but would hold the biosphere at its mercy.

The reviews by Passmore and Thomas inevitably point to the role of the Christian faith in forming Western environmental behaviour patterns, patterns which were to be exported throughout the world by exploration, conquest and colonialism. Attention focuses on the Bible as text and on one particular passage: Christianity teaches that mankind has dominion 'over all the earth and over every creeping thing that crepeth upon the earth'. We ar to be 'fruitful and multiply and replenish the earth and subdue it'.

Naess and Rothenburg (1989, p. 187) point out that the most commonly occurring biblical terms for manking's relationship with nature are 'guardian', 'administrator' and 'steward' and they attack this notion as follows:

> The arrogance of stewardship consists in the idea of superiority which underlies the thought that we expect to watch over nature like a highly respected middleman between Creator and Creation. We know too little about what happens in nature to take up the task.

There is no doubt that a Christian ethic of stewardship (supported by Passmore, 1980, as representing the seed-corn for a new environmental ethic) received a setback from the development in the seventeenth Century of Baconian, mechanistic, science. To Francis Bacon the very essence of science was its enabling and emancipating power for humans in relation to wilderness and unharnessed natural potentials. The logical outcome of this Western ethic was the triumphant period of exploitation which we now call the Industrial Revolution. However, science had also presided over what Thomas (1984) labels 'the dethronement of man', for example, through theories of organic evolution, though even these tended to encourage a view from the 'pinnacle' achieved in the 'perfection' of *Homo sapiens.*

Outside the question of animal rights, into which Thomas enquires very closely, Christianity had few reasons to questions an association with the 'civilizing' influence of resource exploitation until the effects of an Industrial Revolution became manifest. Air pollution had begun in London as early as 1273 and by the time John Evelyn was writing his *promifugium* in 1661 the situation in terms of ill-health and other damage was for beyond Evelyn's subtitle phrase of... *the Inconvenience of the Aer* (see the 1972 reprint)! Aside from blaming Newcastle coal for the problem, Evelyn was a practical environmental manager, suggesting that 'all those works be removed five or six miles distant from London'.

Others who recorded the plunder of resources and the many effects which would now be labelled 'externalities' included George Perkins Marsh (1864), who recorded mainly rural plunder, and Friedrich Engles who, during the mid-nineteenth century in industrial northern England, witnessed the appalling toll of industrialization upon the home, work and natural environments of the new cities. However, urban politics became based upon arguments over the means of production rather than the ends or effects of production. Karl Marx, for whom Engels' observations formed field data, took a characteristically meterialist view of nature and diverted attention away from more spiritual and ethical arguments concerning the use of the environment and of Nature. It was left to unexpected groups, for example the Lake District romantic poets, to reinvigorate a possionate love of wilderness for its own sake. John Ruskin was perhaps unique in criticizing both the political economy of resource development and the impacts it was clearly having upon landscape, flora and fauna (Landow, 1985).

In a recent global overview of the ethics of environment and development Engel and Engel (1990) assemble contributors from faiths other than Christianity: Islam, Buddihism, Hinduism, together with traditional Chinese and African perspectives. Clearly none is much 'better nor worse' than Christianity and the variability is mainly accountable to the role of animal rights and of a dimension which might be labelled closeness to earth'. Another, growing axis to environmental ethics, though not in a spiritual form outside the 'Earth Mother' sects, centres on the role and rights of women in the environment. Women are closer to practical environmental management in many societies and have distinctive environmental perspectives, but both of these potential contribution are generally subordinated in patriarchal societies. Question-nature surveys in the University of Newcastle in the last five years have consistently shown females to be more concerned about environmental issues than males.

Engel (1990) describes sustainable development as representative of the core of a 'new' environmental ethic. He claim (p. 5) that

> Our present political and economic arrangements are only retained because they are perceived to be legitimate, and their legitimacy rests ultimately on the perception that they are ethically justified. History teaches that once this ethical justification is challenged by new moral sensibilities, and legitimacy withdrawn, the arrange-ments are likely to change.

However, we should beware that, in the case of global environmental problems, ethical stances are likely to be yet more diverse than world religions; we cannot take Western, Christian, mechanistic science perspectives as in any way pervasive. Engel goes on to admit that 'It is difficult to make even the most accepted moral principles operational in a world of sovereign and antagonistic states' (p. 5). He states four ways in which an interest in spirituality, morality and ethics can have practical utility:

Table : Robert Arvill's Candidate Environmental Ethics

1.	Integrity	to infuse ecological precepts and a true environmental ethos into your lifestyle
2.	Humanity	to share the earth's resources more equitably with all life on earth today and tomorrow
3.	Determination	to arrest pollution and squalor and to promote quality in your surroundings
4.	Judgement	to choose wisely between competing and conflicting aims and values in order, with humility, to promote the trusteeship of society for the environment

1. it helps explain the role of human values;
2. it explains human motivations;
3. it gives moral guidance to alternatives courses of action;
4. it helps resolve conflicts.

Such an interest, therefore, is not merely a framework for analysing historical trends but a very practical tool in the crucial social context of environmental management. Arvill (1967) was bold enough to offer candidates for environmental ethics in an era where mankind is dethroned by biological science, depressed by the impacts of applied science/ technology, and too far from primitive origins to follow the sustainable patterns of behaviour followed by indigenous peoples.

Modern times : issue-attention cycles

Arvill's canidate ethics may win respect but not a following; Naess's more profound agendas penetrate very little into active environmental management. The dominant resonance of 'Mankind and Mother Earth' in modern times has been, and continues to be an 'issue attention cycle'.

Human beings even when armed with a range of scientific methodologies championing prediction, are notariously poor at anticipatory action unless the hazard signs are very clearly displayed. Human approach a hazard with caution only if they have experienced that one in the past. For these reasons environmental events have tended to power the somewhat jerky progress of modern environmental management; ethics have had little influence despite their potential utility as part of coping strategies. In the twentieth century the rapid and all-pervasive influence of publicity through the media has meant that 'issues' and 'crises' are frequently the main channels through which the public are kept informed about the natural environment and their own impacts on it.

Downs (1972) identified five phases in the 'issue-attention cycle' followed by American public opinion:

1. pre-problem; it exists but is not recognized;
2. discovery and enthusiasm–often prompted by dramatic events;
3. appreciation of complexity and costs of the problem;
4. gradual decline of public interest;
5. post-problem—in the case of environmental issues a long phase with periodic resurgences of interest in the 'solution' (or its failure).

Sandbach (1980) uses press coverage of environmental issues to develop broader, composite versions of the issue-attention cycle, such as the rapid growth in interest in all environmental issues in the late 1960s and the plummeting of this concern in favour of the economy and work after the energy crise of the early 1970s. In the developed world it seems that this composite rise and fall has now smoothed out; the environment it regularly selected as important, despite the condition of the national or international economy. Public opinion, such as that recorded by opinion pollsters and question naire surveys in the developed world regularly lists the environment and its component management problems as a matter of concern. However, within the 'motor' of progress towards environmental management the 'sparking plugs' still consists of individual issues and their attention cycles dead seals, cancer clusters, fish kills and ozone thinning come and go by the week.

Certain issue have, through their widespread impact, had a more profound effect on the progress of managements. Several reviews have been made of the landmark events (which can include action by leading scientists and politicians) of the 'New Environmental Age' (Nicholson, 1987). Nicholson himself selects, from personal, professional experience; the influence of such books as *The Earth as Modified by Human Action* (Marsh, 1864) and *Silent Spring* (Carson, 1962), events such as the wreck of the oil tanker *Torrey Canyon* off the Scilly Isles in 1967, and conferences such as the United Nations Confrence on the Human Environments in Stockholm in 1972.

Other reviewers, such as McCornick (1989) have charted the build-up of pressure for possitive management from environmentalists (i.e. active campaigners, rather than passive operators) in the 'global environmental movement'. Membership figures for pressure groups are obvious sources of data; the point in the late 1980s when these groups, in Britain, overtook membership of trade unions was clearly a landmark to our changing priorities. McCormick uses the device of tabulating the organizations and treaties which chart the jerky progress of the movement at an international level. However, his chapters themselves provide a broader classificatory guide to the growth of environmental issues:

Table : Significant Individuals and Events in Modern Environmental Management

Data	*Category*	*Details*
1864	Book	George Perkins Marsh's international evidence of land and water degradation. Raised the issue of longer-term implications of productive land use.
1956	Book	Thomas's edited compilation constituting and update on Marsh's warnings.
1952	Disaster	London smog. 5-10 December, 445 direct deaths and 4000 longer-term fatalities. Led to the Clean Air Act 1956—UK first developed nation to act.
1962	Book	Rachel Carson's *Silent Spring* revealed the environmental effects of the early, crude persticides such as DDT; established the wide geographical spread and persistence of chemical pollutants.
1967	Disaster	Wreck of the oil tanker *Torrey Canyon*—117,000 tonnes of crude oil spilled and washed on to holiday

		beaches. Drew attention to the dangers of increasing scale of energy sources/trade and inadequancy of government response and dispersant technology. Led to formation of a UK government department (of environment).
1969	Picture	Apollo space programme—lunar landing/widespread 'spiritual experience' among astronauts. Earth-view established in environmental campaigns and advertising.
1973	Conference	Stockholm Conference on environmental issues affecting development. Led directly to environmental policy-making in the European Community.
1979	Book	James Lovelock's *Gaia* further developed the global biosphere concept and hypothesized the mutural dependence of organic material and its habitat. Transcendentalists take up Gaia as a spiritual guide; environmental science uses it to prioritize the global management task, e.g. controls on the loss of stratospheric ozone.
1986	Disaster	Chernobyl nuclear power plant USSR: 50 miles from Kiew, 32 deaths and 135,000 evacuated. Long-term, international health effects. Established, with 'acid rain', the international transport of pollution in the atmosphere. Discussion of risks in a world based upon nuclear energy given a case example.
1990	Book	Clark University's global review in the Marsh (1864, Thomas (1956)... series. First attempt to separate the influence of three centuries of development from natural trends and cycles, i.e. the true impact of makind.
1992	Conference	United National Conference on Environment and Development—'The Earth Summit' in Rio de Janeiro.*

* This is a hopeful entry!

'The roots [largely Victorian]'
'Protection [conservation. wildlife] 1945-1961'
'The environmental revolution 1962-1970'
'Prophets of doom [resource exhaustion, pollution] 1968-1972'
'The Stockholm Conference 1970-1972'
'The United States Environment Programme 1972-1982'
'Northern Hemisphere politics 1969-1980'

'Southern Hemisphere—environment and development 1972-1982'

Table provides a sample of the flesh of issues on this skeleton structure.

Every author is bounded to produce a biased and partial view of the significant developments; the bias of Table is towards events and individuals who have contributed towards academic and legislative progress in the United Kingdom in the modern era. The contents of the table illustrate both the issue-attention cycle on a large scale and the longevity of Down's 'post-problem' stage.

Clearly scores of environmental issues have quickly faded from our attention in the modern era because news editors have discarded them, because they were purely local or evidence was circumstantial or because in an unspecified way human society decided to continue facing the hazard.

Table : Niches in the Pattern of Policy Opportunities

		Scale	
	Individual	*Corporation**	*State*
Agent			
Moral	'home ecology'	environmental	environmental
Persuasion		audits	assessment on policy
Economics	conversion to	production of	conservation
	clean fuels	'green' goods	for-debt
		and technology	tax incentive
Legislation	planning law	litter laws	law of the
	smokeless zones	labour and the	sea
	tree preservation	environment	catch limits

* *We have concentrated upon commercial corporations here.*

We can detect in those events which have had a longer impact the popularity of command-and-control measures in policy-making (e.g. new legislation or new government departments). Such policies react to events; alternatives to command-and-control require anticipatory, precautionary action. The contribution of academic ideas seems mainly to have been to confirm at an understandable level the broader patterns, especially geographical patterns (see Calder, 1991), of human impacts rather than to predict them and to shape precuationary action.

People and Environment: Scales of Interaction

The high content of geographical principles in this book makes the question of scale of measurement, management and policy imperative; put another way, has hinted at roles for 'actors' in environmental concern and remedies, and we need at least a cast list or order-appearance for them.

Johnston (1989) (p. 110) argues a division between individual and collective action in environmental management:

> although individual initiative in the attack on environmental prolems is desirable there are major limits to it, especially within competitive modes of production, and viable approaches to both solving existing environmental problems and preventing the creation on others must involve collective agreements.

Johnston's chosen geographical scale for analysis becomes the nation state but since he also identifies capitalism as the dominant mode of social production we also need to operate on a second collective scale for which the term 'corpo-ration' is appropriate, although it must be given extraordinary breadth to include, for example, non-governmental organi-zations and commercial companies. We see the corporation as intervening between the state and the individual.

Management requires policy: how is policy formed?

There are said to be three ways in which policy on environmental management changes:

moral persuasion (or 'good practice');
legislation (command and control);
economic manipulation.

These could equally well be routes along which policy operators, although Johnston (1989) prefers four types of action at state level:

goal-oriented: planning for the future;
problem-solving: amelioration of the present;
allocative: promoting certain trends;
exploitative: opportunity-seeking, precautionary.

Seeking symmetry we retain the first, triple division and merge it with our inherent triple of geographical scales in Table.

Environmental ideologies, politics and policy

This theme is close to that chosen by Sand-bach (1980) in his-sighted compilation of Marxist and pluralist alternatives in formulating environmental policy at the scale of the state, and his analysis of the roles of pressure groups and political parties. He separates the functionalist, pluralist environmental ideologies of the twentieth century from the Marxist, materialist standpoint. The former, according to Sandbach, is the more political since it often natively reinforces the existing power structures:

> popular ecology, systems analysis, cybernetics, decision theory, technology assessment and cost-benefit analysis could be seen as agents of social control rather than liberation. (p. 26)

There is no doubt that policy-making on the environment must not continue as an uncoupled muddle of the ethics and issues raised in above;

a coherent political debate is badly needed and is inevitable as the decisions needed for long-term environmental management become more profound and hard-hitting. When human lives face profound changes there is bound to be a political dimension but it remains difficult to see quite what this will be in existing. Western societies, even after the rise of their Green Parties.

In the transition from environmentalism to environ-mental politics it is impossible to neglect material interests; even the forerunners of the deep ecology movement (practitioners of what Bramwell, 1989, calls 'ecologism') represented at best a High Tory, landed, privileged axis in politics and at worst a Nazi connection (from which the German Green Party still seeks to distance itself).

It remains difficult, therefore, to see whether environmental politics will turn out to be (in terms of UK political colours) 'blue-green' or 'red-green' Paehlke (1989, p. 273) suggests that the latter is more likely because of the stage of development which has been reached by environmentalists:

> Environmentalism as an ideology is now at a stage of development comparable to that of socialism a century ago. Environmentalism may never obtain a mass base similar to that of conservatism, liberalism or socialism, but it has already transformed the way many people understand the political world. Environmentalists have produced a sociological, political, economic and philosophical literature of remarkable breadth, depth and variety that has significantly affected the political and administrative agendas of most nations of the world.

Paehlke lists ten priorities in an agenda for 'contemporary environmental progressivism'; he also notes a divergence of fundamental proportions from the socialist agenda because 'distributional issues take second place to choice of technology, design of technology and use of technology' (p. 189). He designs a simple axis diagram in which 'left-right' issues are swung by ninety degrees to 'environmentalism–antienvironmentalism'. If readers cannot identify an 'antienvironmentalist' view perhaps they should consider the extremely hostile reaction to Rachel Carson's *Silent Spring* (Hynes, 1989) or the speeches and articles written in 1991 by the UK Conservative MP Theresa Gorman on 'eco-terrorism'! Bramwell (1989) is a little more coherent in her rejection of the ecological movement which she accuses of advocating a return to primitivism and 'concomitant anarchy'.

What these analysis neglect by grouping environmentalists as a political force is the inherent breadth and lack of cohesion in environmental ideology; 'holism' and 'pluralism' are semantically inadequate to cover the spectrum of pressure groups within which environmentalism now resides. The ecologists' theory of niche is perhaps the best guide; each individual has found a component of the movement with which they are comfortable and the lack of dialectic has removed any need for discipline in debates.

John McCormick (1991, p. 35) reviews British environmental politics and bravely attempts a typology of the pressure groups:

> The words 'movement' and 'lobby' imply homogeneity, cooperation, singleness of purpose, unity and steady evolution. But this misleading... There are sectional groups with demands which can often be conceded with minimal public controversy. There are economic and ideological groups. There are functional groups (mainly pursuing economic interest) and preference groups ('united by common tastes, attitudes of pastimes'). There are emphasis groups...and promotional groups.

The struggle of the UK Green Party to convert an increasing sympathy with sustainable environmental management to a political support takes place against this background. Meanwhile conventional political parties appropriate elements of the environmentalists much like a clothes purchaser in the fitting room. It seems inevitable that policy-making in environmental management may have to proceed for the foreseeable future against an incoherent political force field. The irony is, however, that it is unlikely that policies will succeed unless they are the subject of the widest public consultation, almost the equivalent of government by plebiscrite.

Knowledge and Institutings: Defining the Breath of Policy

As revealed in the foregoing sections, one of our yardsticks for recording progress in environmental management has been the connection between events, issues and their interpretation by academic authors *en route* to institutional incorportion. As we discuss, however, the development of active environmental policies depends as much on a sound and unified knowledge-base as it does upon similar qualities of political pressure. If we regard current environmental politics as 'undisciplined' we must throw same insult at environmental science (the irony being that it is the organization of knowledge into 'disciplines' which is much to blame!). A tentative wish-list for environmental futures might well include a sound knowledge-base ('sound' means both accurate and acceptable) and adaptive institutions of learning, finance and law to put policies into practice.

Academic disciplines

Because of ever-increasing specialization in education and research, an economist is expected to be ignorant about glaciers and a glaciologist about economics. So when experts discuss the state of the planet, it can be like hearing a chiropodist and a dentist arguing about a patient's heart condition.

The specialization of academic disciplines has both intrinsic and extrinsic origins; within disciplines progress is driven by very detailed research at locations near 'the cutting edge'. Research is gratifying intellectually and brings rewards for the individual, his/her discipline and the institution. Were we without academic institutions and were they not, currently, so poorly funded, it is unlikely that competition between disciplines would be so well-developed as it is in a modern Western university, for example. Many such institutions have gladly embraced environmental problems as a further opportunity for detailed 'reductionist' reseach but, discovering the inevitable multidisciplinary nature of the topic, have found severe problems of combining breadth and depth; even greater problems then emerge of peer-group acceptance, publication and further funding.

To geographers the quandary is not new; during the Victorian period geography struggled politically to join the growing range of specialisms in British universities. It succeeded mainly because of the service-ability of its knowledge-gathering about a far-flung empire. Halford Mackinder's vision of the subject stressed the interplay of the natural sciences and their joint relevance to an emerging political geography of resource exploitation.

Nevertheless, the holistic approach cannot be said to have triumphed in geography at all; lack of methodological rigour and an unitative specialization to find favour with other disciplines have dogged the subject. Even the integration of geology, geomorphology, biogeography and climatology under the Victorian heading of 'physiography' broke down (Stoddard, 1986) in the face of specialization, and the challenge of linking the physical and human environments was unanswered because both aspects of the subject became prey to the fashion of reductionism and of mechanistic, not organicist, science. If we regard geography as a talisman of holism in academic institutions we emerge with, at best, the impression of a field of knowledge which encourages an appreciation of environmental problems, rather than of a discipline which solves them. One danger is that this appreciation leads to a glib academic self-satisfaction (Newson, 1992a, in press).

Nevertheless, on a more optimistic note, higher education in the western world is now showing signs of a willingness to form interdisciplinary teams and geographers are often towards the core of such groupings. At school leve UK education policy has recently seen fit to develop a National Curriculum in geography and has offered the subject a key role in educating young people about environmental problems and their management. There is no doubt that the effect of the high profile given to environmental education (including TV and magazine coverage) in the last decade has made children highly aware of the problems, if not the solutions, and this is bound to have political and institutional effects in future decades.

Meanwhile methodologists face the continuing problem of defining and making operational a rigorous treatment of both the ontological depth and epistemological flexibility demanded by environmental management; geographers have much to offer this debate.

Practical management: institutions

We cannot blame acedemic leadership alone for an inappropriately structured knowledge-base for the New Environmental Age. If knowledge is to have practical applications these normally emerge in partnership with the institutions of state regulation concerned, for example, with law, finance and technology. Professionals enter these institutions from education and, like researchers, they appear to be performing better if specializing. Governments design sectoral policies, e.g. for agriculture, energy, forestry and water, to cement this separation, perhaps in the hope that 'creative tension' will offer the best policy outcomes an interdisciplinary issues.

Whilst the United Kingdom's Department of the Environment and the United States' Environmental Protection Agency are examples of two kinds of government institution with deliberate interdisciplinary aims, the ideal situation seldom translates into the critical field of administration. Policy-making, when it comes up against what is practicable, is not merely faced by the constraints of the financial resources but by the units by which administration is conducted. These are geographical units of nation states of tiers of local government.

It is interesting, therefore, to consider the fundamental administrative units by which interdiscipinary institutional structures might act. For example, air-pollution management through either legal or fiscal means operates in regions where the air circulation can be mapped, e.g. Los Angeles.

4

Legislation and Pollution in Calcutta

There is nothing new in this. Successive generations of Calcuttans have taken the view that the city's acrid odours and obscured horizons are a recent problem, set against a relatively smokeless past.

However, a much longer history of air pollution is apparent from earlier accounts. By the eighteenth century, smoke was cited, along with heat, dust, humidity, and noisome smells, as one of the attendant hardships and health hazards for Europeans in Calcutta. The city was renowned for its insalubrious air. Calcutta was proudly labelled the 'City of Palaces' and the 'Second City of the Empire', but its architecture was obscured by thick winter mists while its cosmopolitan inhabitants were forced to breath a grey-brown muck. Colonial governments attended to the problem with a concern and level of expenditure which betrayed real anxiety. Calcutta became one of the first cities in the world to adopt smoke nuisance legislation in 1863—only ten years after London, and well before many European and North American cities. A special committee was formed to investigate the problem in 1879, and in 1902 the Smoke Inspector for Leeds, Frederick Crover, was employed at great expense to survey Calcutta's smoke and make recommendations for its abatement. Grover's report gave rise to the *Bengal Smoke Nuisances Act of* 1905, and the subsequent establishment of the Bengal Smoke Nuisances Commission, which carried out a systematic but selective smoke abatement programme throughout the colonial period.

The political urgency of Calcutta's smoke problem was closely bound up with the history and function of the city within the empire of British India. The seat of government until 1911 and the commercial capital of the subcontinent until the First World War, Calcutta housed a high proportion of the European military, administrative and mercantile groups which made up the ruling classes. But for all its imperial power, Calcutta was a city nested in swamps, with longstanding problems of overcrowding, disease, and extreme poverty. Its rapid population increase, with over one million inhabitants by 1911 and over two million by 1941, intensified problems further. In these conditions, the ethos of urban improvement was strong. The dominant European ideology contended that Calcutta was liveable only because the inherent dangers of an Asiatic city had been subordinated to the discipline of scientific control.

But smoke raised a different problem. It highlighted that Calcutta combined two radically different sets of ecological problems—one, the crowded streets and poor sanitation which Europeans associated with colonial Asia, and the other, the social disruption and heavy pollution more familiar from European industrialization. The combination unsettled common stereotypes, causing Lord Curzon to despair that smoke 'makes one forget that this is an Asiatic capital.' Though industrial smoke was not a prominent political issue among either imperialists or nationalists, it was an important focus for social conflict since it posed difficult questions, not only about the nature of urban society and the prospects for industrialization in India, but also the role and responsibilities of the state in the context of environmental degradation. Many of the features which are now axiomatic in environmental regulation—systematic monitoring, reliance on technical experts, technological remedies, and close collusion between industry and bureaucracy—were consolidated under the aegis of the Smoke Nuisance Acts. So, too, it was under the Acts that new techniques for policing industrial labour and disciplining the social practices of subordinate classses were introduced and consolidated. Through these developments the state acquired the capacity to construe and manipulate the quotidian experience of air pollution in an industrial city.

The Incidence and Character of Smoke

Calcutta was uniquely situated to suffer from aim pollution. A centre for heavy industry located close to the Bengal coal fields, the city was host to many types of emissions. Moreover, its topographical and meteorological characteristics tended to prevent the dissipation of smoke into the surrounding atmospheric sink. The combined effect of heavy emissions and poor atmospheric clearning bore directly upon the physical comfort of inhabitants, and many complaints were lodged. Official correspondence before 1900 reveals major smoke inundations had become a routine feature of Calcutta life by the late 1870s. Before considering the social responses to this problem, it is necessary to consider the general incidence of smoke in Calcutta's urban environment.

The perception and incidence of smoke are difficult to treat as separate issues. In general, the darker and stronger-smelling varieties of smoke elicited more comment, even though they were not necessarily the most prevalent or the most deleterious in their effects. Some fuels emitted relatively little perceptible smoke and yet produced compounds harmful to plant and animal life. Smoke, like any other physical phenomenon, is perceived in ways largely determined by conditioning and cultural associations. The extensive burning of drug and other light biomass fuels such as straw and crop residues was a distinctly Indian practice, and served to mark out differences between South Asian and European technologies. Francois Bernier, travelling with Aurangzeb in 1665, complained that the evening meal was typically cooked over a fire of 'cow and camel and green wood' which produced a smoke that was 'highly offensive, and involves the atmosphere in total darkness.' Bernier was not alone in finding Indian smoke repugnant. Since dung and light biomass remained popular domestic fuels in Calcutta throughout the nineteenth and early twentieth centuries, there was ample opportunity for complaint from European quarters. On the other hand, Europeans tended to tolerate and even romanticize woodsmoke from domestic fireplaces. Bengalis were inclined to ignore dungsmoke, but like Europeans, they frequently complained of industrial coal emissions.

Calcutta had well-established markets for wood, charcoal, and dung before the nineteenth century, and there was a lively trade from rural areas to feed urban demand. Dung was carefully collected, often mixed with straw or rice-husks, and then shaped into cakes for burning. Dung-drying was extensive within Calcutta itself: in 1848 the Municipal Commissioners recommended that the drying of dung for fuel be prohibited as a nuisance, though the proposal was not translated into law. Wood seems to have been preferred as a source of fuel where available, but it is possible that deforestation and increased urban demand brought about a greater reliance on dung, straw, and other low-grade biomass fuels. In some contexts, dung was clearly preferred over wood. Dung was not only touted as one of the five sacred products of the cow, it also offered the advantage of a longer cooking duration over a safe flame. Nevertheless, dung was the principal fuel only for the poor; those who could afford to do so purchased wood—and later coal, coke, and gas—for domestic purposes.

Despite the prevalence of biomass smoke throughout the colonial period, it was the dense black smoke from coal which attracted the most attention. The use of coal as high-grade fuel was not entirely, but it was only with the introduction of the steam engine that coal was used on a much larger scale. Steam engines were introduced for river navigation and modest industrial efforts by 1830. Coal did not immediately supplant wood as the primary fuel for raising steam, since unreliable supplies and high prices impeded coal consumption. But in February 1855 India's first proper railway was opened between Calcutta and the Raniganj coal fields, permitting a massive increase in the supply and distribution of indigenous coal. In the decades which followed, Calcutta was transformed into the centre of the Hooghly industrial corridor—an Asian equivalent of the Ruhr valley—with high levels of production and correspondingly high levels of air pollution. With its government mint, municipal water pumps, river vessels, ocean-going ships, railway locomotives, engineering workshops, and the growing number of jute mills and other industrial undertakings, Calcutta hosted nearly every type of steam engine then operating in South Asia.

Early on the British complained of the quality of Indian coal. In his 1867 survey of India's coal resources, Thomas Oldham concluded that Indian coals were high in ash content and normally provided only ½ to ⅓ the heat of average English coal. In Grover's more detailed study of 1903, he found that Indian coals could contain from 14.8 per cent to 47 per cent ash by weight, depending upon the variety and source. Apart from a higher ash content and lower calorific value, Indian coals produced more smoke than English coals, though a small number of clean-burning coals were available. Generally cheapter types of coal smoked more and produced less heat than more expensive varieties. Since most coals in India were found to produce a soft, poor-quality coke, the possibilities for developing a supply of smokeless fuels were strictly limited.

In addition to biomass and coal, a third category of fuels included oil and gas. The use of vegetable oils for lighting and cooking was widespread in the eighteenth century and continued into the colonial period.

5

The Role of Forests

The role of forests in environmental conservation as one of the most important components of the biosphere is well recognised. The forests are the largest, most complex and most self-perpetuating of all the ecosystems. From the point of view of flore and fauna they have the most diverse gene pool. It is in the forests that the natural regulatory processes excel, producing the most stable of all ecosystems. The forests therefore play a vital role in environmental conservation.

Our Hoary Conservation Tradition

The principle of conservation has all along been an integral part of the Indian ethos. This is borne out by our ancient scriptures and historical records. The best in Indian culture was born in the forests. The Aryan civilization was cradled in our forests and sour rishis who evolved the Hindu philosophy, lived in complete harmony with nature and meditated in the peace and serenity of the woods, to give us the supernal values and ideals through our ancient scriptures, the Vedas and Upanishads. Their ashrams were an epitome of man living in close communion with nature, with the trees, birds and animals. "Ahimsa Parmodharma" is a basic tenet of our religion and philosophy. Lord Buddha describes the forests as "a peculiar organism of unlimited kindness and benevolence that makes no demands for its sustenance but extended protection to all beings, offering shade even to the man with the axe who destroys it. "No wonder then, that Gautam sought the shelter of the Bodhi tree to become Buddha, the Light of Asia. The world's first recorded conservation measures were enacted in India during the third century B.C., in the days of Emperor Ashoka whose benevolence extended to all living beings. His edicts on stone, on nature conservation, survive even today. There is now an acceptance of the idea of the oneness of life and of our earth. The survival of man is dependent on the survival of animal and plant life. The hoary tradition of our country in conservation continues even today and we have the inspiring example of the bishnoi community in Rajasthan, Haryana and Uttar Pradesh, dedicated to protecting our trees and wild animals. The recent 'chipko' movement which emanated from Chamoli, in the inner Himalayas, is another striking reflection of this concern in the minds of the people.

Forests as an Important Facet of Environment

The important of forests in the welfare of makind cannot be over-emphasised. In whatever the forests fulfil, the touchstone and measure of their value is human weal and satisfaction. Late Shre K.M. Munshi defined its role beautifully in the words, "There is a balance on earth between air, water, soil and plant. Trees have a great place in the economy of nature. They hold up the mountains, cushion the rain and storms. They discipline the rivers and control the floods. They maintain the springs, they break they winds, they foster the birds. They keep the air cool and clean. They are the guardians of the perennial springs of water. They are the natural defenders of dust storms. They check erosion by wind and water and they preserve the fertility of the soil."

The future of mankind is inextricably linked with forests, both as a national resources and as the strength behind a healthy environment. The ecological perspective has to embrace diverses aspects ranging from sustanance linkage of the rural communities and the demands of a developing economy to the dictates of scientific management assuring sustainable utilisation of the national resource.

Nature has lavishly endowed our country with a rich biotic heritage, with nearly 5% of all known plant and animal species found on the earth. Oure flore and fauna include about 13,000 species of flowering plants, 30,000 species of insects, 10,500 species of molluscs and other invertebrates, 2000 species of fish, 140 species of amphibians, 420 species of reptiles, 1200 species of birds and 340 species of mammals, besides a vast variety of oceanic fauna. No other country in the world, area for area, excels India, in the variety of its biological reserves.

The Forest Crisis

Despite our rich and hoary tradition in nature conservation, and the need to preserve our forests inviolate, there have been many factors which have proved inimical. The grim reality is, India with as high as 15% of the human and 14% of the cattle population of the world, has barely 2% of forests of the globe. The enormous and relentless pressure on our diminishing forests is therefore at once manifest. Nevertheless, of late, there has been a general awakening to protect our forests, which are virtually under a seige. This awakening however has to be translated into reality. "One touch of nature, makes the whole world kin" says Shakespeare.

It would be pertinent to recall an apt observation by UNESCO on the "environment crisis", which is an follows:

> "Imperfect understanding of the natural mechanisms which make possible the maintainance of life on earth; disregard of the unintentional effects of technology, in particular, the various forms of pollution; poor management of the soil, forests and water; unbridled consumption of fossil fuels; uncontrolled urbanisation; the relegation of the rural population to a marginal position; and the crushing of traditional cultures-these are the most obvious and most frequent disadvantages of the change that is taking place in the relations between man and his environment."

In this context, we need to ponder, as to how we could achieve material progress, without impairing the environment. Our late Prime Minister Smt. Indira Gandhi, in her stirring address in 1972 at the United National Conference on Human Environment at Stockholm, advocated "Development without Destruction", as the cardinal principle of planning. Being sensitive to the harm that thoughtless and unimaginative economic development can cause to the environment, through reckless destruction of forests and the resulting problems of soil erosion and floods, she was perceptive to the supreme importance of conservation in planning. Like a seen, she drew upon the fountain of wisdom and insight, from our ancient culture, to rivet attention to nature being imperilled by despoilation.

Permanent Needs the Forests Fulfill

The following are the paramount needs of the country which the forests are required to fulfil:

- Maintenance of environmental stability through preserving and where necessary restoring the ecological balance that has been adversely disturbed by an insufficient appreciation of the role of forests and consequently their rapid despletion;
- Conservation of what remains of the natural heritage of the country through preserving the existing natural forests along with their vast variety of flore and fauna which represent the tremendous biological diversity and genetic resources of the country;
- Checking denudation and soil erosion in the catchment areas of rivers in the interests of soil and water conservation, the prevention of floods as well as droughts and for the control of the premature siltation of costly reservoirs;

- Checking erosion along treeless banks of rivers, in the hot and cold deserts of Thar and Ladakh and their environs; on large stretches of waste lands in the hilly and drier parts of the country; on areas denuded of vegetation by shifting cultivation and on barren sea shores;
- Safeguarding and sustaining the welfare of tribal communities which are almost entirely dependent on the use of various forest resources. Generating productive employment for the large number of unemployed and under-employed people in the rural sector in programmes of afforestation of degraded lands, whether Government or privately owned, and the need for generating forest-based employment for rural artisans;
- Generating productive employment for the large number of unemployed and under-employed people in the rural sector in programmes of aforestation of degraded lands, whether Government of privately owned, and the need for generating forest-based employment for rural artisans,
- Meeting requirements of fuelwood, fooder, minor forest produce and small timber for the rural and tribal populations primarily through the afforestation of all denuded and degraded lands, regardless of their classification;
- Eliminating the pressure of industry on natural forests through the afforestation of all denuded and degraded lands;
- Encouraging more efficient use of forest resources by all sectors of society;
- Providing amenities for recreation and conservation education in urban and rural environments; and
- Creating a people's movement for achieving these objectives.

6

Educational Impact of Projects for Improvement of Rural Housing

Introduction

Housing and environmental conditions in human settlement in rural areas of developing countries are far from satisfactory. According to available evidence there is considerable shortage of rural housing in many of the developing countries. Taking Asia as a whole the magnitude of housing needs during 1985 is given in Table. It may be seen that rural housing deficit is about three times the urban housing deficit.

Table : Urban-rural Population, World and Asia, 1885

(Million)

Regions	*Urban*	*Rural*
World, Total	2198	2750
Developed Areas	928	347
Developing Areas	1270	2403
Asia	943	1931
East	500	682
Middle-south	270	867
South-east	116	318
South-west	57	65

Source: UN Monthly Bulletin of Statistics.

Environmental Conditions

While it is true that the villages and rural settlements in the developing countries of the region are not overcrowded as the large cities and metropolitan areas, in many other respects housing conditions are unsatisfactory. Low cost rural houses usually consist of just one room hut. In India, for instance, some 34 per cent of the rural household occupy only one room.

Inadequacy of accommodation for the family and overcrowding are therefore evident. In many cases, for want of a separate kitchen, looking fires in the living room fill the house with smoke.

The areas surrounding the houses are often polluted owing to back of adequate drainage and sanitation. Latrines are either not built or are insanitary and inadequate to serve the number of people that use them. Potable water supply is generally not available and water for drinking is obtained from wells, ponds, rivers, streams, etc., which are often polluted or are exposed to the risks of pollution.

With few exceptions, rural villages have not been planned. Their layout is generally haphazard or disorderly. The villagees are mostly congested with narrow winding lanes, which become muddy and slushy, particularly during the rains. The villages and neighbouring towns are also not properly connected with good roads for inter-communication and this inhibits their economic and social development.

Several reports and observations have referred to the poor conditions of rural housing as being most important cause of poor health of inhabitants in rural areas. A number of surveys have also revealed that the vast majority of rural households in the developing countries subsist with only the barest minimum of or often without essential housing services and facilities.

Environmental Education Through Demonstration Projects

The NBO is engaged in promoting improvement in rural housing and environmental conditions. Twelve Rural Housing Wings of NBO have also been established in the country for research, training and extension in rural housing and village planning. These wings are located at Chandigarh, Bangalore, V. V. Nagar, Howrah, Jodhpur, Srinagar, Trivandrum, Varanasi, Ranchi, Simla, Madras and Gauhati.

NBO is implementing a scheme for construction of clusters of demonstration low cost houses along with items of environmental improvement. So far 73 cluster demonstration housing projects have been taken up in selected villages in different geo-climatic regions with varying socio-economic conditions as shown in the map of India.

In each cluster demonstration housing project a set of 20 houses catering to the needs of economically weaker sections of the society are put up at lowest possible cost making improved use of local materials and self-help. On a plot of 90 sq.m (100 sq. yards) a house is put up to provide minimum accommodation in a plinth area of 20 to 25 sq. m comprising of atleast one living room, separate kitchen and an a verandah. An additional room can be constructed for future requirement.

A separate built-in sanitary latrine and a bathing plàce are also provided in the house at the near backyard where a cattleshed can also be put up. There is a front yard for meeting the family needs of rural occupations.

Improved used of local materials is made building more durable houses. The aspects related to protection of houses in areas prone to floods, earthquakes, cyclones etc. are also given due attention. The cost of each house is not to exceed Rs 5000 in all parts of the country except high altitude hilly regions where the cost can be Rs. 7500. Alongwith more durable house, items of environmental improvement such as provision of smokeless chulah, sanitary latrine, drainage, bathing place, arrangement of water supply, paving of streets, orderly layout of houses to achieve a density of 60 houses per hectare with provision of open spaces, community hall, biogas plant, plantation of trees etc., is also made in each cluster demonstration housing project.

With the technical guidance of NBO and assistance rendered by the Regional Rural Housing Wings of NBO, large scale rural housing schemes have been taken up in many states in the country such as 25,000 houses in the state of Punjab, 5000 houses in each district of Assam, 54,000 houses in Rajasthan, 75,000 houses in Kerala and 65,000 houses in Andhra Pradesh.

Impact of Environmental Education

As has been stated earlier the cluster demonstration housing scheme is intended to motivate the rural people in improving their built environment. The promotion of informal education of the rural people is therefore the main objective of the scheme. In this paper the impact of the cluster demonstration housing scheme has been briefly highlighted indicating the important practical gains achieved, the lessons learnt and supporting measures that are required to propagate housing and environmental improvement in rural areas have also been identified. Although informal surveys, studies and interviews have been made by NBO and RHWs to assess the impact of cluster demonstration housing projects in improving the built environment, it is rather difficult to make a proper assessment of the impact because of several technical, social and economical factors that are involved such as the new concepts which bring about a change in life style of the rural people, tradition bound nature of the villagers which is deep rooted in beliefs customs, rituals etc., a poverty of the rural population and comparatively high cost of construction of houses and provision of essential services for environmental improvement which are much beyond their affordable limits etc. The process of environmental education through cluster demonstration houses has generated.

(i) Awareness about the innovative techniques of construction of houses at low cost making improved use of local materials and self-help and for environmental improvement in and around the dwellings.
(ii) Participation of the beneficiaries in implementation of the innovations in meeting their housing and environmental needs.
(iii) Proper use of the facilities provided and their up keep and maintenance.
(iv) Skill formation through developing know-how and participation in the construction works.
(v) Training of artisans who had been employed for adoption of innovative use of materials and techniques.
(vi) Feed back of experiences in the use of dwellings and the essential services for environmental improvement.

Practical Cains

As has been found from actual observations, the following positive gains have been achieved through the cluster demonstration housing projects:-

(i) Tidy appearances of the housing cluster put up
(ii) Improved sanitation in and around the houses
(iii) Availability of water supply
(iv) More double houses
(v) More liveable and comfortable dwellings
(vi) Better quality of environment.

In-depth studies are required to ascertain the extent of practical gains achieved over a period of time from the cluster demonstration housing projects.

Lessons Learnt

The survey and studies undertaken have brought forth several lessons that can be learnt in educating the rural people in the improvement of housing and environmental conditions through cluster demonstration housing projects, These include:

(i) Changes in life-style is greately dependent on social and cultural background of local people which should be given due consideration.
(ii) Slow-Change is due to slow absorption of new ideas on account of social, economical and cultural factors.

(iii) Extent of acceptance is dependent on life style of the rural people, the level of technology south to be introduced and the cost of construction to be incurred etc.

(iv) Actual adoption of technique is dependent on the ability of rural people, techniques, new ideas and to put up in practice.

(v) Proper use is dependent on the know-how acquired and the techniques of proper up-keep and the maintenance of facilities and disadvantages of new facilities provided.

Supporting Measures Required

In order to propogate the practical gains achieved and to account for lessons learnt in the cluster demonstration housing projects, the following important supportive measures are required to be taken for further propogation of inovative techniques methods for improving housing and environmental conditions in the human settlement in rural areas.

a. Day-to-day technical advice needs to be provided in the proper use of dwellings and various facilities provided for environmental improvement.
b. Techniques and methods of up-keep and maintenance of dwellings and essential services which are provided need to be imparted to the local population.
c. Financial support by way of loans and subsidiesare required to be made available who intend to adopt these improvements in housing and environmental conditions.
d. Cost of houses and essential services should be brought to affordable level by adoption of appropriate technologies.
e. Feed back of experiences over a period of time should be organised for making necessary improvements and modification taking into account the local situations.
f. Investigations and research in local problems should be undertaken to evolve appropriate technologies taking into consideration the variety of local conditions.

Conclusions

The scheme of putting up clusters of demonstration low cost houses in various geo-climatic conditions with varying socio-economic situations is an important five-year Plan of NBO which is being implemented by its regional Rural Housing Wings. The assessment of the impact of environmental education generated by the scheme has clearly brought out the following:

a. At least one cluster demonstration house should be put up in each district in each state in order to have country-wide impact of the scheme.

b. Wide publicity through audio-visual and mass media should be made to popularise the innovations that have been success fully adopted in cluster demonstration houses.

c. Innovative techniques for building houses employing improved use of local materials and techniques for environmental improvement should be included in the curricula for imparting education to architects, engineers, builders, plannars, etc. as well as to artisans engaged in building construction work.

d. Informal training programmes and exposition at school level should be introduced for propagating impoved housing and environmental conditions.

7

Environmental Education and other Cross-Curricular Themes

Economic literacy is arguably a key requirement of the whole curriculum for young people if they are to understand the causes, effects and ways of tackling environmental problems whether they be on a local or global scale. Economic perspectives should be an integral part of any discussion of environmental issues alongside other perspectives such as, political, social and technological since 'students should be encouraged to examine and interpret the environment from a variety of perspectives. (NCC, 1990). The need to examine the significance of the economic dimension is important for a variety of reasons. Economic factors are a contributory and often major cause of environmental problems. Some of these environmental problems are more serious and concentrated in their effects because of economic factors. Technological solutions to environmental issues are sometimes available but not taken up because of cost factors. The unequal distribution of wealth between the 'North' and 'South' has an influence on the scale of environmental problems and possible solutions. There is a growing recognition that the misuse of the environment has economic costs and an acceptance that when cost benefits we weighted up, only a portion of degraded land can be satisfactorily rehabilitated. Finally, there is a growing acceptance of the need for sustainable development in which conservation and development are planned together.

How can the Integration of EIU into Environmental Education be planned for?

Both EIU and Environmental Education are important cross-curricular themes in the National Curriculum. In order to aid teachers in planning the curriculum, guidance for Environmental Education draws on a model developed in the 1970s, 'education about, through, and for the environment'. In *Curriculum Guidance 7*, teachers are presented with a list of environmental topics for guidance but teaching Environmental Education may best be approached as a series of issues many of which are controversial and in which the importance of economic literacy is a key to understanding. How can EIU be integrated into environmental education particularly in those subjects in which the environmental problems are an important part of syllabuses, particularly Geography and Science? In a consideration of any of the major environmental problems there are a number of questions which can be investigated in relation to these four dimensions.

Planning the Integration of EIU into Environmental Education

(1) What are the indicators of the problem?
(2) How is the problem perceived?
(3) Where is the problem occurring?
(4) What is the scale and rate of the problem?
(5) What are the causes?
(6) What are the implications?
(7) What measures can be taken to avoid, mitigate or rehabilitate?
(8) What is economically feasible?

A Growing Interest in Global Environmental/Developmental Issues

Not until the 1960s was there anything but patchy interest in the environmental dimensions of development. In 1972, the UN Conference on Human Environment in Stockholm was instrumental in bringing countries together to consider the future of the number of studies expressing environmental/development concern notably the Brandt Report in 1980. In the late 1980s, the World Commission on Environment and Development (The Brundtland Report) marked a issues with the move to sustainable development. There is now a general acceptance that there are a series of major global environmental problems. These are:

— global warning;
— damage to the ozone layer;
— deforestation, particularly of the tropical rain forest;
— acid rain;
— soil erosion;
— desertification;
— the threat to endangered species of plants and animals.

How Significant are These Problems?

Each of these global problems are characterized by their scale and complexity, their interdependence, the threat that they pose to the planet and the fact that they require international cooperation to tackle them. There are some clear trends: land is being lost from production at an alarming rate; global levels of carbon dioxide and the ozone levels already give cause for concern; the loss of genetic resources as species become extinct is serious and accelerating; the effects of toxic chemical and other pollutants are significant and increasing; the problem of soil erosion is potentially the most serious form of resource depletion. The problems are world wide and particularly affect the South. Some developing countries appear to be trapped in a downward spiral of interlinked ecological and economic decline. Sub Saharan Africa and Amazonia are often cited as particularly prone to environmental/development problems but there are many other areas affected in both the North and South.

What are the Economic Causes of Environmental Problems?

There are several explanations of environmental degradation from the environmntal development literature which involve economic considerations. One consequence of the economics of production is that entrepreneurs tend to maximise profits in the short term possibly incurring degradation and then invest all or part of their profits elsewhere. External factors acting on production systems can cause or contribute to environmental degradation, notebly could market forces, neocolonialism and the action of multinationals. The terms of international trade are seen by many economists as having caused increased economic dependency and indebtedness in developing nations. Many developing countries spend much of their revenue repaying foreign debt and consequently are less able to afford conservation measures. Timber, minerals and land are ruthlessly exploited to try to generate desperately needd foreign exchange. The unequal distribution of wealth between the North and the South is an important underlying factor accounting for a high consumer demand in the more afluent North, putting pressure on the South to develop their resources. The search for profits and the desire to maintain living standards in the North is resulting in a threat to several endangered species notably the tiger, the whale, the elephant and the dolphin. For instance recent evidence suggests that the Blue Whale population has declined to 450 in the whole of the southern hemisphere. The killing of the whale is not an economic necessity for Norwegian fishermen but whale meat is a traditional part of the Japanese diet!

What are the Economic Implications of these Environmental Problems?

All of these environmental problems have an adverse effect on production, standards of living, quality of life, sometimes including life and death. They have both direct and indirect costs. Soil erosion results in a decline in crop productivity and the indirect costs such as the silting of reservoirs result in an associated loss of water, power and increased flooding. The direct costs are vast, the indirect costs are considerable. For instance in Ethiopia, soil erosion caused by decline in forest cover cuts agricultural production by a million tons a year. Some have local and distant effects; river flooding in Bangladesh, partly caused by the removal of the forest cover in the upper reaches of the Brahmaputra, annually affects 20% of the country ruining crops and causing loss of life. Desertification is one of the most serious problems facing the world and annual loss of land world wide to significant desertification is an area larger than Belgium. It was calculated that, world wide, dry land degradation in 1987 cost 26 billion US dollars a year in lost agricultural production. It is estimated that acid rain costs the German economy 28 billion dollars a year. Crude estimates of the value of crop losses due to acid deposition are calculated to be costing Europe 500 million US dollars a year.

How can the Problems be Tackled?

From the late 1960s, there was a movement for those involved in development to encompass a consideration of environmental issues. The concept of ecologically sustainable development seems to have been first voiced in the late 1960s. Later the world conservation strategy in 1980 and more recently the Brundtland Report (1987) and the Peace Report (1989) gave the concept wider publicity. This approach demands an anticipate/avoid rather than a react and cure approach to development. It demands that the question be asked, 'Is it ever acceptable to engage in actions that reduce the potential of future generations to meet their needs?' (Barrow) Distinctions have been made between sustaintable development and sustainable exploitation. Whereas the latter is about maintaining a dynamic equilibrium between production and consumption, sustainable development is linked to economic growth. It has been suggested that sustainable development should ensure that the poor have access to secure livelihoods and that the distribution of wealth does not become more unequal. The main problem in controlling these problems is the cost factor. It is recognized that the Third World cannot to pay for the environmental policies which the rest of the world demands, yet we still have a situation where net transfers from the South to the North exceed 50 billion dollars a year largely because of interest payment on debts. Some of this money could be used to fund 'debt swap appraoches' which already have been used to combat deforestation in the tropics. For some environmental problems, the technology is available but the economic costs are considered to be prohibitive. For instance, future power stations in the UK (a significant cause of acid rain in Western Europe) will have better pollution control which will reduce emissions by 90%. Most of the world's desertification problems could be reversed with present available technology but at a cost.

This chapter has focused on the relationship between economic and industrial understanding and environmental education. It is argued that a basic economic literacy with an understanding of economic concepts such as opportunity, costs, profit supply and demand, terms of international trade, global interdependence and sustainable development are essential to understand the background to, causes, effects and possible strategies to tackle environmental problems. A balanced treatment of any environmental problem should ensure that these dimensions and themes and concepts inform planning in the secondary curriculum.

Health Education

One common characteristic of the cross-curricular themes is that they can all focus on controversial concerns, the therefore there is considerable overlap within topics such as 'population growth' and 'food production'. Like other themes, the curriculum area of health education has much to offer environmental education.

People's relationship with the environment are interwoven with their personal health and lifestyles. In terms of environmental education it is important to remember these are global relationships involving a complex network of interdependent systems, (ecological, physical and chemical, geological), in which human societies and institutions are components. Human populations make enormous changes to the earth, influencing, by their dependence on particular agrarian economies, the disappearance of important habitats, and bringing about the extinction of many species. Human population growth has a two-fold effect: it fuels both environmental destruction and human destitution. We know that nearly a quarter of humanity lives in poverty, unable to meet basic needs for food, shelter and clothing. We know that there is a relationship between high fertility and high mortality. Contraceptive help is crucial in many countries and yet, only slowly, is the concept of sustainable growth and development gaining ground.

One of the dangers inherent in environmental education is that pupils become so overwhelmed by the enormity of the world's problems that they lepse into apathy or cynical resignation. Too often the environmental problem is presented as the determinant of the human response. For example, increased incidence of UV light from the sun is associated with increased incidence of skin cancer. By examining the power of people to alter the environment through changes in attitude and by concerted effort, the thinning of the ozone layer can be examined in terms of assessing aerosol usage, using CFC free products, and developing policies to limit their use. All of these approaches are within reach of the 'environmentally friendly' school.

There are a number of curriculum approaches which can be adopted to promote health education. The essentially individualistic approach taken in *Curriculum Guidance* 5 provides for health education which is about bodily functions and personal growth, and which has an emphasis on knowledge, attitudes and behaviour of individuals. In examining the balance, between people and their immediate environment, the nine components of the health education curriculum provides numerous opportunities for exploring ideas central to local as well as global environmental issues.

In *Curriculum Guidance 3* reference is made 'to the importance of the spirit and ethos of the school.' The aims, attitudes, values and procedures of a school are fundamental to the success of any health education programme, and profoundly influence the extent to which individual awareness, responsibility and personal decision-making develop. Therefore, the concept of the 'health promoting school' (Harrison and Edwards, 1994) does provide an opportunity to:

> take a wider view including all aspects of the life of the school and its relationship with the community e.g. developing a school as a carring community.
>
> (Young and Williams, 1989)

Teachers who can create a classroom climate in which levels of selfesteem are high, in which there is respect for individual needs, opinions and differences, and in which there are open and trusting relationships, will encourage learning about health and, in turn, enhance aspects of environmental education. Like other cross-curricular themes, environmental educational involves focussing on a wide range of concepts, processes and perspectives. The learning environments, within and beyond the classroom, need to reflect the attitude and values which the school's environmental programme is trying to cultivate.

Pupils' involvement in their own surroundings is important in both health and environmental education. According to the Learning Through Landscapes Trust many school playgrounds:

> are hideous wastelands, following years of institutional neglect and short-term planning: the most under-used educational resource in the country.
>
> (Learning Through Landscapes, 1992).

The Trust is tackling the problem of transforming such school sites. The school grounds provide many opportunities for pupils taking responsibility, for example, by becoming in setting up and maintaining a pond or a wild life area and maintaining records of birds, plants, butterflies, and so on. Such direct experience provides a rich opportunity for young people to care for that environment and to seek to improve it.

One of the components of *Curriculum Guidance 5, 'Psychological Aspects of Health Education*', emphasises mental health, emotional well-being and stress, and thus a 'health promoting school' can seek opportunities to address some of the same criteria as the 'green' school. This can be done by:

- Providing bright, cheerful, purposeful and welcoming displays to celebrate success and to provide a stimulus for learning and further achievements.
- Provision of signs that are supportive in tone and wording.
- Creating resource areas that are comfortable, well lit and well heated.
- Creating safe movement patterns, and places for pupils to keep warm and dry outside lesson times.

Overall an environment that is free of litter, graffiti and clutter, with pleasant eating and toilet arrangement and safe places for everyone's possessions, can provide pupils, in both the 'hidden' as well as the 'formal' curriculum, opportunity to acquire knowledge and understanding of factors affecting mental health and emotional well-being.

Another health component, 'Safety', provides pupils with the opportunity for:

> Acquisition of knowledge and understanding of safety in different environments...of skills and strategies...to maintain their personal safety and that of others.
>
> (NCC, 1990a)

A 'health promoting school' can sell 'dayglo' armbands to young pedestrians, and crash helmets to young cyclists as well as teach the Green Cross Code and offer the chance to participate in crycling proficiency schemes. Much can be done to extend pupils' awareness of road safety and personal responsibility. By using local road safety officers, material from RoSPA, and literature from police 'drink-driving' campaigns (with links to the health component 'Substance use and abuse'), issues like driver fatigue, stress, drug use and other distractions can be highlighted and linked to causes of accident. Pupils can be encouraged to think about risks and risk-taking, accident blackspots, weather hazards, and to learn about emergency first aid procedures.

Health and safety at work is also an environmental issue which has links with both health education and Personal and Social Education:

> The quality and safety of the environment in which working and learning takes place can have a profound effect on outcomes and should be paramount importance to the managers of any establishment.
>
> (Baczala, 1992).

There are EC regulations concerning computer use and aspects of the work situation, such as the quality of the screen and basic ergonomics in the work situation. These regulations have arisen because of rising incidences of repetitive strain injury, eye srain, stress, VDU emissions and links to miscarriage during pregnancy. Pupils could consider to what extent ergonomically designed keyboards and 'mice' have helped to alleviate some of these health problems.

The health component 'Food and Nutrition provides opportunities to consider the implications of there being just three species, wheat, rice and maize, which provide half the world's food. Another four species, potato, barley, sweet potato and cassava, bring the total to three quarters (Lean, 1990). Such dependence on few crops is dangerous to health, and disease spreads rapidly through mono-cultures, well-illustrated by the Irish potato famines of the 1840s which caused a fifth of the country's people to die. Human population growth and the need for increased food production are inexitricably linked. Pupils can be taught to understand that successes in food production have benefited some societies with huge increases in productivity. However, there is also opportunity to consider whether we can afford the resultant losses of species.

Finally, there is an important health component entitled 'Environmental Aspects of Health Education'. At Key Stage 4 the NCC guidance (NCC, 1990b) suggests pupils should:

> understand how legislation and political, social, ecnomic and cultural decisions affect health;
>
> develop a commitment to the care and improvement of their own and other people's health, community and environment.

The opportunity for community action in health, raises pupils' awareness of environmental and political limits to health, but is clearly at odds with the individualistic approach taken in the rest of *Curriculum Guidance 5*. Good case study material for use in secondary schools has been offered by Bainnes (1990) who, far instance, allows pupils to reconcile the dilemma of making farming and conservation more conpatible.

> Education for sustainability is a vital precondition for people's health and well-being for the future...We believe the foundations of sustainable development are built mainly on the way people think, the values they hold, and the decisions they make...
>
> (UNCED, 1992)

More ideas for the classroom can be found in Harrison (1993).

Thus health education for the environment provides a vital context for environmental education. It is clearly the responsibility of all teachers of health education to enable pupils to form opinions and to make decisions about the links between human activity and the environment.

Careers Education

Environmental education in the curriculum is under threat as the cross-curricular themes have no mention in the Dearing Review of the National Curriculum. (Dearing, 1994) Geography, a major vehicle for Environmental Education, is no longer compulsory beyond Key Stage 3. Meanwhile Careers Education and Guidance is a theme that must be found time at Key Stages 3 and 4. Initiatives from the Employment Department and Department for Education confirm its role in the curriculum. All this is at a time when the employment climate and opportunities for young people can only be fully understood in global, ecological terms. The relationship between Environmental and Careers Education can be understood by considering the current provision in schools.

A pupil may experience Environmental Education as elements in many subjects and activities. The support for such a programme depends upon the views of the senior management team of a school and the professional enthusiasm of the staff. There may be a post of responsibility for an Environmental Education coordinator but it is rare that a school has this theme as a key element in its school brochure of gives it prominence in the annual report to parents. On the other hand, careers may have an explicit timetable, or at least a recognisable programme of input. This is supported by the Recording of Achievement process especially with the expansion of Youth Credits. Careers education and guidance is also given status in school by the activities of external agencies such as Careers Services and the priorities of the Training and Enterprise Councils. A school is likely to have a careers guidance post of responsibility with non-teaching time allocated for the work. They may have administrative support and attend meetings of senior management. The activities of the school, linked with industry, are likely to be given publicity as opportunities arise to do so. Despite this there is evidence that the provision of careers education and guidance in schools varies considerably. (Cleaton, 1987 and 1993) Indicators which may measure such provision are curriculum time, resources, qualified staff allocation, policy statements and evaluation systems. The proposition is offered that this patchiness exists because of a lack of understanding of the conceptual basis of careers education. One must examine the, often simplistic and unhelpful, concept of CEG in order to demonstrate a common framework of understanding for careers education and guidance and environmental education.

Principles of CEG

For some years the commonly used conceptual framework underlying careers education and guidance was summarised in the acronym DOTS:

- Decision-making;
- Opportunity awareness;
- Transition skills;
- Self-awareness.

Much curriculum innovation and development was based on DOTS, underpinned by *Careers Education from 5-16* (HMI, 1988) The Education Reform Act 1988 made implicit the role of CEG by placing a statutory responsibility on schools to provide a broad and balanced curriculum which:

promotes the spiritual, moral, cultural, mental and physical development of pupils at the school, and of society,' and 'prepares pupils for the opportunities and experiences of adult life.

Curriculum Guidance 6 (NCC, 1990) identified five components of CEG as follows:

Careers Education, a planned programme in all four key stages;

- Access to information,
- Experience of work,
- Access to individual guidance,
- Recording Achievement,
- Planning for the future.

While the statement of the components is a helpful one, some practitioners still prefer to base their curriculum thinking on DOTS because they feel it offers a clearer conceptual framework.

However, there is an even more profound issue to be explored. The underlying purpose of careers education is crucial. Law (1992) identifies certain concept clusters relating to CEG:

CEG can based upon matching pupils to vacancies.

There is the concept of enabling students to develop their awareness of self and be more self-directed in dealing with opportunities which arise.

Directive work may be undertaken in which pupils are coached for the opportunities which are available.

In networking pupils are taught to make the most of the networks available to them, whether through Record of Achievement interviews of community service.

Finally there is the concept of educating, with a focus on learned behaviour.

In this last idea Law identifies learning place in four stages:

gathering and organising impressions;

checking and understanding points of view;

dealing with problem-solving and decision-making processes;

accepting responsibility in a situation for oneself and others.

A conceptual approach to CEG, which is based on 'educating', may provide the most helpful development pathway. Any other concept would seem insufficiently rigorous to allow young people to analyse the wider world.

The problem arises as to the extent to which these activities are an entitlement which all pupils should experience and how far they are experienced by self-selected groups. This is an issue of curriculum design.

CEG: An Environmental Approach?

If an 'educating' approach to CEG is accepted, then one must define the concepts which pupils might reflect upon the how these relate to environmental education. For example:

- A pupil on work experience at a car plant sees the company's Environmental Policy displayed prominently and reports on the monitoring group discussion.
- A Year 11 Geography lesson on the proposed expansion of a major city airport with local environmental consequences, employment opportunities and impact of tourism.

These examples might be considered aspects of a reflective analysis of careers from an environmental perspective. Crucially, teachers must identifly the values such activities involve otherwise environmental policies may be seen, solely, as 'litter campaigns' in a different form. Schools will need to identify the trends which shape the career experience of pupils throughout their working lives. These perspectives must be built into a CEG programme in partnership with environmental education. Key markers may be:

> Hundreds of millions of people will be seeking jobs that biotech farning and automated manufacturing may make redundent. It will also occur just as multinational companies...increasingly compete for global market shares and employ every device...to achieve that aim.
>
> (Kennedy, 1993)

What is said in schools about individual career opportunity and progression?

> Clearly there exist companies and individuals (chiefly professionals providing high value added services) who benefit...and are keenly positioning themselves to gain further advantage. On the other hand, there are billions of impoverished, uneducated individuals in the developing world, and tens of millions of unskilled, non-professional workers in the developed world, whose prospects are poor and in many cases getting worse...leading to mass migrations and environmental damage from which even the 'winners' might not emerge unscathed.
>
> (Kennedy, 1993)

What schools teach of human ethics, interdependence, cooperation and competition, i.e. education, implies a deep understanding of why our world is changing. There are opportunities to discuss how other people and cultures feel about these changes, what we all have in common and what divides cultures, classes and nations. Moreover, while this process of inquiry ought, if possible, to be tolerent and empathetic, it cannot be value free '...Because we are all members of world citizenry, we also need to equip ourselves with a system of ethics, a sense of fairness and a sense of proportion.' (Kennedy, 1993) The purpose of education, vocational preparation or a broad education for global citizenship, are signposts for an evaluation of the whole curriculum by schools from a careers education and guidance and environmental education standpoint.

Curriculum Design

PSE often becomes a 'slot' for all the bits of the curriculum which could not be fitted into another area. A more rational approach to curriculum design is needed, based around the fundamental values which pupils need to explore to prepare them for adult and working life. One may need to organise a curriculum which is based on a conceptual base which helps the young person, whatever its mode of delivery. The work by Buck and Inman (1993) suggests certain criteria for curriculum planning:

Objectivity and the use of evidence to examine a range of ways of life, encouraging a critical perspective judging the quality and quantity of evidence.

Using Concept which enable the leaner to put experience in categories, organise them and then analyse their knowledge and experience. Key concepts include:

- choise, need, want, division of labour, rights and responsibility.
- participatory and experimential teaching and learning styles which develop skills for independent learning including personal and interpersonal. IT, communi-cation, decision making.

Buck and Inman Identify nine key questions including:

'What is the nature of our rights and responsibilities in everyday life?'

'In what ways are the welfare of individuals and societies maintained?'

'On what basis do people make decisions when faced with particular choices?'

'How do people organise, manage and control their relationships?'

'What is the balance between individual freedom and the constraints necessary for cooperative living?'

These questions explore the core values of our global human culture and encourage further cross-curricular work. Reviewing core values produces holistic curriculum design. In terms of a syllabus one could envisage a sequence of study programmes from 5 to 16 which explore these equestions in a development way. A framwork is constructed for more detailed exploration of specific issues in environmental education and in CEG. One may be freed from the tyranny of a content-driven approach and can educate pupils in the true of the concept.

8

Integration of Ecosystem and Urban Systems

Introduction

Though efforts were made to understand the evolutionary process of urban system and ecological systems in isolation, comparatively less efforts were made to understand the similarity of the process of evolution between these two systems. It is interesting that in the process of the evolution of urban system and ecosystem almost a similar pattern is observed; however with an exception that the urban system lacks the self maintaining capacity (homeostatic mechanism) unlike that of the ecosystem. If the urban system also have this capability then the environmental problems in the urban system would have been minimum. However, to a certain extent this capability can be created within the urban system through environmental planning (a proces in which architects, planners and Economists will have a major say) and for that we should know the similarities and dissimilarities of both the systems in a detailed fashion.

Similarities Between the Evolution of Ecosystem and Urban System

In a natural ecosystem:

1. All the organisms and physical environment are interdependent and related to one another and activity of one element affects the other,
2. The evolution take place in a simple pattern and progress towards a complex and diversified pattern,

3. Changes in one component affect the other component,
4. As evolution progresses the systems become mature and attain self maintaining capability (homostatic mechanism),
5. Stability of the system is maintained through recycling/cycling of components and natrients. These are the main laws of the evolution of ecosystem, though many more functions/laws can also be observed.

Now let us examine how the urban systems evolve and maintain themselves. In devloping urban systems where industrial activity is the 'motor' of development, the development/evolution begins with a single system and gradually it develops into a complex system. For example, when a small industrial unit accompanied by a small set of population starts operating, a small settlement comes up; activities like construction of houses, roads, shopping complex, etc., take place which in turn attract more population, and the increae in population directly adds to increased economic and commercial activity and more industrial units having forward and backward linkage with the earlier unit come into being (which again attract more population) and the momentum takes place in an interwomen fashion.

The above relationship is strengthened in an enduring manner through production-consumption linkage, i.e., all the consumers depend upon the manufacturers and manufacturers depending on consumers (like the food chain relationship in the ecosystem, i.e., the dependency of one species on the other) and both manufacturers and consumers depending on primary resource producer/suppliers. As the momentum goes on increasing, the intensity of activity pattern changes and the entire system (urban system) moves towards a complex and diversified pattern of relationship, but with instability (unlike the ecosystem). This instability is attributed to the by-products/negative externalities (waste or pollution) created both by the consupmtion and manufacuring activities and the waste/by-product thus created is not absorbed in the system in which virgin resources are always in demand and a portion of that resources is steadily converted into waste which continuously get accumulated.

But in an ecosystem, the relationships are maintained in such a way that the waste product/byproduct of one system becomes a supporting factor for the other. For example, in a virgin soil system the rainwater helps initiate the vegetation and the vegetation gives shelter and food to an array of animals and birds and the waste product/by-product of both vegetation and animal help increase the health of soil and that soil again get strengthened though this process for maintaining an enduring vegetative and animal systems and thus progress towards maturity with self maintaining ability.

It is interesting to observe that whereas in as undisturbed ecosystem (i.e., ecosystem without man's intervention) the system by itself maintains stability, the urban system is not able to do so; and not only that the instability of urban system is spread over (in the form of pollution and waste) to the ecosystem and thereby creating total instability as the vicinity of the influence of the urban system progresses so rapidly that it disturbs the smooth functioning of the ecosystem (like transforming green belt areas into housing and industrial areas) and thereby enhance the complexity in both the systems and the total instability is the final outcome.

Role of Environmental Planning

Now let us enquire whether it is possible to create a self sustaining ability within the urban system and thereby maintaining stability of the total system (both ecosystem and urban system) through environmental planning. This can be done, we are able to identify the terminal points of relationships of urban system and the mechanism/process of accumulation and the effects of by-products-wastes. That is,

(a) how the manufacturing activity create and accumu-late wastes and how the waste interact with other systems;

(b) how the consumption activity create and accumulate waste and how the wastes interact with other systems; and

(c) how service activities and infrastructural activities create wastes and interact with other system, etc. When we analyse this problem we will know about the origin (the linkage/terminal points), process of interaction (how it affects the other elements), its different character and manifestations.

One this is done, we will be able to identify the resource value and nuisance value of waste from each terminal point. When we will be able to determine the resource value (through recycling) we will be in a position to find ways to make the urban system absorb that byproduct and thereby help increase the stability of the system. Again, when we will be able to determine the nuisance value of the by-product of the urban system, then we will be in a position to make arrangement to avoid the interaction of the byproducts with other elements in the system which again help increase the stability of the urban system.

To make this concept more clear, let us take the example of an urban system. An urban system operates within the ecosystem and both the systems are related inverteratly. As we did explain above, in an evolving urban system there are three main subsystem which create unabsorbable by-products/waste within the system. They are:

a. Manufacturing (production)
b. Consumption, and
c. Infrastructural activities (construction of roads, buildings, communication networks and transportation).

Let us analyse how manufacturing activity (production) create waste and interact with other systems. Different manufacturing processes in an urban system create many types of gaseous, liquid and solid pollutants. When the gaseous pollutants, mainly pollute air, the liquid pollutants toxicate land, surface and groundwater; and solid pollutants (solid waste) mainly pollute land and water (many of these toxicants are biologically non-degradable). The pollutants thus entered into the urban ecosystem through different linkage points (air, land, surface water and groundwater) now enter into the metabolic system of human, animal and plant systems. Man gets maximum toxicants as the toxicants accumulated in the animals and plants also get into man's metabolic system through food chain mechanism and create disorders. When air and Water pollution create different types of disease in man and animal, in plants they result in significant reduction of production and thus the resource renewability process within the ecosystem is negatively affected. Though to a greater extent intangible, the nuisance value (quantification of negative externalities) of all these interactions can be quantified.

Now, to reduce/avoid the negative interaction of these by-products and the subsequent disorders on man, animal and plants, these by-products can be transformed into useful resources (as the wastes/ pollutants are mismanaged resources). An urban system, as we have stated above, create waste/pollutants through its different economic activities (like production,. consumption and service activities). All these waste/ pollutants can be recycled and convered into resources (both renewable and non-renewable). Recycling of any pollutant is having double advantage i.e. when we recycle a pollutant, we will be able to recover more resources (thereby add to resource stock and less demand on virgin resources particularly non-renewable resources like metal and minerals) on the hand, and reduce the process of non-renewability accuring among renewable resources (like retardiation of plant growth due to air and water pollution) base and thereby, again, add to resource stock. Thus, recycling will become a balancing factor between urban system and ecosytem and if the entire waste created by an urban system is recycled, the integration between urban system and ecosystem become complete and the quantification of by-products become feasible.

These are some of the micro level (i.e. identifying the area and interaction of each elements and sub-systems in the urban system) environmental tools which we can deploy. Through this approach, as show above, we will be in a position to quantify different by-products of the urban system (like air pollution, water pollution and solid waste) and also the process of diffusion and interaction. Understanding of these aspects will pave they way for achieving the 'space-species activity equilibrium' (i.e., in a given space what activity can be undertaken, and what will be the intensity and how much human and other population it can support, and what will be the sustainable resource it can create to support the system and what will be the intensity and the aprocess of by-products/waste created and how these elements are interacting in a comprehensive and integrated fashion).

Integrated Environmental Approach

As we have explained above though both the systems evolve separately, they follow some sort of similar pattern also affect each other; because the urban system evolves itself in space' (i.e. within the ecosystem) and that is why achieving the space-species-activity equilibrium' is the key factor in achieving the harmony between urban system and ecosystem. Besides using the micro environmental tools/ techniques we have shows above, a package programme of macro environmental techniques are to be deployed to obain harmony, between ecosystem and urban system. These are: (a) Space-species approach, and (b) space-activity approach.

(a) Space-Species Approach

Space-species equilibrium explains that what will be the equilibirum relationships between the different species (vegetation and animals including man) and a given space, what will be the optimum level of the population of vegetative species (trees, grass and other cultivation) and animal species (including man) and how both the systems can survive in a mutually benefiting fashion (positive symbiotic relationship). That is, how vegetation helps animals (including men) to survive and animals help vegetation to survive (vegetation provides food and shelter to animals including man, how animals enrich the soil system for the survival of trees and grass through its excreta and decomposition of body and how man help increase the grass and trees). To achieve this, the vegetation productivity (biomass productivity) of the space has to be determined first and then calculate how much animal population including man can survive on that system in an optimum fashion. If once that is done, then the space-resource-species equilibrium can be achieved. Here, the change in population of animals and man has to be adjusted with the biomass productivity (resources): otherwise the system may tend towards disequilibrium (with man in the top of the food chain pyramid and animals in the next ladder).

Further, any artificial inducement to create a productivity enhancement (mechanisation and all other factors introduced by man) in any system will create disequilibrium. For example, when we introduce mechanisation in agriculture, soil health is deteriorated, (due to deep tillage and fertilizers and posticide pollution) and as a result the biomass production is reduced which directly affects the dependent species negatively and thereby create a disequilibrium in the system. Another disequilibrium impetus will be initiated from they by-products of synthetic products introduced into the system. Again, most of the non-biodegradable synthetic waste neatively affect the zoological and botanical species and thereby cause illness and reduction in productivity. For example, the synthetic waste remain within the ecosystem for many years and negatively interact with the metabolic system (including the genetic system) of plants and animals and thereby cause drastic reduction in productivity) (and also cause changes in the community and the food chain relationships) which again results in a reduction in the availability of resources and hence a total disequilibrium.

(b) The Space-Activity Approach

Thus, after attaining the space-species equilibrium (which also imply for resources equilibrium), the space activity equilibrium can be worked out. Space-activity equilibrium exploins how in a given space having a given resource accruability the entire human activity interact in an equilibrium fashion so that both the systems (ecosystem and urban system) co-exist in a mutually benefitting manner. Here, the structure and pattern of activity (housing, industries, roads, other related constructions, their intensity and interacting mechanisms, etc.) has to be examined and the resource support available from that given space also has to be considered. For example, in a given space what can be the maximum different industrial activity that can sustain, taking into account its negative effect on the existing ecosystem and the overall effect on both the systems including its population attraction (through employment) and population support (through income and goods and services), mechanism. Keeping this as a guiding factor, housing, roads and other infrastructure have to be worked out again and keeping in mind their negative impact on the ecosystem and the overall effect on both the systems.

In a space-activity approach, different economic policies which directly or indirectly affect (or determine the intensity and direction of above activities which in turn affect the space-activity equilibriumn) the activity pattern is also included. For example, the investment policy, infrastructure, wage rate, saving, consumption pattern, etc., directly affect the activity pattern and any change in such a policy instrument will reflect on the space activity equilibrium.

Relevance of Gandhian Approach

It is here that the Gandhian approach becomes compatible with the space activity approach. The Gandhian approach emphasis on a local resource base planning. Keeping the smooth process of renewability processes within the ecosystem, i.e., any action which negatively affect the renewability process is not adopted. In the space-activity analysis also, guiding factor is the same. In Gandhian approach the resources within the overall sustainability of existence for all the dependent system (man, animal, plant, etc.). Further, that resource base should be the basic supporting factor for employment, or in other words, the employment planning should be done in such a way that it should not go beyond the resource-population equilibrium. The intensive technological involvement in the production processes which negatively affect both resource-population equilibrium and resource renewability (attributed to effluents/pollutants emitted from high technology involved in production processes) process is avoided. Again, as we postulated earlier, the effect of economic policies and consumer behaviour affect the space activity approach. The Gandhian approach to consumption is also relevant to the concept. That is, a consumption pattern/behaviour should be within the compatible limits of resource availability within a region (or a simple consumption pattern which will suit to both resource availability and ecosystem balance). Hence, in the space activity approach the Gandhian approach (Economic Policies) can play a major role.

Conclusion

Thus, though we have explained a theoretical framwork for intergrating ecosystem with the urban system (after indentifying the similarities and dissimilarities) which have complete applicability only on a 'Virgin Space', and its full implementation is slightly difficult the manner in which we have explained above. However, it can partially be applied to solve the existing environmental problems. For example in an urban system with a space-species disequilibrium, particularly with regard to vegetation, this approach will be useful. Likewise, to control the activity pattern again this can be applied to the existing systems so as to achieve space-activity equilibrium.

However, one important thing to be remembered here is the involvement of experts from many different fields/disciplines. For instance in the process of the implementation of the space-activity approach only an architect can decide/understand how the built structures should be erected in that given space so that aesthetic harmony can be achieved between the urban system and ecosystem. Again when the question of augmentation of vegetation comes in the process of implementation of space-species-approach a botanist/agricultural scientist has to decide about the harmonious combination of vegetation with space and built structures. To decide about the activity pattern of industries; only the engineers and economists can suggest a harmonious combination. Finally when the question of integration of different elements comes, it is the environmental planner who can give the answers.

Thus, it can be summarized that the evolution of urban systems and ecosystems is almost on the same pattern except that the urban systems lack the self-maintaining ability due to their inherent failure to absorb the byproducts/waste within. However, this ability can be inculcated to a certain extent in the urban system through different environmental planning approaches/techniques (and to achieve that a new breed of environmental planners and administrators having multi-disciplinary talents and understanding have to be created to shoulder that responsibility).

Environmental Education in The Universities in Karnataka

The main guiding principles of environmental education are: (1) Environment education must be precise of the economic, technological, socio-political and ethical factors and practices that create ecological imbalance, and (2) The environmental education must depict the relationship between the man and nature as different from the one that has emerged during industrialization. The education must be critical and inventive. Critical means the present social, political, economic and cultural practices where- as inventive refers to cultural ethics for the survival and prosperity of man.

The modernization of industries and the mechanization of mining activity and mineral processing have threatened the natural resources which include mineral wealth, groundwater and the fauna and flora of the region. From the syllabii of the post-graduate courses in various universities it is observed that most of the universities lack the aspect of environment, as the enviroment is very much essential for an earth scientist, chemist, metallurgist, mining engineers. In the present paper the authors have prepared a syllabus for the post-graduate students which shall enable them to understand the environmental impact on the natural resources etc.

The post-graduate education in Karnataka consists of two years duration in different branches. In some cases like Geography, Geology and Mathematics, three years duration course exists in some of the unversities. The syllabii for the post-graduate courses do not emphasise environmental aspects of various fields. The environmental educational problem at postgraduate level must be interrelated with various disciplines like physics, chemistry, biology, mathematics and management. At present there are five universities in the state, but not a single university provides environmental education separtely. The Karnataka University offers Environmental Geology at post-graduate level as a part of a paper in M.Sc. course. The syllaby cover the following:

Man and Earth, Earth processes that affect man-Earthquakes, surficial movements. Man's alterations of environment, gaseous, liquid and solid wastes and their disposal, radioactive waste, water pollution, water resources, projects, coastal installations, managing and environment—the physical system including the oceans. The biologicial system. The above does not emphasise the practical application of the subject. In our opinion there should be thorough practicals of projects for identifying the ecological imbalance of the environment. The students be trained in analysing polluted samples and remedial measures to be suggested for the protection of the environment.

We fell that there should be separate post-graduate courses in environmental management. The qualification for the course must be wide open to all the graduates of natural sciences.

Model Syllaby For Environmental Engineering Course

Air quality, water quality, toxic substances and environmental health, municipal solid wastes, energy, natural resources, ecology and biotic resources, Wastal ecology, Human settlement and landuse, noise pollution, environmental regulations, global environment, economics.

Apart from the above aspects there should be some practical exercises as necessary.

From the above study the following guidelines may be considered for the framing up of a post-graduate course in environmental education:

1. There should be a separate department of environment in the Universities for providing a post-graduate course and also research facilities must be made available to tackle the environmental problems.
2. Every district must be provided with an environmental cell to identify the problems of the region.
3. The environmental cell may communicate with the common man about the hazards of disturbing the environment.
4. In order to protect the environment the post-graduate course is a must in the Universities of India.

ENVIRONMENTAL ENGINEERING EDUCATION FOR MINING ENGINEERS IN DEVELOPING COUNTRIES

Introduction

Mining is a hazardous profession and every year many miners lose their lives through strate falls, explosions, ınundationss, rockbursts and other accidents in mines. Mining operations can also result in hazardous situations for the general public as well and can cause grave demage to the surrounding environment. In the past, mining engineers have not paid much attention to the protection of environment. But growing public concern for environmental protection has forced the governments of most advanced countries to formulate stringent legislation in this regard. In the developing countries, appropriate technologies have to be found which will keep the environmental damage due to mining to a minimum but at an acceptable cost.

In the past, environmental protection has not found place in the curricula of mining engineering courses. The current emphasis on the subject has necessitated the introduction of this topic at the undergraduate level for general appreciation, as well as the development of post-graduate courses on the subject for training specialists. The purpose of this paper is to discuss the topics which should be included in the syllaby for undergraduate and postgraduate courses on environmental Protection in Mining Areas.

Hazards to General Public and Environmental Damage

The hazard to the general public from accidental failures in an industrial plant or facilities was dramatically highlighted by the catastrophic methyl isocyanate leak in the pesticide plant at Bhopal on the might of 2 December 1984, killing more than two thousand people. The health of several thousand persons may be permanently impaired. Similar disasters of a smaller scale, involving general public, have occurred in some mining areas as well. One can cite the 1966 case of Abarfan tip slide in South Wales and the 1972 Buffalo creek dam failure in USA. As recently as July August 1984, working of the huge OK-Tedi gold mine in Papua-New Guinea had to be suspended due to leakage of toxic sodium cyanide in the nearly Ok-Ma river. Limestone mining in the Garhwal Himalayas has been suspanded under the orders of Indian Supreme Court because of the possibility of environmental damage by such mining.

Besides sudden hazards, the mining process causes slow and gradual degradation of environment through discharge of polluted water, toxic gases and dust, deforestation, land damage, and changes in hydrological conditions. The landscape of the region may also be greately altered through creation of tailing dams, waste heaps and mineral dumps. Where blasting in resorted to, noise and blast vibrations cuase damage to nearly structures, accentuate landslide problem in hilly areas and drive away wildlife.

Land Damage due to Mining

Looking at the Indian coel mining scane we find that lamd damage is a particularly several problem. The projections for coal demand show that the output has to be raised from the present 145 mt to 375 mt by the year 2000 AD. The bulk of the increase will be obtained by opening new opencast mines: the share of surface mined coal is expected to go up from the current proportion of approx. 47% to about 60-65% by the turn of the century. Mahendru (1985) estimates that around 3 milion cu.m soil and rock mass has to be moved every day to achieve the target of surface mined coal by 2000 AD. The extent of land damage depends on the geomining conditions, especially on the thickness of seam or seams mined and the quarry depth. For an averge quarry depth of 100m, a stripping ratio of 4 cu. m/t of coal and outside dumps and associated activities requiring almost the same area as that from which coal is stripped, nearly 8 ha of land will be damaged per million ton of coal production (Banerjee, 1982). With the projected 225 mt per year of open cast coal an area of 1800 ha of land would be damaged per year around the turn of the century. By all accounts this is a very large area and so much land should not be allowed to become wasteland. Like the surface mining of coal, the surface mining of other minerals is also increasing and causing serious problems of land degradation. Most advanced countries already have enacted stringent legislations and the developing countries are following suit to protect the environment from such damage due to mining.

Education Mining Engineers for Environmental Protection

Mining engineers of the future must learn to win the minerals with least damage to the environment. The undergraduate mining engineering curriculum should include a paper to give the students a general appraciation of the environmental problems due to mining, and the possible abatement measures. The aim of this postgraduate (Master's level) course should be to turn out spacialists who can plan and undertake measures relating to abatement of environmental damage due to mining.

Environmental sciences is a multidisciplimary science. Small concentrations of pollutants in water and air can be determined only with a good knowledge of analytical chemistry. Pollution disperation in the atmosphere as well as transmission of noise and air blasts are influenced by weather conditions, and therefore, some knowledge of meteorology is also assential. Many other measurements such as particle size and mass, air and water flow rates, temperature and sound level, etc. require a good knowledge of physics. As the affects of environmental pollution are felt by the living organisms—both plants and animals, and the toxicity of an equatic environment is generally expressed in terms of the survival of a specified animal species, the mine environmental engineers should be able to appreciate also the basics of life sciences.

An elective paper on Mining and the Surface Environment has been introduced in the final semestar of the undergraduate mining engineering course at the Indian School of Mines, Dhanbad, from 1983. The syllabus of this course covers amongst other topics, mineral production and population growth, visual impact, land reclamation and subsidence, air and water pollution, tailing dam, noise, airblast and ground vibration, and legislations relating to environmental protection. We are not aware of a similar elective course being offered by any other mining department. The subject of environmental protection is however covered as a part of the general subject of mine design. For example, in Colorado School of Mines, the undergraduate "Surface Mine Design" course covers analysis of elements of surface mine operation and design of surface mining system components with emphasis on minimization of adverse environmental impacts. The paper also covers the environmental impacts.

Graduate Courses for Environmental Protection in Mining Areas

Various mining departments in different countries have introduced environmental protection in their postgraduate courses. In the Colorado School of Mines, the graduate course on "Mine Environment Planning" deals exclusively with anvironmental protection. The course on "Mine Industrial Hygiene" deals with mine atmospheric contaminants and noise pollution.

In the Royal School of Mines (Imperial College of Science and Technology), London, topics related to mining and the surface environment are covered at the graduate level and two of the Masters thesis submitted in 1982-83 were related to environmental topics. The Imperial Collage of Science & Technology has started a separate course for Environmental Technology where one year M.Sc. course is offered. A student taking above course has to take the core courses and then oapt for specialisation in environmental problems related to his special interest including mining. The core course on "Primary Mineral Production and Energy" for example includes "constraints on mineral production, limits to growth, mining and pollution, world energy requirements, fossil fuels, pollutions and energy" etc., and the optional courses on Mineral Production and the Environment" covers topics on environmental impact of mining, waste utilization, reclamation and legislative concepts.

Structure of a B.S. Environmental Engineering Programme

The Middle East Technical University in Ankara (Turkey) offers a 4-years B.S. degree in Environmental Engineering since 1973. This is rather uncommon. The anvironmental subjects may be broadly grouped under two heads of Environmental Sciences (Environmental Microbiology and Environmental Chemistry), and Environmental Technology (Water, Air and Land Pollution Control) and the amphasis in the graduate programmes may be given on either of the groups depending primarily on whether the course in offerred by an applied science faculty or an engineering faculty.

Conclusions

Environmental Engineering education in many universities has started as an offshoot of civil engineering departments. However, where the need of an industry is more specific, as in mining, it would be better to formulate separate and specific programmes. Some universities abroad have already introduced full undergraduate courses in Environmental Engineering but we feel that the inter-disciplinary nature of the subject can be better covered in a postgraduate programme. There is also a need for short-term industry-oriented courses for in-service people who did not banefit from such coureses earlier.

9

The Citizenship and Environmental Education

Environmetal issues are important to young people. Organisations with an environmental focus are among those with expanding membership. Without empowerment, participation and skills of communication, progress can be difficult for young people who wish to work for an environmentally-sound future. Citizenship education is about participation, community involvement, rights and responsibilities, democracy, the law, and the provision of services by voluntary, state or private services. Citizenship and environmental education share many common characteristics:

Environmental Education may be thought of as comprising three linked components:

- Education about the environment (knowledge);
- Education for the environment (values, attitudes, possitive action);
- Education in or through the environment (a resource).

(NCC, 1990a)

This concept transfers well to education for citizenship. If young people are to be encouraged to take citizenship seriously, they need to be included as participative members of the community. School and the local community are stages upon which this participation can be played out. Education about participation is the knowledge or curriculum content upon which aspects of citizenship are based. Without some knowledge, discussion and decision-making are lacking a firm foundation. Education for participation involves values, attitudes and skills (of debating, negotiation and presentation). To persuade others or to consider, seriously, they views of others, demands competence in these aspects of working. It is about involvement in activities of a participative nature using the community as a resource, and people outside the school as community partners.

The aims of education for citizenship are to:

- establish the importance of positive participative citizenship and provide the motivation to join in;
- help pupils to acquire and understand essential information on which to base the development of their skills, values and attitudes towards citizenship.

> Education for citizenship develops the knowledges, skills and attitudes necessary for exploring, making informed decisions about and exercising responsibilities and rights in democratic society.
>
> (NCC, 1990b)

The Speaker's Commission on Citizenship stresses that:

> the opportunity for learning provided by the community experiences will provide an indispensable springboard to encourage sagments to make a voluntary contribution in later life. (HMSO, 1990)

Schools need to make clear to students what they are aiming to do as coherence in the learning process is crucial. Work which combines environmental awareness and education for citizenship has an important role. Similarly there are many links between national curriculum core and foundation subjects and the cross-curricular themes which need to be made.

> If, through the themes of environmental education and citizenship, schools are expected to re-educate society to its responsibilities they will have a key role to play by involving children from their earliest years in learning from their surroundings, using the local environment as a medium for enquiry and discovery and as a source of material for realistic activities. Pupils need to feel free to move into and out of the school building from an early age as part of the whole process of learning.
>
> (Thompson, 1993)

There are many activities which satisfy the congruent aims of education for citizenship and environmental education.

Nursery School

Children focussed on flowers in a project entitled. 'The Darling Buds of May'. After selecting one flower a week to study the children then plant seeds and bulbs and watch them grow. They set up a flower shop in the nursery after visiting their local florist to see how it should be done. They reconstructed Monet's paintings of the garden at Givermy. They visit the bulb fields in Spalding before creating their own flower festival which becomes the culmination of the project. The streets around the nursery are lined with crowds of flag-waving adults and children as a parade of flower floats passes, by, decorated with daffodils and tulips. Alongside these floats, parents, teachers and nursery nurses are accompanied by an energetic group of children, colourfully dressed to represent the flowers and countries of Europe.

Citizenship Concepts: Work and leisure, community.

Environment Concepts: Plants and animals.

(Walters, 1993)

Playground Project

An inner city infant school wants to improve the playground facilities to encourage more diverse and cooperative playtime activities. Teachers collect information by observation, video and questionnaires about the children's feelings and opinions on current and future provision. Meetings are held to discuss feedback and make plans. A grant and other help from *Learning from Landscapes* (Learning Through Landscapes, 1986) is obtained for changes to the playground.

Citizenship Concepts: Community, individuals and groups, use of leisure.

Environment Concept: People and communities, cultural aspects of the environment.

(Centre for Citizenship Studies in Education, 1993)

Key Stage 2, Active Citizens

A class, in a school beside a busy road, decides to tell the local council their concerns about a subway, constructed to provide a safe way of crossing the road, but little used by the children as they find it a threatening environment. They survey opinion by questionnaire and study the problems the subway presents. In English they write prose, poetry and letters to the council complaining of dirt, darkness, graffiti, vandalism and water lying on the surface. By taking action the pupils gain in self-esteem and confidence. They focus on a local concern and do all they can to improve a situation.

Citizenship Concepts: Community, being an active citizen, public services.

Environment Concepts: People and communities, impact to transport on the environment.

(Edwards, 1993)

Secondary School Activity

A school council decides that the school environment needs to be tidier. A survey is conducted of the views of local residents and primary and secondary school pupils and teachers. The findings are used to plan an anti-litter campaign, involving picking up litter, a poster competition, talks by older pupils to assemblies of younger year groups, group work on how best to react if you witness litter being dropped.

Citizenship Concepts: Community, being an active citizen.
Environment Concepts: People and communities, buildings, management of waste and recycling.

(Centre for Citizenship Studies in Education, 1991)

Key Stages 3 and 4, Conservation

The extension of an industrial estate threatens a pond containing protected species. Local schools use the opportunity to debate the need for employment against the desirability of conservation and consider alternative solutions. They work with the council, developers and the fire brigade to re-establish the pond and all its wildlife in a new location.

Citizenship Concepts: Work employment and leisure, public services, being an active citizen.
Environment Concepts: People and communities, endangered specis and conservation, destruction of natural habitats, impact of industrialisation and urbanisation.

(Centre for Citizenship Studies in Education, 1991)

'The Night Shelter Project'

One Upper School and the contributory Middle and Lower Schools work together. Each school conducts its own project work on 'Homes and Homelessness'. All come together on one day near the end of the summer term, at the Upper School, when they share project experience by means of an exhibition and, using waste resources provided for them, they build shelters in groups of four. They sleep out overnight in these shelters. Homelessness is a local issue. Human needs include food and shelter. Follow-up work in each school is varied and covers international, national and local projects, housing provision in the parental home, setting up home independently, rented or purchased accommodation and budgeting.

Resources: Children's Society materials (Children's Society 1991), CSV and Leaving Home Project (Hope, 1989). Local Council, local churches, Police, companies provided materials for shelter building.

Citizenship Concept: Community, being a citizen, the family, democracy, public services.

Environment Concept: Buildings, industrialisation and waste, people and communities.

'The Mineral Debate'

This is a simulation for secondary schools in which participants adopt roles of those with vested interest in whether or not further extractive industry is to be allowed around a town. The County Council's long term plan in to restrict further gravel extraction and an embargo has been placed on the allocation of any further licences to excavate. However, a major notional company has discovered extensive deposits of a valuable mineral. This discovery has occurred at a time of a national recession which has badly affected the local population. Participants debate the issues and the council votes to decide whether the development application should be allowed or rejected.

Citizenship Concepts: Community, being a citizen, democracy, work, employment and leisure.

Environment Concept: Soils, rocks and minerals, uses and management of resources, effects of extractive industries, people and communities, buildings, industrialisation and waste.

(Thompson, 1993)

Key Stage 3—'Industry in Focus'

A whole year group is involved in a weak-long project. Teams of pupils engage in study of nine branches of local industry. Objectives are to increase knowledge and understanding of the economic and industrial world, local environmental, local career opportunities, and political issues. The week starts with presentations from UK Atomic Energy Authority and Friends of the Earth to illustrate conflict existing at national level between industry and the environment. Each pupil visits two of the following local industries: a chemical manufacturing company, a waste disposal firm, sand and gravel extraction, water treatment, supermarket 'greening', organic and non-organic farming, testing involving animals and recycling. The visits are reported and issues raised such as the chemical industry creates smells, increases traffic in thc locality but provides employment. Sand and gravel extraction has had a devastating effect on the countryside but provides materials essential for road construction. Pupils witness the efforts of a responsible company carrying out restoration work. Each pupil will develop indepedence of thought, respect, tolerance and understan-ding of effective action to deal with matters felt to be intolerable.

Citizenship Concepts: Skills of communication and taking action, investigation, reporting, evaluating, decision-making.

Environment Concepts: Effects of extractive industries, water, plants and animals, waste.

(Thompson, 1993)

INFORMATION TECHNOLOGY

Bob Hopkins

There are several examples of lessons and projects that illustrate the use of Information Technology in Environmental Education. They follow the structures first described in the National Curriculum documents for the two disciplines. *Curriculum Guidance 7: Environment Education,* describes the coverage of the subject in terms of education about, for and in the environment (NCC, 1990). Non-statutory guidance for Information Technology describes the development of Information Technology capability across five stands which have recently been defined in two themes. (Dearing, 1994)

Dearing's recent report to the DFE emphasised that information technology is fundamental. Therefore, although many of the ideas described below are equally accessible without a computer. IT can develop an increased awareness of the environment and vice versa.

Learning ABOUT the Environment

A CD-ROM called *Water* (Academic Television, 1993) contains information ranging from skiing to oil spills. A large database may be researched and individual case studies such as Dolphins, The Thames Barrier, etc, considered. Water can be studied from political, industrial, recreational and other perspectives. However, each theme is described with a mixture of video clips, sound commentaries, text and still pictures. The potential of the compact disk is only just entering schools, but as each CD is equivalent to around 500 ordinary floppy disks, they are a significant advance in accessing information.

Learning FOR the Environment

Sometimes ecological disasters happen in the vicinity of the school but more often, a sensitivity to environmental issues has to be developed in our pupils secondhand. A computer simulation called *Fishkill* can illustrate what happens. It offers the opportunity for pupils to roleplay the part of environmental scientists who are faced with an emergency situation. A quantity of dead fish in a stretch of previously unpolluted river are found. To a time-scale decided by the computer, the scientists must decide what to do. They can take water samples, examine the poisoned fish and test water unstream of the disaster. The samples are then returned to the laboratory and tests carried out to determine the cause of the deaths or the degree of pollution. The scenario can be decided or created by the teacher in advance. Pupils may have to prove a case against a factory and its industrial waste or against a farmer's excessive use of insecticide. The problems of proof, of accuracy and of diplomacy all have to be faced and overcome.

Learning IN the Environment

Datalogging is the name given to the computer's ability to record certain changes in the environment. This would normally be difficult if you wanted to monitor a riverside or bat box. The computer would be vulnerable to the elements and far from its source of power. Datalogging boxes such as 'Sense and Control', however, can be set up at the computer and then detached to be used at the work site. They monitor light levels, temperature, pH, oxygen and other environment factors for periods up to two days. Instruments known as light gates could be located at the entrance to bird boxes and the frequency of the arrivals of bluetits to feed young measured. School children, thus have access to the rigorous observations formerly the province of the dedicated hobbyist or profesional. For example, the bacterial activity inside a cowpat might be enough to maintain a temperature above that of the surrounding areas. Datalogging equipment could quickly be set up to test the insulating properties of groundcover in snowy conditions. The kits need to be returned to the computer in a field centre, laboratory or classroom so as to download and examine the results. However, there is the prospect of serious computing in the field.

Theme One—Communicating and Handling Information

The new A1-MI road link provided a good opportunity for a local secondary school to abandon its timetable for some year groups and to devote the best part of a week to investigating the development of industrial estates on nearly land. Graphics programmes were used to design an industrial development, word processed letters sent to obtain the information necessary to develop can parking facilities, and amenity areas incorporating access for those with special needs. Desk-top publishing programms were used to produce the plans and to persuade the local authorities and action groups that the developments should take account of the natural and working environments. IT-produced letters and plans lend authority to voicing matters of concern, advice or protest on environmental issues to politicians, newspapers and planners.

In another example children were asked to follow up their observations of the structure of the daffodil flower with a description of reproduction in plants. A carefully prepared overlay for Prompt Writer on an Overlay Keyboard ensured success in sequencing events for a group of children whose inability to produce structured writing could have made this a difficult, demotivating task. The pupils were not only successful but also highly motivated to take their work further. IT allowed them to concentrate on the ideas under review and be released from the delays involved in normal sentence construction.

There are times when the sheer quantity of information can make searching for evidence of information very difficult. Back copies of the country's newspapers are now available on CD-ROM. This makes it possible to research, for example, the contribution to the nuclear debate made by the *Times or the Guardian* newspapers.

Similarly, no study of the weather at Key Stages 2 or 3 in complete without some reference to past and current weather statistics. The current weather may be monitored by hand or with a datalogger. 'Is this wet for July?', 'What is meant by a miserable summer?', are both questions which require reliable statistics. A database such as 'Pinpoint' on the Acorn or 'Crass' and 'Information Workshop' on RM computers can structures these statistics in an accessible and searchable way. Many of the statistics are already available from meteorological stations around the country, although not always for use on computers. The usual database structure involves records and fields. In the case of weather data the records are likely to be the days and the fields will be the types of statistics gathered for each day. Typical fields might include date, rainfall, wind direction, temperature, wind speed and cloud cover. There is no reason why one field might not be the acidity of any rain that fell during a 24 hour period. The 'Watch' organisation have the necessary kits to make the measurements.

When learning about the environment, database can be created or used to find information on minibeasts, butterflies, animals and so on. Once again the new CD-ROMs have a role to play and two of the first group of CDs to become available include *Creepy Crawlies* which includes details of 70 of the world's most photogenic beasts with text, sound commentary and video clips. The other is called *Mammals* and is a fairly comprehensive view of some of the world's mammals, again with video clips, stills and animal sounds.

One of the best examples of a useful database is called 'Pondlife' (Granada Television). There are three parts to this programme. The first assumes a pupil has approached the computer with a jam jar containing a pond creature. The computer prompts the pupils with questions about the creature such as the number of legs, wing cases and size. From the pupil's responses the computer identifies the creature with a picture and name. The second part of the program is a database of information about any of the identified creatures which are likely to be encountered in the pond environment. The third part of the program models a pond or stream and its behaviour when populated with various life forms and when polluted in various ways (see next section).

An old, yet under-used program is called 'Branch' (Flexible Software) which facilitates the production of branching identification classifications. Pupils are shown pictures of a variety of moths and butterflies, for example, and encouraged to find questions which can be applied to all the butterflies and moths. The 'branching' system will divide the creatures neatly into two groups and teach the pupils some of the distinctions within the generic term 'butterfly'.

Theme Two-Investigating Models and Control using IT

Modelling is the process where the outside world is modelled in some way on a computer screen. The working of a food chain can be replicated on a computer and the affects of pollution on the creatures concerned can be determined without any loss of life. The 'Pondlife' program can be used to model the animal and plant populations in a pond or stream. The computer first asks the user for the dimensions of the pond and the types of vegetation found there. There program goes on to ask for the creatures that might be found there and adds them to the model. When the simulation is ready the species can interact and the way the pond reaches a balance of species is shown. However, the balance can then be deliberately disturbed by, for example, pesticides, flooding and several other factors. The effects are studied in a time sequence allowing dangerous processes to be modelled safely.

Sometimes the factors that need to be manipulated are statistical and the number-crunching can be accomplished very easily by computers. A spreadsheet such as 'PSS', 'Grasshopper' or 'Excel Starting Grid' can easily be adapted to show the effects of culling elephant or seal. Too little and the environment takes over, sometimes with its own brand of cruelty or sacrifice, too many and the population falls into decline.

The laboratory is an excellent place to look for evidence about growth or animal body structure. The same instruments used in the field to monitor temperature or to keep track of the comings and going of bats, can also be fixed up, via a 'Sence and Control' box to record the growth of plants. Such questions as, 'Is the rate of growth affected by the amount of light, minerals in the soil or the amount of water available?', can all be tracked on the computer. Similarly the hypothesis that small mammals are more vulnerable to frost and the consequences of heat loss than larger mammals, can also be tested by looking at the rates of cooling associated with the contents of large and small vessels in the laboratory.

One might also consider the use of computers to capture satellite images from space, to monitor weather fronts perhaps or study 'Landsat' images which can pinpoint changing land use in every field in a country. This is an expensive process for the school. In many cases, however, the expense of IT has already been met. Most schools have access to computers, to datalogging equipment and to satellite images. Those schools without access, often primary schools, could still make use of the facilities via their local authority advisory service or their local secondary schools. At the simplest levels, there can hardly be a school without its own supply of word processors. databases and spreadsheets and all can be used for environmental education.

Environmental Education and Practical Considerations

Conservation Organisations and Schools

There is no better way for children to understand environmental concepts than by becoming in the practical application of the principles concerned, i.e. 'learning by doing'.

Many organisations make opportunities available for pupils to participate in conservation. There are several options which are easily accessible to schools, with fruithful relationships to help children understand the importance of the links between global and local issues. Pollution, transport, overpopulation, loss of habitats and decreasing biodiversity are reflected in the school's immediate environment. Pupils can also learn to challenge the economic assumptions which usually dominate the arguments put forward about how one should care for the environment. They can come to appreciate that conflicts of interest will arise.

The global effects of environmentally-harmful activities must be understood so that pupils appreciate that the issues do not just involve Britain. Friends of the Earth and Greenpeace are campaigning organisations which collect data on international topics as diverse as the disposal of radioactive waste, overfishing in the North Sea and Brazilian mahogany production. The World Wide Fund for Nature privides schools with information on how wildiife is being affected by human activities. There are many ways in which children can be helped to do something about these issues through such organisations, who are always keen to expand their youth sections. They provide material for pupils to carry out projects, arrange events and join sponsored activities. Children can become better informed in their conversations with friends or family about how to adjust their lifetyles to be less harmful by using less water and electricity, eating fewer of the endangered species of fish, recycling materials, etc. The scenario presented by these organisations can be overwhelming so it is important to relate them to what children can do in their own sphere to contribute towards the solution. Too much bad news on its own can make children and teachers feel powerless and without hope, which is counter-productive.

On a national scale there are other organisations which can provide schools with valuable support. The Learning through Landscapes Trust is an organisation set up to help schools make better use of their grounds for conservation. They run regional conferences for teachers to give them practical advice. The Young People's Trust for the Environment and Nature Conservation is also worth contacting, as in the Council for the Protection of Rural England. The latter has commissioned a national report on how much of our countryside is being lost to development. Their 'Agenda 2000' provides valuable background for teachers whose pupils are investigating the effects of mineral extraction for example. If a school in England requires funds to set up a practical environmental project in its grounds, then English Nature has a grand scheme available, administered nationally from their Peterborough headquarters.

Locally there are many conservation organisations which schools can call upon to provide evidence of environmental situations closer to home. The Young Ornithologists' Club (the junior RSPB), the Wildlife Trusts (WATCH) and the Bat Conservation Trust (Young Batworker) all provide newsletters, posters and projects for children and help them to make a contribution to protecting the environment. WATCH, for instance, has carried out valuable ozone and water quality projects. It is important to represent these issues as topical, controversial and exciting, with plenty of graphics to catch youngsters' imaginations. These junior groups place their emphasis on practical action as opposed to textbook identification. The children who plan to specialise later in, for example, ecology or botany, can be guided onto the right track by such organisations at an early stage. Children are encouraged to gain practical knowledge via enjoyable, group activities such as a badger watch, a guided bat walk using bat detectors or a tree-planting event. As well as having fun, the children are acquiring cross-curricular skills which provide an excellent base for reaching attainment targets in Geography, Science and Technology.

Many conservation organisations help schools to see the environnment as as opportunity rather than a problem. For example, taking on the management of a piece of land within the school grounds as nearby is an excellent way of putting environmental theory into practice. Some schools may feel daunted by such a challenge but should be encouraged by the example of the case study in the next section of this chapter. In Northamptonshire, the Countryside Services branch of the Country Council helps many schools and community groups to set up what are known as 'pocket parks'. These are areas of land which are owned and managed by local people with access for everyone to enjoy peaceful recreation in a manged, conservation setting. Pocket parks can be havens for wildlife as well as people, and through them children can regain that contact with nature which many have lost. Thus schoolchildren learn the principles of natural succession, population dynamics and habitat creation from the local pocket park. They also learn how to explain these principles to others, which may mark the start of a long-term commitment to protecting the environment.

For those Northamptonshine schools which do not have their own parks, there is sometimes one in a bearby village or town. A strong emphasis is placed on the educational benefits when a pocket part is set up and an invitation is issued to local schools to use it as an extra classroom. Scouts and Guides can gain conservation badges there and Duke of Edinburgh Award candidates may use them for their studies. Parents and governors may become involved in weekend work parties with a common, worthwhile goel of helping the school and providing an attractive amenity for the neighbourhood.

The benefits to the pupils are, clearly, many. There is the physical one of healthy fresh air and exercise, which many children may lack because of their increasingly, sedentary lifestyle. There is the mental stimulation of satisfying their intellectual curiosity about environmental processes processes which are actually being promoted by the children themselves. Watching their experimental comfield turn into a blaze of summer colour, or toads colonising their newly-created pond can be awe-inspiring for children. Because they are practically involved, their understanding is likely to be the greater.

Emotionally and socially, there are also many benefits to be gained by schools from undertaking a practical, conservation project. Although some children may be too young to understand, they too have the opportunity to respond to the spiritual dimension of life which contact with birdsong or the process of metamorphosis may engender. Teachers may benefit too. Such feelings could be brought into English if older pupils are studying, for example, Wordsworth's poety and his views on nature.

In addition, all can benefit from a sense of pride in what has been achieved, the team spirit that has been fostered and a growing sense of responsibility for the environment, which is one foundation of a complete education. A very positive statement is being made to the outside world about whatr the school's values, are, and everyone feels reassured that such values are being upheld.

A more tangible boost to the school's image may come in the form of an environmental award. Several conservation organisations are now making such awards available to schools, for example, Anglian Water's 'Young People's Conservation Award', Shell's Better Britain Campaign', The Tree Council and many of the country Wildlife Trusts.

When a school embarks upon a wildlife area or pocket park it must decide on which conservation organisations to establish a working relationship with and how to recognise and avoid pitfalls.

Two of the most important aspects of such a project are to appreciate the long-term commitment or sustainability of the scheme needed to ensure success and gain secure tenure of the land. The pocket park should be handed on to each new generation of pupils to care for. It should be a project which, in one sense, is never complete. Anoter important principle is to involve the wider community, creating a valuable link with the school. It is very easy to forge ahead with an excellent project, only to have it neglected and forgotton in the summar holidays. Therefore, it is vital to bring in as varied a mix of local people as possible, to share the care of the site throughout the year. This means that if the area is in the school grounds, there must be public access, which may not be acceptable to some schools. The alternative is a system of key-holders which might be complicated, hindering spontaneity.

Once a group has been set up to manage the pocket park, it is advisable to appoint a co-ordinator or leader who can liaise with the various conservation bodies and keep everyone informed of progress. The British Trust for Conservation Volunteers provides excellent resource packs and books and has field officers in most countries. The Shell 'Better Britain Campaign' produces a free guide which is available to all schools. It offers useful advice on how to get started on environmental projects. Sometimes, there are county-based services, employing people who have experience in supporting projects. In Northamptonshire, which pioneered the idea of pocket parks, there is Pocket Parks Officer who provides advice, support and grant-aid, where needed. Other counties may obtain help from environmental or tree officers or the local Wildlife Trust. The Sussex Wildlife Trust has been particularly active in promoting pocket parks, following Northamptonshire's example.

The next stage for schools is to prepare a five year management plan with a description and evaluation of the site as it is now, objectives for the future and a schedule of work for achieving those objectives. Site plans and species lists can be included. The plan may be as simple or complicated as the school desires but it does need to be an easily-understood, working document which can be passed on when the main organiser leaves the school. It is important to get the opinions of a cross-section of the school and wider community, to establish ownership of the project before the plan is written. Again Wildlife Trusts, English Nature or local authority officers may be able to help with this.

Part of being successful in any venture is anticipating challenges or difficulties and preparing for them in advance. Environmental education projects can be susceptible to vandalism. Advice on how to combat this can often be gained from the ranger at the local authority country park. Toughened perspex for interpretation panels, metal bars in gates and entrances which block motor bike access are devices which have to be considered. Finance needs to be thought carefuly, so that a project can be properly completed. The British Trust for Conservation Volunteers regularly updates a list of organisations which will provide grants to schools and conservation groups. It is wellworth schools affiliating to the Trust in order to have regular access to this and other useful information.

Another difficulty may be maintaining momentum once the novelty has worm off. One solution may be to form a network with other groups carrying out similar environmental projects, in order to exchange ideas, materials and motivation. As established group, which knows the ropes, can act as 'mentor' to a new group, awakening their own enthusiasm, as well as giving practical help to the 'novices'. Such networks are being set up in some countries by the national organisation ACRE under their 'Rural Action Scheme'.

We are fortunate in having a wealth of very active conservation organisations in this country which schools can call upon to help them promote environmental understanding action. One must hope that future governments will make an equally strong commitment to environmental education and provide the necessary resources to enable schools to the take up the challenge.

Creating an Education and Community Environmental Resource

This is a case study of a large environmental project conducted by the staff and pupils of Nicholas Hawksmoor Primary School with the help and involvement of the local community. The development dependent upon cooperation between many diverse groups and organisations that came together to create an area of considerable local importance.

The main objectives of the project were to-fold:

(a) To provide a conservation area for use by the pupils of Towcester as an educational resource. The town lies in an intensely cultivated farming area; patches of woodland and pond that remained as isolated corners of the landscape have mostly been cleared and drained. Access to the remainder is difficult as it is not within easy walking distance and is likely to be fenced. Landscaping of the town's open spaces has left few areas where the children may observe and study wildlife in its natural habitats.

(b) To provide a valuable leisure amenity for the local community. Towcester has developed rapidly in the last decade. Unfortunately provision of leisure amentities has not kept pace with the building of new houses and the town's population of some 6,000 people is left without a public park. The Pocket Park provides a much needed area for quick relaxation.

The Pocket Park occupies land adjacent to the school field. It lies in an area designated by Towcester Town Council for development as a riverside walk. This is a linear park providing a walkway between the town's new leisure centre on the edge of the town and the shopping area in the centre. However, the land here is of a particularly marshy nature rendering it unsuitable for traditional landscaping but most suitable for the creation of a pond and wetland conservation area. Towcester Town Council most generously offered free use of the land to the school in recognition of its possible use as an educational and leisure resource. A small management committee was set up in April 1991 to coordinate the project.

A complete survey was first undertaken by the children. Aided by a governor of the school, who is a civil engineer, they measured and 'levelled' the area. This involved children using a veriety of mathematical measuring equipment to define the area and map its features. The children then drew their own scale plans for its development. This work introduced the children to the concept of proportionality in a relevant and meaningful way. Surveying and producing plan drawings taught the children complex skills and gave them an understanding of the difficulties encountered by civil engineers and others on major building projects. It also highlighted the importance of achieving on major building projects. It also highlighted the importance of achieving the right answer in a calculution. From the children's work a master plan drawn up for the park's development.

Care was taken that native Northamptonshire species were included in the planting scheme. Existing features were retained and new ones created to ensure that the maximum variety of natural environments would be available for study. These included a small lake, 125 metres of native hedgerow, a small copse or woodland area, spring flowering and summer flowering meadow and a wetland. The managment group were determined that the park should be accessible to all, including the elderly and less able. A kissing gate was installed which was specially designed and constructed to allow the passage of wheelchairs and pushchairs. Hard paths were laid to facilitate mobility by these groups and wide, angled platforms constructed to enable observation and study of the pond by people from their wheelchairs. The creation of the lake was felt to be beyond the scope of our volunteer workforce so a professional landscape contractor was employed to carry out the major construction work, thereby ensuring the success of the project. Funding for this was provided by a Pocket Park Grant, a scheme initiated by Northamptonshire County Council.

These grants cover three- quarters of the cost of development; one quarter is met by Northamptonshire County Council, one by South Northands District Council, another quarter is provided by the Countryside Commission and the remaining quarter must be found by the Pocket Park Management Committee. In our case this extra quarter was supplied by the Town Council. Once the scheme has been realised adivce and assistance is available from a Pocket Parks Officer to ensure correct maintenance and management.

Construction work began on site in July 1991 and quickly created the pond and paths. With the aid of Towcester Fire Brigade the pond was filled. Anglian Water had given permission for water to be drawn from a nearby brook for this purpose. The water provided was thus already rich in pond life forms and was not contaminated by the chemicals present in tap water.

Groups of children from the school, helped by members of the local community, then began the work of planing. Every child in the school grew their own wildflower plant from seed and planted them in the park. For the younger children this demonstrated the life cycle of plants, the necessity of creating the right conditions for growth and the importance of continued care to ensure the plants' survival.

In the Autumn of 1991, Year 5 and 6 children planted young trees in the area which will, in time, become a woodland. Research into tree species by the children gave information on which trees to plant and the planting distances between them. Precise and detailed measurements of the growth of these trees has continued providing children with a database of information on growth patterns for their further studies.

That same Autumn, one group of Year 5 and 6 children sowed the meadow, first dividing the land into metre squares and weighing the seed to ensure the correct quantity was used. The children then prepared the ground and sowed the seeds. This involved them in calculations of weight and area ground measurement and ratio.

During the winter months a 'Hedgerow Planning Day' was timed to coincide with National Tree Week and was very well attended by children, parents, grandparents and other community groups. Around fifty people planted over 1,500 trees and shrubs to form a native Northamptonshire hedge around the perimeter of the park. They also set hundreds of bluebell bulbs and cowlips.

Since the completion of the major planting and landscaping the children have been responsible for a large part of the maintenance work in the park. This has included keeping the base of trees and hedges free of weeks, hay making in the meadow and pond clearance. They have also worked to keep the area free of litter. A maintenance plan has been drawn up to ensure that the park is developed fully and safely. This provides a yearly cycle of clearance for pond and paths, hedge trimming and tree pruning. It also provides a planned timetable for moving the meadow to ensure the continuance of a variety of species and for regular weeding and watering of the whole area.

The area is now used by all pupils in the school from nursery age to Year 6. Nursery children are currently monitoring the changing seasons and how they affect the flore and fauna. Year 3 pupils are pond dipping and recording the pond life forms present. Year 4 based their project on weather observations in the park. Year 5 is studying the growth patterns of the meadow with the use of quadrants. Year 6 regularly use the area as a stimulus for their art-work. They have recently produced close observational drawings and paintings, one of which won a first prize in the 'Britain in Bloom' competition.

All ages use the park as a practical base for their maths and science work. Because the park in situated adjacent to the school grounds, this makes regular visits easy to organise on a daily or hourly basis. With the aid of a grant from the British Trust for Conservation Volunteers, the Pocket Park Association purchased 'First Sense' measuring equipment for use by any group, school or community, working in the park. This equipment allows sensory probes to be sited in soil or water which record temperature, humidity, light, etc. The probes then feed this information directly into a computer to produce charts and graphs. Recent use of the system by Year 2 and Year 3 children enabled quite complex analysis to be undertaken by relatively young children.

The park has also been the setting for community art classes, led by the deputy headteacher. The resulting paintings were then put on display in the town's Leisure Centre. Frequent visitors to the park include elderly residents of a nearby senior citizens' residential home, and physically and mentally disadvantaged young people from a local Day Care Centre. Other local schools and youth groups including 'Beavers' and 'Brownies' have also used the park for both educational and recreational purposes. Through out the summer it is used by families living in the locality, for walking or, often, as a site for a picnic.

Funding for projects such as these is often a major stumbling block. The group approached both and national organisations for financial support, spreading their net widely. Though often unsuccessful, this has resulted in donations from many different sources. These have included the 'Shell Better Britain' campaign which provided a 'set up grant', Macdon alds Hamburgers who provided wildflowers, and a local charity which donated a bench seat. Approaches to local businesses resulted in many small gifts of money and equipment. The park has benefited from affiliation to the British Trust for Conservation Volunteers who have provided expert help and advice, loans of equipment and a financially advantageous insurance scheme. The Nicholas Hawksmoor Pocket Park Association is now a fully registed charity which enables it to draw on many other areas of grant aid.

Since its completion the park has been the recipient of many awards and commendations. It won the Smith and Allebone Shield, a scheme run by the Northamptonshire County Council and the Northamptonshine Wildlife Trust jointly, in recognition of the children's knowledge and understanding of conservation issues. In 1992 the school was proud to receive a gold medal in the Queen's Anniversary Trust Awards as one of over 6,000 schools from Great Britain and the Commonwealth which were entered for this award. Only six primary schools achieved this accolade. Children and staff travelled to St Jame's Palace to receive the award from Her Majesty the Queen and the Duke of Edinburgh. Understandingly, this was a most memorable day for all concerned.

10

The Environmental Education and Core and Foundation Subjects

Coming to have a view and to articulate it in a satisfying fashion is the beginning of a sense of ownership of an issue. Of all classroom subjects, English is the one where the fullest response can be made, in private and public ways. Sometimes a poem or a story read in class will impel a pupil to write their own poem or story in an exploration of personal feelings. However, such responses may not come at once. Feelings take time to be worked through before they surface in a child's consciousness. Unfortunately, today's curriculum demands can work against this reflection, but the words of Grace Nichols, commenting on her own poem *Forest,* are salutary:

> Reading back the poem I was surprised at the line, 'And we must keep Forest' because in a way, it reflets my own concern about the preservation of our forests. But I didn't set out to say this at all in my poem. I wasn't thinking of making people aware of the importance of keeping our forests. It just came out in poem. This is what makes poetry exciting for me. A poet can discover things in her own poetry. It's like going on an adventure. You don't know quite where the poem will take you because it has a living mind or spirit of its own. So one of the most important things in writing a poem is to tune in to the feelings of the poem, to listen to that still small voice in the poem, instead of forcing it to say the things you think it ought to say.

Pupils can of course be presented with environmental matters in more prosaically-rooted language work. Here too, the scope for classroom development is very wide. Questions about the environment evoke strong feelings, where they be concerned with road-widening or rain forests.

Environmental matters may seem siimple, especially when they appeal so powerfully to our emotions, but the issues are more problematic. Often genuine dilemmas are involved, like the competing claims of convenience versus conservation, or utility versus aesthetics, and the best outcome is by no means always clear-cut. Change in the environment is not necessarily bad, or even where some initial damage is done, greater good may eventually result. On the other hand, although all environments change, there are those who argue that we should preserve things as they are and repair any damage. There are significantly different points of view here that need to be explored through debate and discussion.

The English classroom can usefully bring together such work. Often this is best done through cross-curricular planning, with pupils collecting evidence from work in other classroom subjects, like science or geography, and bringing the results to the English classroom. The presentation of such evidence, and the arguments that stem from it, need to laid out in a lucid way, and for this the English classroom provides the best forum. Students can work in small groups on different aspects of a question and bring together the various strands in whole class presentation and debate. Class groupings can be arranged so as to foster the individual abilities of everyone in the class, so that each pupil, however they may have fared in more knowledge-laden subjects, feels able to make a contribution. Thus, a pupil may have difficulty with the science or the statistics of an environmental issue, but be able to give convincing rhetorical expresion to their feelings. If words are their strength, they can be placed with scientific and mathematical colleagues so that the group produces a richer and fuller response than any of them could have managed alone.

Implied here is the extension of the sense of personal responsibility from the domain of private behaviour to the public. In making that move, we are asking pupils to work out their position on larger environmental issues, albeit in the safety of the classroom setting. Clearly we want our pupils, as embryonic citizens, to develop a sense of public responsibility. The step is thus an important one, and as children become more aware of environmental issues, we will want to bring to their notice some of the threats that endanger the environmental. The sinister aspect of the world described in Patten's poem is that whatever 'it' is that is spoiling the world is invisible. Pupils can be a sked to find examples of destructive things that are being put into the environment, from nesspapers, magazines, and from what they are learning in other school subjects. Such information can be put together in the form of a collage, made up of media articles, pupils' own findings and poems and stories they have written themselves. Such contemporary material, displayed in classrooms or school corridors, will help to keep environmental issues in pupils' minds.

Alternatively the devastated world of Patten's poem can be compared with poems that depict a less blighted nature. Grace Nichol's peom *Forest* whould be an appropriate contrast. Pupils might go on to work in groups to compile a set of poems and prose on the theme of humanity's treatment of nature, which could be the subject of a dramatized presentation to the whole class, or to a class of younger pupils in the school.

Popular classroom texts like *Z for Zachariah* reinforce the theme of an environmental destroyed by man, and pupils react powerfully to such texts and the discussions that they provoke. Factual material can be brought in to supplement the discussion, and the work given a practical outcome for a greater feeling of engagement with the issues. Pupils engaged in this sort of work may be writing to local MPs and newspapers, or designing and distributing leaflects to raise public awareness about an issues. For older pupils project work can provide a focus systematic work on an environmental issue about which they feel strongly.

Pupils being asked to respond to material like this are also entering the period of adolescence, when issues are taken with great seriousness. This is often particularly the case where there is damage or suffering to innocent creatures. Consider, for example, the strength of pupils' reaction to Brown John's poem *To See the Rabbit* (Brownjohn, 1983). As teachers we have a responsibility to ensure that our pupils do not take too much personal responsibility for environmental damage over which they can have no direct control. Many of the things currently being done to the environment are outside the scope of the ordinary person. They result from commercial exploitation, national and global political decisions. Very often we do not hear about these matters unitl things have deteriorated too far for much rescue work to be done. Adolescents can be encouraged to explore and voice their judgements and feelings on these issues, but should be protected against over-assumption of guilt.

Much of the material on environmental issues that we give our pupils is strong stuff, and we need to balance its impact by reminding them of the limits of their personal responsibility. It is one thing to regret pulling down the hawthorn glade, but quite another to feel you might have prevented the destruction of Tweyford Down. Things have got more complicated since Wordsworth's time. We can, however, help our pupils to express their reactions to environmenal issues in appropriate ways. These ways will, as suggested above, include letters, petitions, collages, poems, plays and stories. They will show pupils making something out of the powerful feelings evoked in them as they reflect upon the environment. The strength and the delicacy of expression that such feelings can evoke is here illustrated by a poem taken from a collection written by pupils at beaumount Leys School in Leicester in poetry workshop sessions spread over a week in March, 1994.

A Fiery Fish
Imagine a flexible nugget of gold
Or silver, its orange glittering.
Shaped like a darting bullet
Ricocheting off the shiny walls.
With scales, layered like an onion
And an open mouth, gaping like a cave.
They say it lived in a glass, water land
And had a seven second memory span.
This beast diet out with mankind
But it lives on, it is a legend.
(*Nick Brookes, Year II*)

Mathematics

Mathematics is not an exercise carried out in isolation, a kind of ill-defined limbo. One operates in an environment; the class or work room in which one sits, the sounds that are a part of the process of which intrude, the people one works with, are all part of the working environment. At the same time, the mathematics in which one is engaged could well be a tool one could use, either to make an examination of the environmental in which one lives or to make an impression upon it. One needs to examine both of these aspects of the relationship between mathematics and the environment.

There are schools where it is possible to enter a room where mathematics is taught and not know it until the subject is announced. There are classrooms with wooden shelves groaning under the weight of rows of identical dusty textbooks. There are corridors devoid of any kind of decoration or display. Down these corridors and into these rooms pass children who expect and are expected to engage with mathematics. They will spend a lot of their valuable learning time in an environment whose main effect is to depress and stultify. If we want children to appreciate the aesthetic beauty of mathematics then we need to create for them a working environment which is full of this beauty. There are many very attractive and stimulating posters that can be used to decorate corridors and walls. Mobiles of solid shaped can be suspended from any ceiling. Most importantly, all available wall space can be covered with children's mathematics. There can be no environment more stimulating to learning than one where both the subject and the learner are obviously held in high esteem. If the external surroundings are ugly and uncared for this will, almost certainly, be reflected in the internal responses of the child. A primary school teacher reading this may well challenge the description of a school devoid of displays to stimulate. However, let them be assured that they exist, and have been reported upon. However, there is less obvious, yet potentially more damaging environment that can have a profound effect upon children's attitudes to mathematics. This is one created by people who clearly do not enjoy mathematics, who cannot perceive any value in it beyond its being a tool and who are quite prepared to state proudly that they are no good at it. We must do everything in our power to ensure that this mental environmental is as positive as we can make it so that the children receive every encouragement to engage with mathematics. The best teachers of art clearly enjoy being artistic, teachers of English read and cherish literature. It is to be hoped that all teachers of mathematics enthuse about their subject and can be seen getting pleasure from using elegant mathematical processes.

So, having created as effective a learning environment as we can, we must use the mathematics we have learned to inform us about the wider community outside and to enable us to make some impact upon that environment. The physical environment in which we live is an immensely complex three-dimensional structure. As we move through it the shapes of which it is made up are continually changing their size and position in relationship to us, the observer. Children can obtain great insights into aspects of space and shape, such as similarity and enlargement, by investigating what happens to the relative positions of trees, buildings and so on when they travel past them. It is possible to simulate this in the classroom by asking pupils to put five or six objects on a table in the middle of the room. They can then walk around the table and sketch the objects in their relative positions from different points of view around the table. If the table is then cleared and the pictures, together with the objects, are given to another group, then they can be asked to try to replace them on the table in their origional positions. Another activity which forces children to examine carefully their surroundings is getting them to draw panoramas. On a residential visit a group of children might be taken to a good viewing point such as the summit of 'Catbells' in the Lake District, each with a compass. They could then be allocated a ten degree are and asked to sketch what they see within this arc. When the pupils return to base they could draw out their portion of the view on large sheets of paper, taking care to ensure that each side of their section matches with those of the neighbouring sections. The whole set of views could then be mounted around the walls of one of the workrooms. The mathematics required is not great but the pupils will certainly have studied the view from the top very carefully indeed.

Children can also examine the make-up of both natural and man-made objects and try to see how their mathematical structure relates to their efficiency and effectiveness, or not as the case may be. The links between the growth patterns of trees, the structure of a dendelion flower and and Fibonacci sequence can lead to extremely rich investigational situations. There is no need to visit the Alhambra in order to see how geometric forms and structures can be combined in breathtakingly beautiful ways. In fact, by examining the geometry of the man-made structures in which we spend our working days, the links between aesthetics, mathematics and fitness for purpose can be investigated.

Environmental problem-solving is clearly one area where there is vast scope for mathematical activity. A task such as creating a garden, a pond or a reserve for wild life will require the use of the kind of which should already by developing under the heading of 'Using and Applying Mathematics'. The practical skills or measuring, estimating and calculating will obviously be as much in evidence as servicing skills. However, weighing up of the priorities, the gathering of information to inform decisions, and the creation of a balance between theoretical and realistic outcomes will call for a sophistication of thought which is not too often required in the carrying out of specifically mathematical tasks. The task does not have to be on the scale of those outlined above. There are many problems that can be set to find efficient ways of packaging items for sale where more attention, from an environmental point of view, is payed to the kind of material used. An investigation into the whole area of wrapping and packaging could yield a lot of insights into the amount of waste we experience during the very ordinary activity of shopping. The concept of 'cost' can be made to take on a much greater significance if environmental considerations have to be taken into account. Encouraging children to take a closer look at their surroundings, asking them to make judgements about the efficiency of transport systems, waste disposal systems, heating systems, manufacturing systems, recycling systems will not only force them to look critically at their environment, it will also require them to develop skills in the collection, handling and display of data as well as using statistical analysis techniques. The mathematician, like the scientist, cannot operate in a vacuum. This is not to say that there is never a time when we can do mathematics for its own sake. Wrestling with a purely theoretical piece of algebra or a combinatorial problem is an immensely rewarding activity, an apportunity to hone our intellect. However, there must also be a time when we take this intellectual capability and apply it to the solving of problems in the world in which we live. We have to make our own small contribution to the creation of a physical and mental environment where we can live at ease and use appropriate mathematical processes at will.

11

The Science Education

Despite many statements of intent and well-meant attempts to heighten the profile of science, the response in terms of numbers of students at all levels opting for science subjects has been disappoining. This peculiar, British antithesis has a considerable bearing on what follows. On the one hand, it is claimed that environmental education furnishes suitable means for introducing science in a user-friendly fashion, which ought then to assist recruitment to examinable science subjects in the later years of school and beyond. At the same time, a significant proportion of those inspired by environmental education subsequently encounter difficulty when attempting to pursue that interest in higher level courses, because of the science content. The common ground would appear to be that there is an important difference between the 'science' experienced via environmental education and the science in subject-specific disciplines, including environmental science, in further and higher education. The difference is that environmental education is highly selective in its references to science, usually from an issue-based approach, whereas formal encounters ith the sciences proper, involves exposure to markedly different language, values and procedures from those underpining other areas of the curriculum.

As has been widely acknowledged, science in intellectually demanding, requiring progressive acquisition of its distinctive mores and methods, whereas much of the so-called science in environmental education is actually partiol scientism. This is not to deny its utility, but the distination should be recognised if there are not to be misleading consequences at a later stage, to the detriment of both the student and their perception of science. Following the Toyne Report, this difficultry is no longer confined to primary and secondary curriculum development. As a provider of an under-graduate degree programme in environmental science, certain obsevations are tendered about the relationship between environmental education and science. Students choosing this course wish to have more than awareness. They intend to study in depth and breadth and to gain employment as practitioners. Meanwhile, there are numbers of primary and secondary pupils with aspirations to attain similar goals. Successful candidature depends largely upon their choice of examination subjects. In order to make good decisions, the questions of the place of 'science' in environmental education needs to be better understood.

This 'top down' approach is of direct relevance to environmental education in the primary and secondary phases. The science in 'Environmental Science' is essentially derived from the established disciplines. However, the scope and purpose of environmental science is not only different from that of traditional science subjects, it is also is some respects contrary to their way of looking at the world. Environmental science is holistic rather than reductionist. It necessarily involves explicit secrutiny of not ony natural systems, but the interactions with human systems. Moreover, from the point of view of the latter rather than the forner, environmental science—as a problem-solving enterprise—seeks solutions that have more to do with the decision-making conscious, animate beings than the outcomes of chemical physical processes. As such, the domain embraces rather more than pure science is intended to, or is able to deal with. There are also many aspects of science that are not necessarily pertinent to the conduct of environmental science. This awkward overlap between science proper and environmental science has to be negotiated with considerable care if neither is to be misconstrued.

The contribution of science to environmental science is simultaneously conditioned by the context from which it has been dervied, i.e. the paradigms of science, and the context in which it is employed, within the realm of environmental science. Much friction and misunderestanding arises from failure to acknowledge this relational consequence. From the point of view of environmental science, its demands upon science are relatively straight-forward:

What is the natural world composed of?

How is it organised?

How does it behave?

How has it developed?

Conventionally, this would be delivered as study of the atmosphere, lithosphere, hydrosphere and biosphere. With explicit or implicit adoption of general systems theory, most frequently manifest in the guise of models of ecosystems and biogeochemical cycles, the systemic structure, functioning and dynamics of the natural world is thereby approached. Alongside inputs from biology, chemistry and physics, the spatial

(Geography) and temporal (Earth history) dimensions are also well to the fore. There is usually consideration of the natural world at a variety of scales, from sub-cellular and sub-atomic, to global. The pure science subjects yield vital understanding about processes, in terms of transformations of energy and matter. In addition to this 'content' there is also desirable inclucation of certain fundamental attributes of science. Although the principles of chaos, catastrophe and uncertainty are now having some influence, most thought is firmly in the logical-positivist tradition, emphasising objectivity in observation, consistency in experimentation, precision in measurement and logical interpretation of results against the structures of hypotheses, laws and theory. Complimentary practice in the use of information processing technology is *de rigueur* as an adjunct. The intention is to develop modes of behaviour akin to those of pure science, whether or not the phonommon in question can be so described. For example, the topic of soil erosion embraces more than pure science but its comprehension, including the conspicuous 'human dimensions' is felt to be enhanced by adherence to the *mudus operandi* of science proper. In order to complete the groundwork, attention then turns to the character, structure, functioning and dynamics of the human systems that impinge upon the natural world, seen as the 'environment'. Happily, the concepts of general systems theory can usefully (though not exclusively) be employed for this too, but science otherwise has little to contribute. Instead, geography, history, economics, sociology, business studies and political studies are to the forefront in this element. The crux of environmental science is then the interactions between human and natural systems. The relationships may be seen as dependence, partnership and dominance; the process of development and its impacts for both the environment and mankind. In this, the role of science is ambivalent and, in practice varies according to the outlook of the particular course team. The interface between natural and human domains is now being actively engaged by proponents of both natural and human science subjects, the way forward having been demonstrated for example, by the re-unification of human and physical geography in recent years. Hence, as the focus at last of integrated study, such issues as floodplain management, or deforestation, are being so much better illuminated.

Thereafter, environmental science proceeds to deliver its particular benefit in terms of intervention in the dynamics of the situation, attempting to manipulate processes to the advantage of the future of both natural and human systems. That is, the concern shifts from understanding to 'management'. This is the ultimate justification of the subject and the reason many wish to obtain qualifications in it today. Most courses correspondingly offer the opportunity of eventual, applied specialisation, for example land resource development, waste management, pollution control and wildlife conservation. The fundamental sciences contribute accordingly, with chemistry and physics notable in waste management and pollution control, biology in pollution control and wildliffe conservation. The environmental scientist though, has to grapple with the problem of how knowledge and wisdom is to be translated into materially effective action. For this, detailed study of the frameworks, procedures and mechanisms whereby decision-making is accomplished are called for. Students need to acquire the appropriate skills so that information is reported, communicated and marketed to entrepreneurs, regulators and policy-makers. This represents an emergent area as yet imperfectly developed, but warranting contributions from management, as well as politics and media studies. Of course, the recommendations to decision-makers incorporate the findings of science and those making the case need to be suitably equipped to draw sensible conclusions from them. In case it be thought that the cause of science is somehow diminished, there is desperate need both for 'boffins' who are more aware of the downstream utilisation, and consequence of their products, and 'green' managers similarly informed of the upstream science of their decisions. In this respect, a sea change of attitude is in prospect, if recent, key statements of policy are to be believed, that may bode well for the employment prospects of some environmental scientists. (HMSO, 1990 and 1994) Whilst it can be seen that science is integral to environmental science, it by no means constitutes all of the curriculum. Intending candidates ought to posses at least one pure science (physics or chemestry) at advanced level, (preferably, biology too), plus another drawn from a wider range than hitherto appreciated. This might be geography, geology, history, economics, sociology, business studies or politics.

The character of the science that is needed, has been most clearly set out in another recent government publication (Brawn, 1992)/ It is correspondingly vital that the earlier phases of primary and secondary education stimulate interest in science. Pupils will only be adequately prepared if Science, and other subjects, are incorporated into curriculum design and delivery.

Design and Technology

Technological development is about changing or controlling the human environment to enhance survival or improve the quality of life. Developments, such as the invention of the steam engine and car, have had far-reaching effects on both rural and urban landscapes. Even apparently, minor improvements such as the invention of the chainsaw opened the way to rapid deforestation. Although this created economic gain it often lead to ecological imbalance and loss of rain forests. In the past technological 'improvements' were usually introduced without considering their effect on society and the environment. Consequently, control over changes has been one of the strongest motivators for increased efforts to understand technology. (Layton, 1993)

It is not sufficient to teach pupils technological skills and concepts. One must also consider the possible consequences. Pupils should not feel that technological change has created complex and major environmental problems that are beyond the influence of ordinary people. Design and Technology can demonstrate that there are opportunities for taking action to improve or conserve environments. Additionally pupils are given an approach for evaluating their environment, methods for appraising different solutions and some of the skills needed for intervention.

The Importance of Including Design of Environments within National Curriculum Technology

Unfortunately the potential in design and technology for pupils to evaluate and improve environments may not be realised because of the proposed changes to the statutory Technology National Curriculum. The particular reference to environments in the first Design and Technology Curriculum (DoE, 1990) has been omitted. (NCC, 1993) In addition a reduction of attainment targets may mean that teachers concentrate on the planning and making process with little input on identifying needs and evaluating products which is recognised by Environmental Education guidance as providing the real opportunity for pupils to explore environmental issues through Design Technology. (NCC, 1990a) Consequently, teachers will need their awareness raised as to how design and technology might include worthwhile activities that will meet the advice of Environmental Education guidance and ensure that pupils do more than examine and make artifacts.

Evalauting the Quality of Environments and Suggesting Improvements

To create or improve a product or environment effectively, existing ones need to be examined in a focussed and structured way. For example, an evaluation of the local park might start by producing a detailed map and description of the physical features and facilities. Having identified the requirements of the children, their careers and other adults who use the area, the function, aesthetic quality, advantages and disadvantages of each facilitry can be discussed. Each suggestion can then be evaluated in terms of time, cost, materials and skills required with the intention of producing a design to improve the park. The project could be extended by including a requirement to provide facilities for visually impaired and physically disabled children. Although it is unlikely that the pupils will be able to implement many of their proposed changes, the activity will enhance their ability to look at and evaluate a familiar locality carefully.

Opportunities to Create Positive Change

Many pupils fail to recognise that they can care and improve the environment. They also feel that intervention is beyond most adults. Plans can identify, both what is immediately possible, as well as what could be done when they become adults. Young children might evaluate and design familiar environments, e.g. their homes and schools. Older pupils can study localities which are more complex and unfamiliar. However, young pupils can, successfully, examine small businessesses, and challenging opportunities for the older pupil can arise from studying the home or school.

Primary school children might look at the design of their own bedroom and discuss what features they like or dislike in order to suggest improvements such as rearranging furniture or storing toys. They might also design the ideal bedroom within a specified budget using furniture catalogues and wallpaper books. Older pupils could research and produce designs for specific needs such as a kitchen for an arthritic or wheelchair-bound person. Another project could involve pupils finding out about 'environmentally friendly' products, modern methods of heating and insulating buildings in order to improve practice in their own school or to design a home for the future.

Recently more schools have been involving their pupils in enchancing their own school grounds. The pupils have assisted in evaluating the existing facilities, producing plans for improvements, raising funds and helping with some of the installations. The raises pupils' awareness of the quality of their surroundings and that it can be enhanced. (Jarvis, 1993) Improving the school and its grounds has also frequently lead to an increased sense of belonging, more responsible behaviour and a general reduction in litter, graffiti and vandalism. (Mares and Stephenson, 1988) A series of small projects rather than one major enterprise are easier to finance, can cater for several groups of children over the years, and are more realistic about staff resources and commitment. Even where there are limited grounds or where the land is taken up by playgrounds and sports pitches, there may be opportunities to plant trees on boundaries or small woodland areas, provide hanging baskets and potted plants, or add murals and sculptures to the walls. Other successful projects have included establishing chequer-board gardens, wild flower meadows and butterfly gardens. Pupils can design additional equipment such as benches, shelters and climbing apparatus, facilities to attract birds and ponds. (Anon, no date; Cantrell, 1989; Mares and Stephenson, 1988; Young, 1990) As a natural resource changes, so ongoing monitoring and maintence is esseintial, creating further opportunities for technological projects. These might include setting up a nature trail with an associated information pack, pond cleaning and creating eye-catching litter bins or posters.

Using Energy and Resources Efficiently

The carefully use of non-renewable resources should be practiced as part of technological activities. Pupils must learn to use materials economically. Efficient use and control of energy is also essential in the design and creation of mechanical and electrical products, not only for economic reasons, but also with respect to environmental considerations. When evaluating and designing such products, pupils should be encouraged to take into account the merits of using renewable energy sources and how different cultures have solved similar problems. For example, in the past some intermediate technological solutions in the Third World have been treated with disdain, whereas they are efficient solutions, well suited to the environmental resources of the locality. Examples are the use of bicycle trailers in Sri Lanka and the small-scale hydros (micro-hydro) on fast flowing streams in Peru and Zimbabwe. (Budgett and Meakin, 1993) These successes are in contrast of some 'modern' Western techologies, which were developed to suit conditions of temperature zone ecosystems and subsequently created great environmental damage when imposed on other, usually tropical, environments. (Farvar and Milton, 1973)

Balancing People's Different Needs

'Finding solutions to environmental problems has to take into account the fact that there are conflicting interests and different cultural perspectives.' (NCC, 1990b) These conflicts of interest may arise between different groups of people using the same location, between short-term and long-term interests, between economic progress and the need to conserve the earth's limited resources. As designing and evaluating products for specific needs is an essential part of design and technology, pupils can be helped to empathise will people of different ages, societies and cultures and recognise their varying requirements. They may also learn that it is not always possible to find an ideal solution.

Pupils planning improvements for their community can be helped to recognise that their local streets are probably intended to give efficient access to people in vehicles, on bicycles and on foot. Some will be travelling through the area, whereas others will want to get to shops and other buildings. Improvements for pedestrians, such as widening the pavement, providing road humps to discourage speeding cars increasing the cul-desacs and safe crossings, may not be popular with cars users. In order to cater for all users, plans may need to include a fast route with pedestrian foot-bridges, or mean improving public transport.

Other conflicts can be explored by designing a zoo. Pupils' will have to choose between the demands of the public to see animals clearly, and the needs of the animals for a suitable environment. They may balance taking animals from their natural environment and the need to educate people to care for animals. Conservation of the ecological balance in natural environments may be weighted against improving the breading rate of rare animals.

Other projects might include investigating the conflicts between the concreate industry needing gravel and the environmental damage created by large scale quarrying. (Jarvis, 1991) The costs and benefits of using fertiliser on farming and fishing in South American coastal areas, balancing the differences between the various interested parties involved in building a windfarm and weighing up the pros and cons of limiting deforstation in Northen India also offer scope for discussion. (Campbell et al, 1991)

Through such activities pupils may appreciate some of the factors influencing how technological development is changing their local land world environments. The approach and skills provided in design and technology should enable them to evaluate these changes and help them to begin to recognise what they might do it influence the outcomes.

History

> 'Our situation is no longer shaped environment, rather it is increasingly we who are doing the shaping and often disastrously so,' (Worster, 1989)

This change in our relationship with the world in which we live, work and play has raised the environment to the top of the modern world agenda. Talk is of a 'global village' and debate is increasingly focussed on crucial worldwide environmental questions relating to climate, patterns of technological and enonomic development and demographic trends.

This means disappointingly little to history teachers at present. The relationship between history and environmental education is not readily accepted nor its potential fully explored by history teachers. This is in part due to teacher prejudice but also to the relative newness of the emphasis on world-wide environmental concerns. It takes time for such concerns to filter into the curriculum. There is no long tradition of links between history and environmental education in British education as there is with other themes such as EIU and citizenship (Kerr, 1994a and 1994b). Accordingly, many history teachers have a narrow conception of environmental education. The relationship between people and their environmentals is deemed important but it is perceived as the responsibility of other areas of the curriculum notably geography and science. This outdated view is compounded by the lack of detail in *Curriculum Guidance* 7 on potential links between history and environmental education (NCC, 1990d).

If environmental education is to be part of the concerns of school history then history teachers must be persuaded of its relevance to their teaching. They need, above all, to be convinced of the overlap in aims and purposes between history and environmental education. A useful starting-point is to raise teacher's awareness of two developments in environmental education. First, the growing interest over the past twenty years in investigating environments in the past. Second, the important role played by such historical perspectives in informing the debates our modern environment. The environmental has evolved as a significant branch of history over the last two decades, driven by developments in North America. Environmental history has attracted a growing band of historians, geographers, ecologists and anthiropologists intervested in the historical relationship of nature to human society (see, for example, Worster, 1994; Cronon, 1992; White, 1985). They have investigated fundamental issues over time such as population expansion and exhaustion of energy resources and produced much evidence on the social and economic determinants on the changing environment. Research has shown how:

(1) perceptions of the environmental have shifted over time;
(2) all environments present choices about how they are fashioned—what choices are made and how they are portrayed is dependent on the culture of the societies involved;
(3) two trends are behind the transformation of the world's environment namely, the increase in European population and its movement across the world and the rise of capitalism and the modern industrial economy;
(4) the evolving relationship between humans and the environment is very much about prevailing values and value systems.

The reconstruction of past environments has also been marked by a strong moral concern and desire to use the findings to inform social action and decision-making about 'the kind of world we want to live in' (Demeritt, 1994). Put more simply, the desire has been to use the lessons of past decisions about the environment to inform present decisions and future choices about the planet. Thus environmental history is playing a vital role in educating people about how the decisions of past societies have shaped not only the world in which we live but our view of that world.

Awareness of such developments can help transform history teachers' perception of and approach to environmental education. Environmental education as environmental history is a much broader and more readily acceptable working definition for history teachers. It dovetails with the central aims and purposes of history teaching. History is well placed in the curriculum to make a valuable contribution to this broad view of environmental educational in schools and to help pupils to develop the knowledge, understanding and skills which will enable them to participate in present and future environmental challenges.

Closer examination of the guidance for environmental education reveals the overlap with history in the knowledge, understanding, skills and attitudes to be developed and the approach to learning. The three linked components of environmental education (education about, for and in or through the environment) are present in the programmes of study in history. History offers a unique opportunity to put these components in historical context and help to understand present approaches to them in the light of past experiences in other periods and cultures.

The approach to learning in the guidance document and its aims are equally familiar to history teachers. Environmental education is centred on the interpretation of evidence and the formation of rational arguments and judgements based on evidence, often concerning controversial issues. The central aim is to help pupils to develop skills and attitudes in handling evidence, in order to clarify their own values, and encourage 'informed concern for and active participation in resolving environmental problems' (NCC 1990d). This dovetails with the aim of learning in the National Curriculum for history.

There is sufficient overlap to suggest that environmental education can be integrated as part of learning in history in numerous contexts across the key stages. The central question for teachers is how can learning in history help equip pupils with the knowledge, understanding, skills and attitudes to contribute to:

> informed and active participation...in the protection of the environment and the prodent and rational use of natural resources?
>
> (Council of the European Community, 1988)

It is not enough to assume that pursuing the History requirements will prepare pupils for their choices and responsibilities in environmental education. Successful integration requires history teachers to think through the implications of developing the broad view of environmental education as a natural part of the process of learning in history in the classroom.

History can assist best through a process of learning that helps pupils to develop a critical respect for the evidence related to environmental issues and how it is constructed and used. Above all, it includes helping pupils to understand that the relationship between human societies and the environment and the choices and responsibilities of the individual in that society to the environment is ever changing. They should also understand that choices and responsibilities about the environment are heavily influenced by social, economic, political and cultural factors. They should come to appreciate that different interpretations of the relationship between society and the environment (*Curriculum Guidance 7* is one such interpretation and the government white paper 'This Common Inheritance' (HMSO, 1990) in history lead to different questions and alternative ways of seeing things. It requires careful thought and planning in each context. There are a numer of steps history teachers might take to develop this process, notably to:

(1) identify the scope that particular areas of history provide for integrating components of environmental education as part of learning in history;
(2) establish for those areas lesson intentions to help pupils to achieve the Attainment Targets in history and appreciate the interrelationship between environmental issues and social, economic, political and cultural determinants;
(3) resource the lessons and identify appropriate teacher interventions for learning;
(4) assess the outcomes in terms of pupil understanding of environmental issues in modern contexts, preferably moving from personal and local to national, international and global contexts to encourage wider understanding of issues.

This might be achieved as follows:

Context. The teacher decides that nineteenth century Britain offers the opportunity to investigate the impact of the coming of the railways on the urban environment (focusssing particularly on the impact on the built environment and on living and working conditions). This context can be covered at Key Stages, 2, 3 or 4 often with a local perspective.

Lesson activities. The teacher designs activities to help pupils to:

- form opinions from a variety of sources on nineteenth century Britain about the relationship between the coming of the railways and the changing urban environment and investigate how interpretations are related to the selection and use of resources;
- compare and contrast those opinions with their views about the impact of the motor vehicle on urban environments in modern Britain;
- consider their views of modern Britain within the wider context of the spread of the motor vehicle as an international and global concern.

Resources and teaching. The teacher selects a range of sources showing different interpretations of the impact of railways on the urban environment of nineteenth century Britain (these highlight the social, economic, political and cultural determinants behind the decisions about where to locate railways in particular urban environments. Such decisions produced winners and losers as evidenced by the saying 'living on the wrong side of the tracks'). The teacher then ascertains pupils' ideas about the impact of transport on the urban environment for these will affect the way pupils will approach the historical context and the evidence presented to them. The teacher turns these ideas back to pupils to enable them to review their own thinking about the impact of transport on the urban environment.

Assessment. The teacher introduces sources with different views of the impact of motor vehicles on the urban environment in modern Britain to ascertain how far pupils are able to transfer the knowledge, understanding and skills developed in the historical context to a modern one. Finally, the teacher introduces sources which highlight the impact of the motor vehicle in other urban areas across the world (for example South America, North America and the Far East) in order to encourage pupils to consider the issues in moderm Britain within a wider global context.

This is not an easy process to develop. There is no guarantee that pupils win transfer their understanding of nineteenth century Britain to question the influences on the role of the motor vehicle in urban environmental change in modern Britain or will then be able to see the issues raised within a wider global context. It is vital that that transfer is encouraged if learning in history is to equip pupils with the necessary knowledge, understanding and skills to make informed choices about environmental issues. It is a learning process which encourages pupils to develop a critical analysis of society and of the changing relationship with the environment within it. Our rapidly expanding world presents major challenges in the choices and responsibilities facing future generations concerning environmental issues. The health and safety of the planet rests on those challenges being met through considered and informed debate at all levels. Environmental history warns us of the increased risk of our cumulative actions. The potential for irrevrsible damage to the planet is greater than at any time in the past. It makes you think but it should also make you act.

12

The Geography

Geography is an environmental study *par excellence,* Within its disciplines, maps are the most distinctive and particular means by which geographers express themselves, setting out facts and suggesting explanations. Maps of all kinds represent environmental relationships, past and present, direct and indirect. They are purposefully selective, stylised portrayals of a real world which consists of a mosaic of natural and man-made environments. Within these many and varied environments individuals and groups, cities and nations work out their most effective ways of living.

All environments are created and sustained by processes, some natural and some generated by human actions. Natural processes produce climates and vegetation climaxes. Processes generated by human actions create for example, global markets for the producers and consumers of oil, coffee, bananas, sugar, aluminium and steel among a myriad of others. They also establish different kinds of economic, social and political systems. World thematic maps in atleases may be thought of as environmental summaries, records of the stages reached in different parts of the world by these many processes working in conbination to produce the conditions of human life and work.

Larger scale maps, such as the Ordnance Survey 1:50000 Landranger series, represent environments in finer detail. Such maps attempts to portray complete landscapes, everything one can see on the earth's surface, in a given area. At this scale the interactions between environmental conditions and human activities are more clearly demonstrated in the schematic picture of landscapes and townscapes one is given in the maps. It is illuminating to think of a familiar area of countryside, for example, as a kind of precipitate, in the chemical sense, of natural and human events and processes, which have worked and which continue to work together, to create what we see today. These processes include the hedged fields, prairie landscapes of modern arable farming which seems to be replacing them, and set-aside land. Industry too leaves its mark of change in the mines, quarries and power stations, new and long-established factories and areas of derelict industrial land. Villages and towns show their distinctive regional and national characteristics and link to transport and communication systems. Along with tourist areas, maps record all these events and so offer rich sources of raw materials for environmental education.

Some possibilities for developing environmental themes may be considered under the main aspects of geography to be included in the National Curriculum interpretation of the subject. This discussion complements ideas put forward in the NCC Curriculum Guidance booklets, especially Number 7 *Environmental Education.*

Geographical Skills

The skills developed through school geography courses include those of systematic observation and recording, especially in the form of maps. It also includes their interpretation, the use of photographs, various kinds of graphical representation and the use of satellite images by older pupils. These data-gathering skills are used by geographers to seek out and interpret environment information.

Local surveys which sharpen pupils' observations of environmental quality are very important. It is easy to take familiar environments for granted, as being 'normal'. It is the business of the geographer to help children look afresh at their surroundings and encourage them to ask questions about what they see around them. For example children could be asked to consider the visual impact of a street or shopping centre and consider whether they find them attractive or capable of improvement. They might go on to note the condition of pavements, the design of street furniture, shop fronts and advertisements, the condition of paintwork, incidence of graffiti and so on. They might question whether these things have to look as they do or whether their design could be improved. This kind of enquiry can lead into discussions about who might make the improvements and the likelihood of any suggestions being accepted and carried out. Further, pupils could explore the ways in which local residents or shoppers may be able to influence those responsible for the local environment. It may be found that environmental issues in the wider world are echoed in those closely related to the local area. The effective management of traffic is a global problem yet local aspects of it are eminently mappable at the school gates. At continental or world scales some recently published atlases provide a wealth of information and ideas for environmental enquiry.

Aspects of geographical study: Places and Themes

All places are environments. The first purpose of geographical education is to help the growing child acquire a bank of accurate information about 'where places are and what they are like' on a local, national and global basis. Such information is part of the essential framework within which environmental issues can be discussed constructively. In reality there are no exclusively local environmental issues or problems. All have to be examined in the widest relevant context. A debate about the expansion of roadstone quarrying in the East Midlands, for example, has to take account of the distribution of suitable rocks, often in areas of high scenic value. A locality like Charnwood Forest in Leicestershire is visually attractive and of mineral important. The requirements of Britain's road-building programme have to be taken into account and related especially to the development of new routes. These include, for example, access roads to the Channel Tunnel and to the Humber Estuary which are growing in importance as gateways to Europe. Questions about whether road-building solves traffic congestion may also be debated.

Studies in Aspects of Physical Geography

Our technological, urban civilisation is just as dependent upon conditions and process in the natural world as were our hunter-gatherer ancestors. However, our dependence is dangerously less obvious.

One useful way to study physical environments in rural and urban areas is by investigating local relief and drainage patterns and their relationship to building. All villages and towns are located and developed partly in response to relief and drainage features. In all but the flattest towns there are perceptible variations in height which can be used to trace the course of streams even though these may now run in pipes or culverts. Street names, large scale maps, interviews with residents, and old editions of O.S. maps can all help with this fascinating detective work.

Studies of People and Their Environments

The most influential environments within which most people live, work and are governed are human forms and systems of economic, social and political organisation of a formal or informal kind.

One example of a contemporary, all-powerful economic environment is provided by the Russian aluminium industry. The workers' life expectancy is about 47 years. Their living and working conditions are appalling. The aluminium they produce is sold at about half the price of the next-cheapest producers, Australia, Canada and Venezuela. Yet even these countries are low cost producers when compared with Britain, Germany, the United States or Spain. The Russian industry's effective environment is its countrys' absolute need to sell aluminium in a competitive world market to obtain foreign currency. No other circumstance, natural or economic, is more important for that country.

Environmental Studies

All aspects of geography draw together under this heading and one is reminded that human actions are inescapably related to the well-being of the natural world.

Perhaps the most powerful idea to be developed under this section is that of intervention. All aspects of human life are about intevention. Merely by eating, drinking requiring clothes and other facilities, and producing waste even one family or village must make demands upon the modify the systems of the natural world. How much greater then is the impact on the environment of a growing megalopolis such as Mexico City, which is predicted to reach population of 25 millions by the year 2020. The magnitude of the task of supplying water and food to so many people in one place and disposing of their waste products is staggering. It is also unprecedented in the whole history of the human race.

There are many other kinds of intervention. By substituting roofs and streets for farmland, growing towns produce an instantaneous run-off of rain into rivers exacerbating existing flood control problems. The replacement of natural vegetation with crops over most of the habitable earth has lead to a dramatic decline in biodiversity with unknown, long-term effects. Extraction and burning of fossil fuels produces toxic discharges into the atmosphere which may contribute to the 'greenhouse effect'

There are many examples of this kind. Geography and environmental education teach us that human beings must learn to understand and moderate their interventions in the natural world if the human race is to survive. 'Spaceship Earth' is neither an inexhaustible nor an indestructible resource.

Modern Foreign Languages

Before the advant of the National Curriculum, modern foreign language programmes often reflected environmental concern and the resulting contribution to students' knowledge about our environment has traditionally been quite significant. Sixth form studies would include topics such as polution, tourism, beauty spots, the climate of the target language community. At other levels, materials reflected this interest, for example, the Collection Vecue reader about the massacre of baby seals (Lezy in eds. Buckby and Buckby, 1985).

Environmental awareness-raising was not statutory and it could be argued that 'positive' outcomes were incidental rather than pre-planned.

Nevertheless, modern language courses have long included a focus on environmental issues.

National Curriculum Expectations and Approaches

Modern foreign language studies are expected to contribute in a planned way to the development of knowledge, understanding and skills in this important domain. With regard to acquisition of knowledge about the environment (NCC, 1990), Areas of Experience of Modern Foreign Languages Programmes of Study include Everyday Activities (*Area* A), The World Around Us (*Area* C), the World of Education, Training and Work (*Area* D), The International World (*Area F*), all of which afford opportunities for study of environment-related content. NCC guidance (1990) stresses all aspects of the curriculum contribute to environmental education, MFL programmes offer opportunities for study of climate patterns in other countries, of ways of life, of people and of their communities.

Textbooks already offer opportunities for exposure to environment-related content. McNab and Barrabe (1992a) present a unit on animals with students reading about the possible extinction of elphants and preparing posters that promote elephant welfare and protection. In the same work, appreciation of the earth's riches is also promoted (McNab) and Barrabe, 1992b) and comparisons of daily life across the globe are facilitated. Mary Glasgow Publications' *French-for the National Curriculum* includes a students' book and cassette devoted to the environment. (Hurren, 1993) Other recently produced course books provide similar opportunities and for post—16 study, this trend is maintained, for example, with the subscription series *Thematique/Thematisch* (Mary Glasgow). There is no shortage of material. In addition, opportunities for 'real' experience also exist, for example, the log of oceanographer Jean-Louis Etienne available on Minitel via Campus 2000 (*Langauge World,* March 1994).

The Challenge to Teacher of Modrn Languages

National Curriculum proposals (DES, 1990) focussed on the contribution that modern languages could make by suggesting that learners would be able to talk and write about issues of interest and concern to themselves, including environment. Cross-curricular activity could be organised by languages departments themselves, though inter-departmental projects or through the teaching of other subjects in the target language. The proposals suggested that the second would be the most appropriate response. (DES, 1990).

With the final proposals, the relationship to other areas of the curriculum was re-emphasised. Students of modern foreign languages should be offered the change to explore links with other subjects and to develop knowledge, understanding and skills related to environmental education (DES, 1991). Working with other subject departments in strongy encouraged, in single lessons, in a series of lessons, on joing projects or in Key State 4 short courses. Examples of such cooperation have been reported, but pressures on teachers often leave little time for such creative planning. Unwillingness, to engage in cross-disciplinary projects (Gayford, 1993) may account for some of the lack of development. Nevertheless, this may become more readily achievable, with post-Dearing revisions, as links with other subjects as Key Stage 4 become more accessible in the slimmer core curriculum.

Modern languages lessons have the potential to develop knowledge, understanding and skills related to cross-curricular dimensions and themes. *Modern Foreign Languages Non-Statutory Guidance* (NCC, 1992) offers pollution as a topic for study in Key Stage 4 with focus on daily routines, health and fitness, industry, advertising, international organisation, designing and marketing all featuring as contexts for the study of the topic. However, the section on differentiation in the *Guidance* offers a Year 10 target group an extremely challenging example of a unit of work, a worthy aim, but one must examine how fruitful and realizable this is in practice. The scenario described seems more attainable in Year 12 than in Year 10. While reading and listening tasks are possible at this level, it is hard to envisage many 14 to 15 year old learners being able to use another language in detailed discussion of dangers to the environment unless more time is devoted to the study of the foreign language. There is the danger that students who struggle to express views, for lack of language, may suffer demotivation and develop negative attitudes not ony to the language but also to the subject matter. Teaching environmental education through the foundation subject may limit opportunities for understanding where students' subject achievement levels vary greatly.

One must consider how successfully environmental issues can be covered in language lessons that are conducted predominatly in the target langauge. With the Dearing Review, first language study in Key Stages 3 and 4 can be restricted to 315 hours of instructions, with some learners restricted to 262 hours. In this time, it is no easy task to promote language proficieny and integrate cross-curricular themes such that learners speak and write about them with purpose and success. In addition, second language courses receive less time, possibly as little as 180 hours. Given the demands for success at GCSE, there may be a temptation to pay lip-service to the environment, possibly to resort to taken lessons on an environmental problem. However, since the prescribed areas of experience focus on the world around us and the international world, environmental education is integral to the Programme of Study. The issue cannot be passed over.

In the Programmes of Study, emphasis is placed on the development of knowledge, understanding and skills. These can be gained through collaborative, problem-solving and data-gathering approaches in real or simulated cross-cultural contexts. However, students should also be helped to acquire attitudes and values needed to protect the environment (NCC, 1990) and be encouraged to participate in the resolution of environmental problems. Many courses seem to involve a focus on the problems associated with the environment. The dangers of a series of gloom-laden topic-based units of work have been explored (Gayford, 1993). Rather than focussing on the problems of the environment, perhaps modern language teachers should seek to explore the environment as seen by speakers from other cultures in order to 'develop an appreciation of the natural, built, social and cultural environments' (Gayford, 1993) of the communities speaking the target language. This appreciation would represent a considerable contribution to general education, whatever the students' level of achievement in the foreign language.

Approaches and Strategies

The development of positive attitudes to the learning of languages has long been a concern in secondary schools. An obvious strategy is the educational visit abroad, planed jointly with a history or geography department. While useful, this does not affect all students equally. MFL teachers have striven to foster a positive appreciation of the value of a foreign language to the comprehensive development of all learners. This aspiration should inform approaches as teachers seek to promote respect for the beliefs of other peoples, greater cross-cultural understanding and concern for the global environment.

The *Non-Statutory Guidance* (1992) lists topics in MFL that focus on environment in Key Stage 3 and key Stage 4: on forms of travel and their affects on the environmental, energy sources used in the home, waste disposal, noice pollution, products used in the home. Within the latter, scope exists for the exchange of information with partner schools in the target language community. Schools could exchange survey information on products used in the home, on recycling practice, on examples of successful attempts at environmental protection in the home. Such activities could assist not only the development of attitudes but also of skills, such as gathering and evaluating information, entering it on a dabase and working cooperatively with others.

The atmosphere of the department also contributes must to a

developing appreciation of the richness of our environment and the need to work at its enhancement. Attractive, regularly maintained displayes, respect for resources used in the classroom, respect for differing points of view, promotional posters in the target language, commitment to the creation of a pleasant working environment (Thomspson, 1993). These qualities, when regularly evident in classroom life, carry messages about the value of students' own surroundings. Such respect for the immediate environment promotes attitudes that help students address issues and establish a growing sense of environmental responsibility which can be shared with speakers of other languages.

Art

Following the identification of Environmental Education as a cross-curricular theme, the more detailed guidance given on its development (NCC, 1990a; CCW, 1992a) recognized the potential contribution of art of this area of teaching and learning. As the Welsh Advisory Paper points out, 'Environmental Education is frequenly at its most powerful when it is approached through the art of humanities. Providing pupils with opportunities to learn in and from the environment can involve 'sensing'... and shaping materials... to create and express impressions and feelings'. (CCW, 1992b)

This and similar statements are welcome in that they recognize art as 'the missing component in environmental education' (Adams and Ward, 1982b) and acknowledge the major role which art education can play in developing the knowledge, understanding, awareness and action needed to improve the relationships between citizens of the future and their environment. But as they stand, such statements, even when supported by detailed case studies and suggestions for teachers (see, for example, NCC 1990b), are insufficient. If teachers are consistently to create effective teaching-learning experiences for their pupils and themselves, a deeper understanding is needed. both of art and its relationship to the environment.

Here, as elsewhere, the key to understanding the contribution which art has to make to the curriculum as a whole is a changed perception of art itself as an activity. Art can be viewed as a synthesis between two opposing tendencies, which may appear to be in opposition but art in fact complementary. The first is characterized by an individualistic approach, with an emphasis on creativity, originality and expression. The second tendency is to emphasize the social nature of art, which is seen as an activity rooted in tradition, but centred on investigation, exploration and communication. In Europe and America during the present century there has been a strong tendency to value the individualistic approach over the social, so that in education the potential of art as a means of investigating, experimenting, discovering and communicating has been underestimated and under exploited.

As the Statutory Orders for Art in the National Curriculum imply, however, there is a need to redress the balance, to recognize that developing knowledge, understanding and the ability to communicate through investigation is as important a part of art education as the expression of feelings, ideas and themes through creative activity. (DES, 1992; Adams and Ward, 1982c)

Investigation and Communications

All learning is carried out by way of exploration and diaogue with the world around us, whether it be with people, books, toys, machines, objects of art, music or the wider environment. Art as an activity has its foundation in visual exploration and investigation. This is clearly recognized in the current National Curriculum, where the Attainment Targets and Programme of Studies for art based on the development of visual perception (ATI) and visual literacy (AT2). Visual perception is the ability to observe; to see with understanding, both the real world and what is remembered or imagined. Visual perception, together with the skills of analysing and recording what is observed, underlies the more complex skills of visual literacy, which is the ability to 'get information from what we see... to understand at a conscious level the visual language used within a particular culture' (Zimmer and Zimmer, 1978).

Visual perception and visual literacy can be developed only by investigating for ourselves what is around us, and responding to what our environment (including works of art) has to communicate. As the examples provided in the National Curriculum show, visual exploration of the wider environment is an essential part of this process. If such investigation, analysis and recording are linked to environmental education, they can provide the basis of visual experience from which not only art work, but information, opinions, values and action can develop (Adams and Ward, 1982a).

When designing and making, the artist or craftsperson carries on what is in effect an investigative dialogue with materials and the developing workpiece, whether it be painting, drawing, sculpure, pottery, textiles, woodwork or whatever. In the course of this dialogue, new possibilities arise and are exploited: the process is one of constant experiment and criticism, modification, acceptance and rejection. 'Every good work of art...communicates the sense that something in it has been newly tried. The artist is always in training' (Scharf, 1962). This is no less true of pupils in school as it is of established professional artists, and when the work undertaken has the environment as its focus and subject-matter the interchange becomes a three-cornered one, with the artist exploring both the environment and the developing work simultaneously, using each to explore the properties and possibilities of the other.

This being, so, it is to be regretted that the detailed advice in *Curriculum Guidance 7* fails to identify visual investigation through art as the major means of gathering knolwedge and information. Three linked components of environmental education are identified: education about the environment (knowledge); education for the environment (values, attitudes, positive action) and education in and through the environment (a resource). (NCC, 1990c) The role of art in the second and third components is clearly charted; but in spite of the development work of the Art and the Built Environment Project (Adams and Ward, 1982a), it has no place in the first. The guidance is that sufficient knowledge about the environment can be developed through scientific, technological and geographical investigations. This narrow approach to finding out about the environment makes sense only if the beauty or ugliness of our environment is of no concern. If we care about the environment and wish to improve it, an essential part of what we have to learn about it concerns its visual quality, both what it is, positive and negative, and what it might become.

There is extensive literature on the visual quality of the environment, much of which is concerned directly with helping the reader to develop the visual perception and literacy needed to view it critically, understand what it has to offer and how it might be conserved or improved. Much of this has been addressed to architects and planners, but some of the older work, which has achieved classic status, is a very valuable introduction and source of ideas for teachers interested in exploring environmental education through art (or vice versa). Particularly useful and accessible are Fairbrother (1974) on the landscape and environment as a whole, and Cullen (1971) on the urban 'townscape'. The ideas of Cullen and others, applied in the context of secondary and sixth form art courses, form the basis of the Art and the Built Environment Project (Adams and Ward, 1982a), which provides a very useful resource for teachers, using the processes of visual exploration and critical appraisal to develop a synthesis between art and environmental education. Extending the same approach to include the primary sector and the wider environment is the most obvious way to develop the use of art work as a means of communicating the findings of investigations and ideas for improvement and conservation.

Creation and Expression

The emphasis which has been placed here on the more social aspects of art as a means of investigation and communication should not be read as devaluing its role in developing individual creativity and expression. In a balanced concept of art, the two are seen as working together, not in conflict. A useful viewpoint in thinking about the creative-expressive dimension of art in relation to environmental education is one which contrasts objects of art and work of art (Wollheim, 1980). Put very simply, the idea is that the object or art, the actual physical object which the artist or eraftsperson produces, is distinct from the work of art, which is seen as the response of the spectator to the object; the meaning and emotion which persons create for themselves as a result of seeing and interacting with the object. The significance of this idea in the educational context is that it emphasizes the importance of what is learned, felt and experienced by the artist through the process of making the object, and by the spectator through the process of interacting with it visually. The point is made that at gives us the opportunity to evoke intuitive, emotional responses, as well as rational ones, through visual rather than verbal language.

One of the simplest and most direct ways to evoke such responses is by way of symbols. Examples with which children may already be familiar are those used by conservation groups: the giant panda of the World Wildlife Fund and the avocet of the RSPB, for example. Others which have been used to represent threatened wildlife in Britain include the badger, hedge-hog and wild orchid. Similar images, particularly if simplified from a representational into a graphic form (as the panda and avocet have been), can be used to represent environmental and conservation issues locally, provided that those to whom the message is addressed will immediately 'read' the symbol and recognize its significance. Powerful messages, particularly messages of protect, can be conveyed by violently contrasting images, which may combine the representational with the symbolic. One famous example coupled a photograph of a Palladian mansion and its park with a tyre track, brutally superimposed in black. The proposed motorway across the park was never built.

The imaginative-creative approach is also useful when pupils are investigating and expressing a concern for environments such as tropical rain forest or high mountain wilderness, which they cannot experience at first hand. Ideas and images to evoke mood and personal response to such environments and their plight can often be derived as much from the fantasy of Henri Rousseau as from the clarity of Ansal Adams' photographs, but whatever sources are used, effective work will both depend on and develop pupils' visual perception and literacy.

As a final example, art made in and from the environment offers an approach to personal response and creatively which seems to be very much under-exploited at present. This related to the 'Land Art' of the 1960s and 70s, but is much smaller in scale and usually more decorative and ephemeral. The outstanding exponent of this art form is Andy Goldsworthy (Goldsworthy, 1990), who uses material from an environment to create an object of art within it, which may last only for a few hours, but which is recorded by photography. Using Goldsworthy's photographs as stimuli, public and teachers with no previous experience, working in school grounds, gardens and the landscape, have consistently produced remarkable and beautiful results. Work of this kind provides what is in some ways a paradigm of the relationship between art and environmental education. A feeling is generted of contact with and empathy for the earth, which can help both pupils and teachers to the realization that mankind is not above the environment, nor in control of it, but is a part of it and all the changes which it undergoes.

Neither the problems nor the solutions are new. Nearly half a century ago, Alan Jarvis wrote:

> Because day in, day out, we see so much, and because so much of what we see is familiar, our sense of awareness of our environment...becomes blunted. We see, as we live, by habit...The result of the indifference of the vast majority of us to our visual environment is the increasing degradation of our surroundings...Herein lies the vicious circle whereby each generation is forced, in self-protection, to shut its eyes to the environ-ment...The circle will be broken only by increasing our own and our children's awareness of our surroundings and, having learned to seem them, by being determined to change them.
>
> (Jarvis, 1948)

The problem is still with us, but so is the vision to confront and solve it. In doing this, the partnership between art and environmental education has a central, not merely a peripheral role.

Physical Education

The National Curriculum Council's publications, *Curriculum Guidance 7* (NCC, 1990) and *Physical education in the National Curriculum* (NCC, 1992) virtually exclude Physical Education as a possible contributor to environmental education. One would suggest that this results from a lack of understanding from enviromentalists about the nature of physical education (P.E). which extends beyond the purely physical. The publication of *Curriculum Guidance 7* predated the statutory orders for P.E. which include Outdoor and Adventurous Activities, and this may partly account for the scant references to it in the document. The narrow interpretation of the aims of P.E. in the statutory guidelines compounds the situation. Careful reading of both documents reveals the possibilities for environmental education. These possibilities can be more explicitly stted to show where P.E. can:

> Provide opportunities to acquire the knowledge, values, attitudes, commitment and skills needed to protect and improve the environment. Encourage pupils to examine and interpret the environment from a variety of persectives physical...political... technological...aesthetic, ethical and spiritual.
>
> (Curriculum Guidance 7, 1990)

In order for P.E. to succeed in making a valuable contribution to environmental education, each department needs to seriously examine its curriculum, question its current practice and attention it gives to environmental issues. Teachers need to reappraise their own attitudes towards recreational use of all environments and decide to what extent these match the school policy statement on the environment. An environmentally friendly approach by the department would force teachers to adopt teaching strategies that include environmental awareness and work towards developing, in students, a positive attitude towards creative use of the environment for sport and recreation. An audit for environmental education in a local school revealed that the P.E. department through they bore no responsibility towards it. (Bishop, 1992)

A large percentage of school P.E. takes place out of doors in spaces that science and geography might exploit for environmental education. Outdoor exercise is an important factor in making physical activity enjoyable for many participants. A sense of awe, wonder, freedom and the pure enjoyment of open spaces are enshrined within the aims of outdoor and adventure education. The growth in demand for recreation spaces of a diverse nature in the countryside has resulted in the formulation of guidelines, planning laws, Parliamentary Acts and strategic plans to give all users access. Giyptis (1991) suggests that the large number of people wanting countryside recreation must work together to more strongly advocate flexible schemes, which are environmentally protective and positive, otherwise:

> they could lose out to increasingly—and unnecessarily-powerful and articulate protectionists.
>
> (Glyptis, 1991)

Physical education teachers have the opportunity and responsibility to help students develop positive attitudes to the environment as consumers so as to ensure that they maintain and increase access to the countryside and urban open spaces for recreation and sport.

Education Through the Environment

Effective school policies start from an audit of the whole school environment. This should include the indoor and outdoor spaces for P.E.; changing, storage, display and access areas. Often these are neglected in schools and present an image that does not value the quality of the environment for physical activity. It would be comparatively easy to improve the general apperance of, and provide adequate facilities to maintain the cleanliness of the area, e.g. mud scrapers and adequate paved entrances to playing fields. Well-maintained notice and information boards would further enhance the environment and could include information about environmental issues as they relate to sport in particular. Physical educationalists have to provide far more than a physical experience if they are to succeed in developing active lifestyles in students. The whole experience is important and creating clean and welcoming venues which challenge the traditional sweaty, masculine image is a major factor in the success of modern facilities. Schools need to treat this issue seriouly.

Physical education can contribute to playground development projects through all key stages. Work in this area could easily and profitably move beyond the traditional design and technology boundaries. Students could become involved in resolving the tensions between creative and destructive use of the environmental for recreational and sporting use. They might consider the conflicting demands and agree solutions that go some way towards satisfying all users.

Education about the Environment

Sperle and Wilken (1991) state that:

> compared to other sources of pollution, such as industry, sport certainly contributes relatively little to the harmful effects on the environment. However, this does not relieve it of the obligation to minimise the burdens it places on nature and the environment as far as possible.

Personal experience leads the author to suggest that few sportspeople seriously engage in the debate concerning the impact of recretional and sporting pursuits on the environment. It is generally accepted that there is a need for substantial growth in facilities to meet present and future demands. The environmental impact of providing these facilities, many of which are intrusive and require large tracts of scarce land, is at present inadequately debated. It is important that users of facilities need to develop a critical awareness of the issues pertaining to increased provision. This could result in more appreciation of the view of others and raise the importance of environmental considerations in sporting developments to the benefit of all. Within normal lessons, teachers could interweave a dimension that raises the issue of students as consumers of leisure and considers how all activities affect the environment to some degree. The following are some of the questions that could be posed to raise awareness:

Can/should playing fields be landscaped into the surrounding area?

How far do sports buildings intrude into the environment and what needs to be done to improve their apearance?

Are such changes affordable?

What factors determine the type of structure, its site and the materials used?

What are the concerns about floodlighting facilities?

Why do golf course developments attracts so many objections?

Can noisy leisure pursuits like motor racing and shooting be accommodated in an acceptable way?

How can national sporting festivals be made more environmentally friendly (e.g. London Marathon, Wimbledon, British Grand Prix)?

What level of change to the existing environment is permissible for recreational and sporting use?

Are new activities like Ambush! (a combat game) creative or destructive uses of the environment?

Do the advantages of taking part in water-based sports outweight the disadvantages caused by their impact on water courses?

Physical Education staff could build up resource packs to provide interesting case studies for inclusion in Personal and Social Education modules or environmental education events. The development of sports facilities within urban areas provides frequent, local examples of the tensions between participants and residents and would provide excellent starting points to consider the questions posed above. It is important that teachers go further than 'explore the potential for physical activities within the immediate environment' (NCC, 1992) and consider both the impact of these activities on the environment and others in the community.

Education in the Environment

In Finland the 'Move on behalf of Nature' National Campaign is trying to emphasise the importance of physical activity in nature as a context for intellectual, ethical and aesthetic growth (Vuolle, 1991). Telana (1991) reports that in Nordic countries the natural environment has been found to be an important motivating factor for physical activity. In Britain the Outdoor Education Movement has emphasised for impact of outdoor and adventurous activities on the development of the individual across the social, psychological, moral, aesthetic, intellectual and physical domains. Humberstone (1993) provides a critique of the diminution of Outdoor Education within National Curriculum documentation. In order for teachers to go some way towards accessing the potential benefits in personal growth for their students, they need to again, go beyond the guidelines in the Programmes of Study for Outdoor and Adventurous Activities which concentrate on safety matters. Not until (and only in) Key Stage 3 is any appreciation of or respect for the environment, mentioned. This utilitarian approach to the outdoors, sidelines the importance of introducing students to the aesthetic and emotional experiences that the natural environment offers. The sense of exhilaration and humility which so many experience are not mentioned. Importantly, it is from this perspective that students will be better able to appreciate the delicate balance between use and abuse of the environment. P.E. teachers, alone, can approach all their outdoor education from this standpoint, ensuring that all students have the opportunity to experience natural and remote environments that are likely to arouse aesthetic and emotional responses. Crucially, teachers should encourage students to reflect on their outdoor experiences from this perspective. This is more likely to affect the attitudes and future actions of students.

Conclusion

There is a strong case for increased environmental education within P.E. The aim of all departments should be to promote environmentally friendly behaviour within the framework of practising sport and related activities. The starting point will be to critically examine their current physical working conditions and departmental statements concerning the environment.

Music

Music is a powerful artistic medium through which pupils can be encouraged:

- to express their ideas and views about the environment;
- to examine and interpret the environment from an aesthetic perspective;
- to become aware of and curious about the environment and to participate actively in resolving environmental problems.

(NCC, 1990a)

Music is also a consumer of rare timbers, a source of pollution, and a weapon of psychological warfare. It can be shown how and why music can and should contribute to environmental education.

There are at leat three reasons why music should make this contribution. The first is music's communicative power. In the West, pupular performers such as Bob Geldof and Band-Aid, Sting and Paul Simon have made millions of people aware of the effects of environmental issues in Africa and South America by means of recorded music. Briceno and Pitt

(1988) however, include descriptions of projects, run typically by young people, in rural India, Africa and South America which show the importance of live music, dance, drama and poetry in informing rural communities of environmental threats. Tobayiwa (1988), deploring the intrusion of European educational methods in Zimbabwe, recalls the value of learning through songs:

> We learnt the alphabet in song, learnt how to spell in song. We even learnt to speak English in song. Our teacher knew how to reach us.
>
> (Tobayiwa, 1988)

Secondly, because music is not a static medium it can illustrate environmental processes which change over time such as:

- cycle—the water cycle and acid rain;
- ecosystems—the disequilibrium caused by deforestation;
- layering—atmosheric layers and climatic change.

The following quotation might inspire a composition in three movements or a musical collage about climatic change:

> The earth's climate changes. It is vastly different now from what it was 100 million years age when dinosaurs dominated the planed and tropical plants grew at high latitudes; it is different from what it was even 18,000 years ago when ice-sheets covered much more of the northern hemisphere. In the future it will surely continue to evolve... In part the evolution will be driven by natural causes... But future climatic change...will probably have another comparably important source as well human activities.
>
> (Schneider, 1990)

Almost uniquely, music can model the nature of change, however slight or sudden. Key Stage 3 and 4 students could experiment with ways to represent qualitative change, e.g. metamorphosis, mutation, and pollution, by a change of instruments, rhythem or tonality. Quantitative change as in growth, or increased pollution, or decreased resources could be represented musically by an increased pollution, or decreased resources could be represented musically by an increase or decrease in one musical element such as loudness, tempo, or pitch. As students discuss and try out ways to model these changes, they will be developing their understanding of environmental processes and musical elements. *Music in the National Curriculum* (DES, 1992) in each Key Stage refers to composing music in response to a wide range of stimuli, including 'everyday sounds', 'sounds from the environment' (Key Stage 1) and 'compose a piece on an environmental theme' is a Key Stage 3 example.

A third reason for music to be part of environmental education is for the sake of music itself. In spite of the wealth of environmentally inspired music in the Western orchestral repertoire (by e.g. Debussy, Delius, Elgar,

Mendelssohn, etc.) music was nearly left out of *Curriculum Guidance 7.* It finally appears in a drawing of a bit of paper tacked on to the last page before Appendix 1. In view of this add-on status accorded music in the minds of the working party, music coordinators must actively promote music as an expressive medium and participate in cross-curricular teams. Primary music coordinators will find Wheway and Thomson's (1993) *Explore music through geography* invaluable for work with non-specialist colleagues. It is full of simple and clear composition tasks and listening suggestions with titles such as *Sounds of town and country; Timespan; Graval pit*, a composition project about the effects of mineral extraction on the local environment; *Recycled paper, Rainforest,* a Key Stage 2 rhythm layering activity; and more. *Explore music through science* in the same series is also very helpful. For Key Stage 3, Ellis's (1987) *Out of bounds,* is a very good source of materials and musical projects on environmental issues such as pollution and nuclear energy. These projects will enrich the status of music in the curriculum if music staff work in teams with other subject specialists. Royle et al., (1993) describe in detail a Year 8 collaborative music, geography and Welsh project based on the Braer oil-tanker disaster off the Shetland Isles. This project had environmental, economic and industrial understanding and citizenship education components.

Curriculum Guidance 7 (NCC, 1990) gives several examples of environmental projects in which music could play a part. For example, the Key Stage 2 project involving links with Nigeria could have included music in the artistic exchanges. In *The Nature Trail* (NCC, 1990b) for Key Stage 1, the children were blindfolded to them focus on listening to sounds such as their footsteps, and on feeling textures such as tree barks. After the trail, instead of the visually mediated follow-up activities suggested, they could have continued to work with sound, and, as the *Non-Statutory Guidance for Music in the National Curriculum for Wales,* suggests:

- selected and tape-recorded, or sampled, the sounds;
- selected sound sources e.g. body sounds, instruments, sticks and pebbles, to imitate the sounds heard;
- made up new words to a know tune to recall the walk;
- incorporated the sounds into a class sound picture.

(CCW, 1992)

They could have modified the popular *Ant Trail* activity, for example (see Leicestershire Arts, 1992). The trail is drawn on a large sheet of paper and the regions where certain sounds (e.g. footsteps on different surfaces, road noises) were heard are shown. This forms the score. The children decide, in small groups perhaps, how to make the various sounds encountered including the sound of the children themselves. One group then makes the children' sound as someone slowly points with a finger they way along the trail. As the finger enters each region, each group makes appropriate sounds with or instead of the 'children's group'. Many variations can be made to this basic idea and it can be adapted for any environmental setting, e.g. city centre, seashore, school building.

The NCC document does not develop the idea but the examples imply a progression from simple description and recording of environmental states and events at key Stage 1 through the identification of environmental changes, to determining potential problems and proposing solutions to them by Key Stages 3 and 4. The awareness of the conflict between environmental and economic issues and the need to find compromises becomes more prominent in the later key stages. Students will find many ·ways to express such conflict through music.

Music ABOUT the Environment

The examples given up to this point have been mostly music about the environment and it is easy to find examples of Western music which apparently represent aspects of the environment. Walker (1990), however, traces the history of this controversial idea back ot Plato and warns strongly against the temptation to apply this Western musical belief to the music of other cultures. Key Stage 3 and 4 students could have a present day version of the nineteenth century debate about representation in music, and find 'pure' and representational musical extracts to support their arguments.

Music FOR the Environment

Music's capability to express and arouse emotion can be used to the full in environmental education in composition and listening work. Groups should be encouraged to discuss the issues involved and express their views in the music. They could prepare variations to suggest the attitudes of, e.g. road builders, car users, local people and environmentalists to a new motorway (and see *Gravel pit,* above). The roles of songs and actions in getting clear messages across could be explored.

Music IN and THROUGH the Environment

Both in and through the environment. music is a culprit. It pollutes the environment in supermarkets and city shopping malls. People have filed court cases against their music-loving semi-detached nighbours, where musical taste, boredom thresholds and preferred volume levels were incompatible. In schools, antagonism between musicians and other staff about sound levels is not unknown. There is scope for reserach, role-play, debate or real life negotiation here where the domains of citizenship and environmental education overlap. As for music through the environment, older students could find out more about the sources of raw materials for instruments and debate the use of rare materials, such as ivory, ebony, resewood and mahogany. This may culminate in an improvement played entirely on recyclable instruments made from paper, cans and, with care, glass.

Religious Education

And God saw everything that he had made, and behold it was very good (Genesis, 1.31). So ends the first part of the Genesis narrative, the description of the completion of the heavens and earth—how God created all living things and planted a garden eastward in Eden, a garden destined to be ruined when man and women ate from the tree of knowledge. The magisterial severity of the biblical pross and its poetic fire still has to power to strike awe into an older generation. Who, for example, can easily forget the picture of Adam and Eve walking in the garden during 'the cool of the day' shortly before all hell is let loose? (Genesis, 3.8) While such scenes currently continue to resonate in a collective cultural memory, it is doubtful whether they will do so for very much longer. Religious echoes are fast fading. Biblical prose has little impact on a generation of children whose collective ignorance in all areas of belief would, in earlier times, had detonated a national scandal. (McKie, 1993)

Voices from the new right do in fact define the present state of religious education in Britain as a national scandal. (Burn and Hart, 1988) While this assertion may, or may not, be true, the generation of a state of moral panic fuels the development of a 'back to basics' agenda. (Cohen, 1972) An examination of this agenda is important because I would argue that it seriously threatens good teaching in the areas of both religious and envircnmental education. Moral panics invariably breed scapegoats. Currently the blame for falling standards, both intellectual and behavioural, is pinned upon teachers, who are castigated for failing to do what everyone else in society has half forgotten, namely, behaving by codes underpinned by Christian ethics. Such an analysis precipitates a rush to put old wine into new bottles. The positive attributes of sound, Bible-based religious knowledge are revisited by those who find virtue only in the past. (Jeal, 1994) While such attitudes seriously set back the cause of intelligent religious education, they threaten environmental education with extinction. The latter is viewed as new-fangled fiddle-faddle, because environmental education is not deemed to be a proper subject. In this context the 1993 Dearing Review of the National Curriculum is ominously silent concerning cross-curriculum themes. (Dearing, 1993) The Dearning mission of slimming down a bloated curriculum. begin to appear as a cover for a return to curriculum orthodoxy based on subjects.

The intellectual incoherence of the 'back to basics' movement should not full teachers into understimating the potential threat. It has often been remarked that ideology is proof reason. The potentially destructive force embodied in 'back to basics' can be demonstrated by working through a concise case study.

Let us pursue the rationale for biblical teaching in terms of linking the Genesis story within an environmental topic, tackling the theme of creation Practical, professional issues confront the teacher at every turn. Firstly, regardless of the age range envisaged, what is the status of the biblical narative? In a multicultural society, the Bible is now one sacred text among many. Secondary, if the Genesis story is to be treated as poetic fable or sustained allegory, how does this stand against a backdrop of Bible literalism, currently thriving and spreading far beyond its breeding grounds in the southern states of America? Evangelical fundamentalists do, however, have a point to make. If, in re-warking the Genesis narrative for younger children, the text assumes the qualities and attributes of a 'fairy story', what is to stop children thinking of the Bible as one long fairy story? The problems increase with older children. Linking scientific and allegorical explanations together makes the latter appear, at best, whimsical, and at worst, stupid. Perhaps the best contemporary commentary on the perils of peddling Bible stories without very careful consideration is offered by a ten year old girl, whose hand shot up after listening to the sentence which begins this chapter. 'Please, sir,' she said, 'how do we know God is a he?'

This pupil's perceptive response deserves attention. Significantly they student, wise beyond her years, is interacting with the text. This in itself is wothy of commendation rather than repression. Indeed, interaction is welcomed by teachers, most of whom are all too accustomed to the apathetic boredom displayed by the majority of students when confronted by 'traditional' R.E. The idea that pupils will suddenly and reverentially change their learning and behaviour modes because the Bible has been involved, is sadly mistaken. The naivety of this perception is matched only by the notion that hell fire and damnation can be revived in the interests of curbing crime. (Key, 1994)

So, what is to be done? Tossed about in the confusions and uncertainties of a post-Christian (Gilbert, 1980), decidedly secularized society (Chadwick, 1975), there is a strong temptation for R.E. teachers to succumb to despair. Like John Bunyan, it is difficult not to hear all too loudly and insistently the mocking voices of Doupt and Despair. As pollution rises and the ozone layer dwindles, environmentalists may well share similar doubts and anguish. I wish to argue that in the face of pervasive anxiety, considered action provides the best form of therapy.

Therefore in concluding this chapter I have three objectives:

- to set out the defining qualities of Religious Education;
- to demonstrate where R.E. and Environmental Education should overlap and, on occasions, integrate;
- to offer information as to where relevant sources can be obtained.

The Defining Qualities of Religious Education

The pace of secularization in Britain has meant that for some time there has been utter confusion regarding what constitutes religious education. While this debate is properly ongoing, teachers may find it helpful to keep in mind the following points. Religious education is:

- ultimately and intimately concerned with spiritual issues and questions;
- it confronts students with the possibility of a God (or some kind of divine presence) active in the world and not to be relegated to the side lines of history;
- it is essentially concerned with exploring beliefs and values and how these determine decisions and behaviour.

Such a definite and challenging framework tends to make teachers feel uncomfortable. It certaintly helps to explain one of the unacknowedged rituals of school life, namely an agitated headteacher behaving like Coleridge's Ancient Mariner, 'stopping one in three' by the staff room door when an R.E. lesson requires to be covered. Many teachers shrink from the task for a variety of reasons. Quite apart from feelings of mutinous despair at losing a precious 'free' lesson, experienced professionals are unsure of R.E., often in terms of both knowledge and skills. Because they are unsure in these areas, they have genuiwe anxieties regarding their own personal integrity in teaching what they, and others, find confusing. (Patten, 1994) Acknowledging the possibility of a God or a divine presence in the world is an intensely personal matter. Personal belief, or lack of it, does not however preclude teachers from intering into a serious consideration of values and behaviours. It is precisely at this point that colleagues working across R.E. and environmental education need to make common cause.

Religious Education and Environmental Education: A Common Agenda?

Before being abruptly consigned to the dustbin of history (Baker, 1993), the National Curriculum Council undertook pioneering work in areas of cross-curricular themes and dimensions. NCC *Curriculum Guidance 7, Environmental Education*, has been extensively referred to in this book and I have no wish to be unnecessarily repetitive. However, in setting out appropriate and relevant Skills and Attitudes for students to acquire in studying Environmental Education, the NCC authors are providing significant action points to which R.E specialists should pay attention. *Curriculum Guidance 7* stresses the need to promote within students:

appreciation of, and care and concern for, the environment and for other living things;

independence of thought on environmental issues;

a respect for evidence and rational argument;

tolerance and open-mindedness.

These points are worth quoting in full because they uncerringly replicate skills and dispositions identified at national and local levels in the R.E. field. (Wilson, 1993 and Northants LEA, 1987) Here the common cause is made explicit. Collectively these skills, attitudes and dispositions provide the means for cooperation between and across the two curriculum areas, not least in terms of pupil profiling and records of achievement. Giving priority to skills and attitudes is one way of additionally underscoring the importance in R.E. and environmental education of active learning. Doing things with children is in most cases, preferable to preaching at them. For this reason I am hesitant to be too prescriptive in terms of defining curriculum areas and content. In terms of my own planning and teaching, however, I have found a single sentence from the *General Thanksgiving* to be a useful organizer. 'We bless you for our 'Creation', 'Preservation' and all the 'Blessings' of this life.' (ASB, 1980) Whether ascribed to a divine inspiration or not, these three headings provide key starting points for integrated R.E. and environmental education across the age range.

Access to Resources

When considering the current interest in returning to formal teaching, one is tempted to suspect, pessimistically, that the problem of resources is exerting an undue influence. How much quicker, safer and cheaper, for example, to tackle 'Creation' by reading the biblical narrative (*Education,* 1994) as opposed to involving children in creating a wild life garden, planting trees, bulbs, plants, or enbling them, in some way, to create and care for their immediate environment.

Third world problems are all too often our problems and money—its management and exchange is often the linking theme. Many secondary schools operating under schemes of developing financial management are handling budgets running into millions of pounds. Increasingly they are managed and assessed by criteria applied to a medium sized business. In this context, the ethics of financial management and wealth creation are certainly as relevant as the depletion of the rain forest.How the issues might be linked is explored in excellent teaching packs and materials from Oxfam, Traidcraft and Shared Interest.

In conclusion let us examine 'Blessings', the counting of which is greatly undervalued in terms of sustaining our individual and institutional mental health. If the world itself strikes you as quaintly old fashioned, substitute 'celebrations'. OFSTED has recently observed that many schools fail to celebrate enough and that negative teacher expectations significantly contribute to pupil underachievement. This lengthy contemporary thesis was some time ago elegantly summarized by Henry James, who wrote in 1879, 'Smalll children have many more preceptions than they have terms to translate them: their vision is at any moment richer, their apprehension even stronger than their...producible vocabulary. Perhaps, therefore, our greatest sin in consistently to underestimate our children, in particular to underestimate their resilience, their talents and their potential to save our world. Many children I work with have an intuitive grasp of what was written by a nun in the seventeenth century, whose words sum up the spirit and point of this chapter:

> With all its sham, drudgery and broken it is still beautiful world. Be careful. Strive to be happy.

13

The Global Environmental Trends

Slightly more than a decade age, in June 1972, the United Nations convened a major intergovernmental conference on the Human Environment at Stockholm, Sweden. It was undoubtedly the most important environmental even of an international character that took place during the past two decades and to a great extent set into motion a process through which international issues and concerns were to be discussed, reviewed and analysed.

When the Stockholm Conference was first proposed by Sweden in 1968, the industrialized countries in general reacted favourably. This is not surprising since interest in environmental issues in those countries was high. The activities of numerous citizens' groups and non-governmental organizations continually focussed the attention of the general public and politicians to deteriorating environmental situations. Many groups took the streets to protest, and especially in the United States, environment and Vietnam became two of the major issues with which the youth rebelled against the establishment. These pressure groups and several scientists started to publicise critical and emerging environmental issues, some real and others not so. At the crest of the environment movement, the Earth Day attracted an estimated 20 million participants in the United States alone.

In contrast to the favourable disposition of the industrialised countries, the reactions of developing countries to the Stockholm Conference when it was first anounced, were mixed, and the favourable reactions were lukewarm at best (Biswas and Biswas 1982). Interest in the environmental concerns were not as high as in the West, and there was a general feeling that the environmental problems were less of a priority compared to the real problems facing them, alleviation of poverty.

By the time the Stockholm Conference took place, many of the initial concerns and doubts expressed by developing countries were alleviated sufficiently for them to participate in the gathering. This turned out to be fortuitous since the Soviet Union and the rest of the Eastern Block of nations (with the exceptions of Romania) did not take part because of the conflict over the status of East Germany. Eventually 113 nations participated.

The Stockholm Conference agreed on a Declaration and an Action Plan. The Declaration consisted of Proclamation and 26 principles. The proclamation was somewhat general and put man firmly as the central focus of any equation by stating categorically that "of all things in the world, people are the most precious".

The conference undoubtedly raised the environmental consciousness of the world and sensitized public opinion. The Conference itself and the simultaneous Environmental Forum, organized by environmental pressure groups and other non-governmental organizations, together constituted one of the largest international gatherings ever held.

Looking back, more than a decade latter, the Stockholm Conference appears to have been more of a success than many realized at that time. Its timing was right: it was held when the environmental movement in the West was at its peak, and developed countries were willing to provide funds for international environmental protenction and management. It established an institutional machinery, United Nations Environment Programme (UNEP), as the environmental conscience of the UN system and also to look after the events following the Conference.

Many of the major environmental trends of the present and of the future, for example, ecological disturbances caused by the pursuit of short-term benefits in the development process, reasource impoverishment, and environmental degradation as a result of population growth, are not new, but have long been recognised as serious problems. What is new, however, is the accelerating pace and scale of the problems. New, too, is the recognition of their interrelation-ships, which mean that they can be understood and dealt with only within the overall framework of the web of causes and effects that bind them together. It also means that they can not be resolved by further fine tuning of traditional responses. In this sense they are of a wholly new character and require not only their understanding and development of new attitudes and perceptions, but also new modes of management responses, a fact that was clearly recognised at the Stockholm Conference.

The various environmental issues will be discussed herein under three broad categories: interrelationships between people, resources, environment and development; rational use of natural resources, and new patterns of development and life-styles. These categories, however, are not discrete: they too are interrelated.

People-Resources-Environment-Development

An analysis of the report of the United Nations Conference on the Human Environment (Anon, 1973) will indicate that though there was reasonable understanding at that time of the interrelationships between population, resources, environment and development, the approaches adopted in the resolutions were basically sectoral. Since that Conference, however, our understanding of the development processes has been enhanced greatly. This, to a certain extent, was facilitated by the holding of subsequent major United Nations World Conferences (Bucharest 1974) Food (Rome, 1974), Human Settlements (Vancouver 1976), Water (Mar del Plata 1977), Desertification (Nairobi 1977), Science and Technology for Development (Vienna) and New and Renewable Sources of Energy (Nairobi, 1981) (M.R. Biswas 1974, 1975, 1977, 1978 a,b, 1981). Through the preparatory processes undertaken for these conferences as well as through the discussions during the conferences and the subsequent implementation of their recommendations, man's understanding of the complexities of development processes has evolved further. For example, it is now better recognized that development is a multidimensional concept which encompasses not only economic and social activities, but also those related to population, the use of natural resources, and their resulting impacts on the environment (Tolba 1982).

While the interrelationships concept is not novel, the need for rapid development and technological advancement has meant that, very often, whatever knowledge of interrelationships was available tended to be disregarded. However, attempts to solve seemingly technical problems such as desertification, loss of productive soil or deforestation have indicated that emphasis should be placed not only on such physical factors as climate, soil type, modes of cultivation or land-use patterns, but also on diverse factors including demographic trends, types of technology used, levels and distribution of income among the population, consumption patterns, cultural habits and educational levels of the inhabitants, etc. Without such a holistic approach, actions taken to solve specific problems may give rise to several other unintended side-affects, the sum total of which could even be worse than the problems initially addressed. To some extent, this can be explained by the fact that the nature of beneficiaries often tend to be different. Much of the benefits of the original action tend to accrue to a more educated and powerful section of the population, whereas the adverse side-affects, to a large extent are borne by people who do not have a power base and as such as not in a position to influence the socio-economic decisions which affect their own lives and life-styles.

Population

While it may be difficult to forecast the future precisely, one fact is certain: world population will continue to increase for a few decades. The rate of population growth is unlikely to slow appreciably, and most of this growth will take place in developing countries, which will face challenging problems resulting from rapid urbanization. According to United Nations estimates, world population is expected to increase from about 4,415 million in 1980 to about 5,275 million in 1990. The population growth rate in developing countries will in all probability drop slightly from the 2.2% a year rate recorded in 1975, but even then, in absolute terms and using the slowest growth scenario of any international study carried out so far, the number of persons being added annually to the world's population will be significantly greater at the end of the decade than it is today. The past trend of increase in the share of developing countries in the world's population is likely to continue: from 66% in 1950 to 72% in 1975 and about 75% in 1990. The population growth rate in developed countries will in all probablity decrease from the 0.7 percent rate observed in 1975. Because of better health care facilities, the present trend of life expectancies at birth in developing countries is expected to continue to increase. Similarly the migration of rural population to urban areas will continue during this period in both developed and developing countries.

While it is comparatively easy to make the general forecast of population trends, it is more difficult to predict many factors which influence population trends, i.e., fertility, life span, mortality, or migration. Information on population trends is one of the fundamental prerequisites for considering other major environmental trends since basic requirements for food, shelter, energy, minerals, education, employment, etc. depend on population levels.

Interrelationships

Several studies were carried out during the past decade which attempted to relate population to resources availability, environmental degradation and development. Some studies, like the Limits to Growth (Meadows et al. 1972) model, predicted that both population and economic growth must cease by the year 2000, otherwise society would overshoot and collapse. Such studies are now generally discredited, however, since the models developed were simplistic, inadequate, based on faulty understanding of the problems, limited or even faulty data and considered a very high level of aggregation. Those models failed to reflect accurately the important interrelationships and continual feedbacks between people, resources, envvironment and development. What is necessary during the next decade is a more positive approach to development which adequately reflects these interrelationships. There is still a great potential to expand the ability of the global ecosystem to support more people by judicious combination of making more productive and rational use of the earth's available resources and by a more equitable distribution of the benefits of various production processes. Since the carrying capacity of the earth is not infinite, development plans should take full advantage of the potentials but at the same time must be aware of the constraints imposed by the life-support systems.

The study of interrelationships between people, resources, environment and development is important for three major and interlinked reasons. First, it is increasingly evident that development efforts, at all stages of growth and in countries having different social, economic and cultural backgrounds, institutional infrastructures and availability of natural resources, tend to produce systemic effects at national, regional and global levels that have a cumulative impact on the overall productive process and the attainment of long-term development objectives. Second, it is also increasingly evident that such systemic effects result from strong interactions between economic, social, demographic and physical factors. Third, since the exact causal links between these interactions are at present unknown, there is considerable uncertainty with regard to the likely long-term impact of such systemic effects and, consequently, attention has largely focused on the risks of negative impacts, even though the probability of positive impacts is also quite high. Taken together, these three considerations suggest the need for a more constructive approach, emphasising that the study of interrealationships should clarify causal linkages and identify points of leverage so that appropriate integrated policies and programmes can be adopted to start a cycle of positive impacts in terms of attaining both developmental and environmental objectives, and ensuring that development can be sustainable over a long-term basis.

The critical issues are not so much the rate of population growth and the insufficiency or the unavailability of natural resources, but rather the uneven geographical distribution of population relative to the carrying capacity of land and the inefficient and irrational use of natural resources. Consideration of these fundamental issues broadens the scope of analysis from resource depletion, environmental degradation and population growth to include resource redistribution and transfer, environmental management that encourages more rational use of resources, development of appropriate technologies, and population movement. Environmental management of this kind would require better understanding and co-operation among, as well as within, nations, since ultimately the interrelationships between the four areas frequently extend beyond national boundaries. In the final analysis, the problem of interrelationships becomes a collective responsibility of the entire international community.

Many of the conceptual issues associated with the interrelations between people, resources, environment and development have been clarified during the 1970s and are undoutedly better understood and more widely recognized at present than they were at the time of the Stockholm Conference. Understanding of the interrelationships is still incomplete, however, and much work remains to be done during the next decade to analysis the underlying complexities, identify their policy implications and use the resultant knowledge successfully in operational contexts, so that the development process can benefit from an integrated approach, rather than the sectoral approach which is all too common at present. Techniques and means will have to be developed not only for devising intersectoral policies and programme at the national, regional and global levels, but also for ensuring their affective implementation. Such developments should finally lead to rational resources management and effective environmental protection. Major structural changes may be required, including resource transfers between nations to promote a more equitable sharing, development of alternative life-style, and fundamental shifts in international economic relations.

Rational Use of Natural Resources

Resources are the life-blood of any society and the development process is sustainable only if it is underpinned by the continued availability of natural resources. Availability of natural resources, however, is not enough: countries should be in a position to utilize them effectively, which in turn depends on their ability to apply technology, as well as on the availability of funds for capital investment. There are many countries at present which have a rich resources base, but are still underdeveloped due to their inability to apply technology to transform resources and/or to lack of investment funds, a situation which is largely attributable to constraints imposed by social, economic and institutional structures both within and among the nations. During the next decade, attempts must be made to use the available natural resources successfully for further development, while at the same time ensuring that this foundation of the resource and environmental base on which development itself depends is not undermined.

Consumption of natural resources, both renewable and non-renewable, has increased in recent years. Developed countries consume the bulk of the world's natural resources, and irrational use patterns have greatly contributed to the deterioration of both the resources base and the quality of the environment. This is a trend that needs to be reverse. Furthermore, developing countries should not imitate the wastful consumption patterns of developed countries, Renewable resources will remain renewable only if the ecological principles underlying their sustainability is respected, and similarly non-renewable resources can be rendered renewable at least to a significant degree, by practising conservation and extensive recyling.

Food and Agriculture

Let us consider an important natural resources sector—food and agriculture—which is generally considered to be renewable. It is, however, renewable in terms of production only if properly managed. Acceleration of désertification, salinization, loss of productive soil, or loss of genetic resources, can significantly reduce the over-all level of production. To provide adequate food and nutrition for the world's population during the next two decades, food production would have to be doubled by the year 2000. There are some natural constraints, such as availability of good agricultural land and adequate supply of water which have to be considered in any planning process. Beyond these constraints, however, man dectates the pattern of development. If the strategies followed are ecologically sound and viable, it should be possible to increase agricultural production as required. Food is a net product of an ecosystem, and as long as the ecosystem remains healthy, it will continue producing food. However, improper management practices can undermine the agricultural system in a various ways (Biswas, 1984, Biswas and Biswas, 1979). Since this is a vital sector, possible future environmental trends will be explored briefly.

Food is a fundamental basic need; it is imperative that its production be increased and its distribution improved, both to meet the anticipated population increase during the next decade and to improve the nutritional status of the malnourished people in developing countries, who according to World Bank estimates are likely to increase in numbers from 400-600 million in the mid-1970s to around 1300 million by the year 2000.

Since most of the good agricultural land available is already undercultivation study projects an increase of only 4 percent in cultivated land during the next two decades), much of the increase in required food production will have to come from increased yield. While there is much scope to increase agricultural yields in most developing countries, the fact, still remains that the number of people to be supported per hectare of arable land will continue to increase from the figure of about 2.6 observed during the early 1970s. Currently most strategies to increase yields place major emphasis on energy-intensive inputs and technologies such as fertilizers, pesticides herbicides and irrigation without concomitant emphasis on the long-term implications of continued use of such policies. In many cases, such strategies, which evolved during the era of cheap energy have already started to produce diminishing returns. Even though it is now universally accepted that the era of cheap enery is over, this fundamental fact is still not fully reflected in agricultural develepment policies. There is now considerable uncertainty about the overall impact of changing hydrocarbon prices on agricultural production during the next decade, and their eventual implications for the global environment, a fact that needs to be studied carefully. The uncertainty further extends to be ability of farmers to maintain and expand agricultural production while attempting to shift away from energy intensive inputs.

Intensive land, increased use of marginal land and continued dependence of agricultural production on climate will probably mean that the variability of food supply will increase markedly during the next decade. The real price of food will continue to increase, and it now appears that the agricultural and trade policies of a small number of exporting and importing nations will play an increasingly dominant part in determining the quantities of food available for trade and aid, as well as their prices on the world market.

Such development trends will have important implications for developing countries. Their overall requirement for imported food is likely to grow although at the same time the share of the world grain market of food-exporting developing countries is likely to grow from the level of little more than 10% recorded in 1975.

In principle, the environmental implications of future agricultural development are manageable, provided appropriate strategies are adopted. The future environmental trends will affect land, water, inputs and ecosystetms, all of which, in turn, will have impacts on agricultural development.

Desertification

While during the next decade new lands will be brought under cultivation, some of the existing land will undoubtedly undergo soil deterioration due to four principal problems: loss of top soil, loss of organic matter, deterioration of soil structure and build up of toxic chemicals and salts. All these developments would reduce agricultural yields.

Many signs of stress that can be observed at present also affect soil availability, as well as its quality. The magnitude of the problem of desertification and the urgency of countermeasures to reverse the existing trends can be realized from the following estimates.

— The process of desertification is accelerating at great speed, and as a result some six million hectares of productive land are being lost, and many more are deteriorating to close to zero productivity, every year;

— On the southern fringes of the Sahara, some 65 million hectares of once productive land have become desert during the last 50 years;

— Some 600-700 million people, nearly 14% of the world's population, live in threatened drylands, and of these about 60 million are immediately affected by desertifications.

In addition to desertification, current trends indicate continued loss of good agricultural land to urban and industrial development. Increases in urbanization and suburbanization have accelerated the permanent loss of rich and alluvial soils, and in the industrialized OECD countries, urban land area is growing about twice as fast as population. An important future environmental trend could be the expansion of villages onto fertile land. There are already signs of the this occurring in many developping countries, and the trend is likely to accelerate during the next decade.

Deforestation

Expansion of agriculture is a primary cause of derorestation at present, followed by demand for fuelwood and forest products. If present trends continue, it is estimated that both forest cover and stocks of commercial-size wood will decline by 40% during the next two decades in developing countries. From the environmental viewpoint, the potential impacts of this loss would be reduction of biological diversity and changes in climate and in soil and water regimes.

Biotic diversity is not only an important indicator of the ecological health of the planet, but also an essential storehouse for genetic materials for developing new crop varieties and medicinal drugs. While extinction has been the normal fate of virtually all species, the magnitude of deforestation projected in coming decades could mean that the rate of natural extinction would be trivial when compared to man-made extinctions, which will occur primarily due to loss of habitats.

So far as climate is concerned, the main potential impact of deforestation could be increased levels of carbon dioxide. While much of the carbon dioxide in the atmosphere comes from the combustion of fossil fuels, recent studies indicate that carbon stored in biomass is decreasing rather than increasing. Net decrease of biomass volume would imply carbon dioxide build-up in the future though present estimate of the amount vary considerably.

Water Resources

It is not only important to use land more rationally but also. It is imperative that water resources be used more efficiently during the next decade. At present, on a global basis, nearly 80% of all water used is for agricultural purposes. The need for irrigation is clearly indicated by the fact that even though only about 15% of the world's cropland is irrigated, it yields from 30 to 40% of all agricultural production. It is estimated that by the end of the present decade, in 1990, the total area irrigated in the world will increase to 273 million hectares, with 119 million hectares of this total in developing countries. More and more water will be necessary for irrigation. Thus, for developing market economy countries only, it is estimated that 22.2 million hectares of new land will be brought under irrgation, requiring 438 billion cu.m of additional water. Certain parts of the world have already started to face water shortages, and the situation is likely to become worse in the future if current trends continue.

This assumes, of course, that the existing pattern of efficiency of water use will continue. At present, on a global basis, 1.3 million cu.m of water is used for irrigating crops, but for this 3 million cu.m of water has to be withdrawn. This means that 57% of the water withdrawn is lost. The 43% of this water reaching the field is not all efficiently used. Over-irrigation is endemic, which not only constitutes wasteful use of a valuable resource, but also contributes to development of adverse enviromental problems such as salinity, waterlogging and rise of groundwater tables. These side effects reduce the yield of the very land which irrigation, at substantial investment costs, was supposed to make more productive.

As water requirements for agricultural, industrial, hydroelectric power generation and other purposes increase, there will be increasing demands for further water resources development projects. Competing demands for limited water supplies or discharge of effluents to water-courses which would reduce water quality, and hence their potential use, could give rise to international conflicts, especially in the 148 of the world's important river basins that are shared by two or more countries. Similar tensions could arise in relation to coastal fisheries and offshore drilling. Accordingly, it is essential to codify guidelines for management of natural resources shared by two or more States.

The present decade has been proclaimed by the United Nations as the International Drinking Water Supply and Sanitation Decade. While both the United Nations Conference on Human Settlements and the United Nations Water Conference endorsed the target of clear water for all the world's population by 1990, on the basis of the present trends and of a realistic assesment of the future, this target is unlikely to be achieved, even though the number of people, both urban and rural, having access to potable water and sanitary facilities will undoubtedly increase tremendously.

Fertilizer Use

Where the various inputs such as fertilizers and pesticides, used to increase agricultural yield are concerned, the future environmental impacts will stem primarily from their more intensive use. The use of fertilizers per unit area is expected to increase in all regions during the next 10 years. The consequences of this increased fertilizer use are expected to be more serious for aquatic than for terrestrial systems. The adverse impacts may occur from the leaching of fertilizers to lackes, rivers and coastal systems, which could contribute to eutrophication. Much of the nitrogen currently entering surface waters—in the United States of America more than 70%, according to an estimate, is from non-point agricultural sources. Furthermore, the presence of nitrates in drinking water supplies is dangerous to children under the age of three. Fortunately, however, levels of nitrogen that may pose hazards to human health, about 10 mg nitrate/1 water, are relatively rare, even in countries having high rates of fertilizer utilization.

Improper use of fertilizers could aggravate the problem of soil fertility. The atmospheric effects of fertilizer use are still still not well understood but it has been reported that nitrous oxides from fertilizer application could deplete the ozone layer in the stratosphere. If this turns out to be a serious issue, future developments could present difficult choices between increased agricultural production and depletion of the ozone layer.

Pest Management

Despite the growing interest in integrated pest management which could reduce use of pesticides, their application will also probably increase over the coming decade. From an environmental viewpoint, the problems to be expected are somewhat similar to those witnessed in many parts of the world, during the 1970s even though their magnitude and intensity could be different. These are:

- Increasing biological concentration of persistent pesticides as they move up the food chain;
- Development of pest resistance to pesticides;
- Destruction of the natural enemies of the pest, which further reduces the total cost;
- Emergence of new pests which may not have been serious earlier;
- Impacts on human health due to contacts with persistent pesticides.

Energy

As noted earlier, present agricultural practices are heavily dependent on energy inputs. Energy is an important natural resource, whose availability is a pre-requisite for any development. The supply of energy, both commercial and non-commercial, is likely to remain an issue during the next decade.

Much emphasis is currently being placed on the possible future environmental impacts due to increased emissions of carbon dioxide resulting from the combustion of fossil fuels. It is anticipated that carbon dioxide emissions in 1990 will be about double those of the mid-1970s. While scientistis generally agree that emissions of this magnitude will not have major impacts, there is growing concern that, if such trends continue, accumulation of carbon dioxide in the atmosphere may cause climatic changes in the early part of the twenty-first century. According to some projections, continued deforestation and energy-related emissions of carbon dioxide could increase the concentration of CO to approx. 600 ppm by about the year 2030. While the scientific community increasingly accepts the likelihood of possible global warning from such an eventuality, there is no possible way of confirming its validity, timing or specific impacts. Much work remains to be doen on this question in the future.

Increasing use of coal during the next decade could contribute to serious environmental problems, most of which could be limited if proper control measures are undertaken. Without such control measures, mining could create large-scale land degradation, including destruction of natural habitats, land subsidence and water pollution through acid mine drainage. Without adequate control systems, coal combustion could contribute to emission of atmospheric pollutants like sulphor dioxide, nitrogen oxides, particulates and trace metals. Such emissions could increase ecological and health hazards, including the problem of acid rain (Holdgate et al., 1982).

Increased use of nuclear power would raise different types of environmental problems such as reactor safety, nuclear waste disposal and international security.

The major source of non-commercial energy is firewood, and it is not an inconsequential one: the total energy derived fuel wood in 1974 was about the same as from hydropower. Nearly 90% of global firewood consumption is in developing countries where the use of firewood is at present related to the level of economic development. The least developed countries and areas within countries tend to use the most firewood. According to FAO estimate, firewood requirements are likely to increase at the rate of 2.2% per year resulting by 1994 in a fuel wood shortage of 650 million cubic metres annually in wood-poor countries.

Increased requirements for fuel-wood are an important cause of deforestation, with its attendant environmental problems such as destabilization of nutrient cycles, soil erosion, decline in soil fertility, and diminished capacity of soil to retain water (and hence often increased flooding). Accordingly, the organization and proper use of systematic fuel-wood plantation programmes in the future would, while meeting an essential need of the rural and urban communities, make a positive contribution towards environmental improvement (El Hinnawi and Biswas, 1981). What is essential is to organize and manage the supply of the so-called non-commercial fuels with a veiw to sustaining, and if possible augmenting, their supply as well as improving the efficiency of their use. With respect to the latter, the role of women is the most crucial one, since they are principally responsible for gathering firewood and water and are in charge of household cooking. Increased efficiency will be greatly facilitated by providing training to women in the use of improve devices for cooking and heating.

The possibilities of switching to new sources of energy during the present decade appear to be limited (El Hinnawi et al., 1983) and to a great extent the energy crisis for most countries, is a problem of oil. Kerosene is widely used in rural areas for lighting purposes, and diesel is essential for transportation and irrigation. While certain oil-intensive activities like further mechanization in agriculture and use of automobiles do provide some scope for conservation in developing countries the potential is somewhat limited, certainly significantly less than in the developed countries.

Marine Environment

While there appears to be little threat to the open ocean waters at present, coastal waters and enclosed or semi-enclosed seas are receiving increasing loads of pollutants, primarily as a result of man's activities on land which inject matter into rivers, coastal outflows and atmospheric fallout on the oceans. The coastal areas are of critical importance for the well-being of marine biota, on whom future food supplies may increasingly depend, and for human health, for it is here that man is directly exposed to contaminants from bathing and from seafood. Continuing assessment of the significance of present trends is essential for the proper management of these areas. Alternative courses of action must be identified so that they will be available when it becomes advisable to reduce the injection of critical pollutants into the seas from key sources. A more rational approach to the development of coastal zones would pay heed to the need to protect areas identified as critical for breeding and development of marine biota, yet these same coastal areas can be expected to become more crowded as a result of projected demographic growth, together with competing demand for agriculture, industry, transportation, tourism and other development sectors.

New Patterns of Development and Lifestyles

Throughout the history of mankind, lifestyles and development patterns have never been constant, but have continually evolved and changed with time. Furthermore, lifestyles and development patterns at any specific time vary from one country to another, and often there are significant differences between different parts of the same country.

Present lifestyles in advanced industrialized countries can be characterized by several factors, among which are intensive use of resources, high capital investment, high rates of tehcnological developments, low rates of population growth, comparatively low developments, low rates of Inflation, and the availability of a trained pool of personnel to carry out various functional tasks. Majority of the developing countries, on the other hand, have higher rates of population growth, low consumption of resources, high unemployment and underemployment, scarcity of capital (except in oil-exporting countries), high illiteracy rates, and often an agriculture-based economy with strong income inequality and widespread poverty. Overall economic growth and attempts at modernization of various sectors, which were expected to provide better equality and to democratic developing societies, have on the contrary often helped to accentuate economic and socio-political polarization.

Rural Development

The majority of the poverty-stricken people in developing countries live in rural areas, and their incomes are mostly directly linked to the agricultural sector. So far, the concept of "trickle-down" development has failed to improved their lifestyles to any appreciable extent. It is this sector which needs modification, and the present patterns of growth need to be drastically changed during the 1980s. Such modifications however, can only take place if the rural poor, and especially those who are landless or have very small holdings and who constitute the core of the rural poverty problem, are specifically condisered to be the important beneficiaries of any development strategy. It is not going to be easy to reverse the past and existing trend, since the rural poor are often illiterate, unemployed or underemployed and in poor health, and thus often are external to the decision-making process which selects developments strategies that affect their lives. Future development efforts will have to consider not only the total benifits accruing from a project, but also how the benefits are distributed. Any development, in which the distribution of benefits is markedly skwewed, so that they accrue porimarly to a select group of elites , is bound to be unsatisfactory and unsustainable on a long-term basis. Narrowing disparities in the distribution of incomes is likely to improve the environment.

There are many reasons why rural development has not been more successful of far. They include:

(a) Higher rates of population growth, which mean that the meagre productive assets owned become more fragmented in successive generations;
(b) Lack of education and training, which means that not enough information is available as to how the meagre assets of the rural poor can be used more effectively and productively;
(c) Poor health due to unavailability of adequate food and nutrition, lack of potable water, sanitary arrangements and health care facilities;
(d) Weak links to the organized market economy, i.e. lack of access to credit, essential inputs and improved but appropriate technology, problems with marketing of products, etc.;
(e) Use of resources and the environment, for sheer survival, in ways which are unsustainable over the longer term.

Poverty and Environmental Degradation

The presence of widespread poverty is often the cause of serious environment deterioration in developing countries. When reinforced by accelerating population growth, it contributes to the continual erosion of the resource and environmental base from which people must earn their livelihood, thus completing a vicious circle which is proving difficult to break. To meet their desperate immediate basic needs for more survival, the rural poor have no other option but to cultivate marginal land which is prone to heavy soil erosion, graze their livestock on land that is becoming barren from overuse, cut shrubs and trees for fuel-wood, thereby reducing the stability of soil and water regimes, and burn dung which otherwise could have improved soil fertility. Trapped in conditions of absolute poverty, their actions contribute to the further deterioration of the ranewable resource base, making their plight even more desperate with the passage of time. Thus, many of the world's most severe environmental problems are in part a direct consequence of extreme poverty, and it is neither likely nor realistic to expact that impoverised people living at the margin of existence will consider the long-term sustainability of the planet at the cost of their own survival. Without determined attempts to improve their living conditions through further development, the situation is unlikely to get better. This is a major trend that needs to be reversed as soon as possible, before damage becomes too extensive and irreversible, so that the renewable resources base of this planet can be conserved, and wherever possible ehanced for the good of both present and future generations. As the recently issued report on Global 2000 (Barney, 1980) by the United States Council on Environmental Quality has concluded: "Only a concerted attack on socio-economic roots of extreme poverty, one that provides people with the opportunity to earn a decent livelihood in a non-destructive manner will permit protection of the world's natural systems. Nor will development and economic reforms have lasting success unless they are suffused with concern for ecological stability and wise management of resources".

Appropriate Technology

Development depends not only on people but also on the resourses and technology they have access to, and the environmental framework within which these are utilized. Developments, both in the industrial and the agricultural sectors, should not necessarily mimic western models and technology. They should be closely related to the resource base of individual countries, which needs to be assessed and then efficiently developed on a long-term basis for the good of the maximum number of people, and with due regard for the environment. During the next decade, it is essential that biophysical resources be mobilized effectively so that the goods produced, industrial and agricultural, are less extravagent inthe use of resources, do not contribute to environmental deterioration, and improve the overall quality of life.

By itself, technology employed in the service of development is neutral, but how it is used can determine the success or failure of a project. Choice of technology depends on a variety of technical, social, economic, environmental and political factors, and many times what may be considered to be the most appropriate technology in one country could turn to be most inappropriate for solving almost identical problems in another. A review of the history of modern development will often indicate that straight transfer of technology from developed to developing countries has often created more problems than it has solved. While South-South technology transfer through technical co-operation between developing countries makes a great deal of sense, it should not be axiomatically assumed that such direct transfers will present no serious prolems. Developing countries are not all the same; they are often at different stages of development and may have different social, economic and institutional backgrounds.

To the extent it is possible, appropariate technology for developing countries sould be labour-intensive. While this point has received the attention of many planners and engineers for a long time, attempts to use labour-intensive techniques on a continuing basis can be best described as timid and half-hearted. The few successful examples of this approach have been due to the determined labour of a handful of dedicated individuals, and were mostly isolated efforts. Even in these few cases extensive documentation of the techniques used, their costs, effectiveness and public acceptance, and other relevant information are not readily available to others who may wish to use similar technology. Very little has been achieved at implementing such successful techniques at national levels. The virtues of appropriate technology, in short, are more often preached than practised.

Many instances could be cited of socially and environ-mentally inappropriate technology being imported to developing countries, through either bilateral or multilateral aid programmes, without critical appraisal. Foreign consultants and contractors are often used to plan, design and implement projects. In the majority of these cases, they are not fully familiar with the prevailing social, economic and cultural norms of the developing countries concerned, and accordingly they often use criteria which are based on the experience and knowledge gained in the advanced industrialized countries which may not be application locally.

Same attention has been paid during the past decade to elaborating the concept of environmentally sound and approparlate technology, studying the problems and methodology for producing such technology, and developing criteria and methodologies for selection of the best results. However, the application of these concepts in an operational context leaves much to be desired, and needs to be accelerated.

There has been some discussion in recent years of the question of nonwaste or low-waste technology, which can be defined as the practical application of knowledge, methods and means so as to provide the most rational use of natural resources and energy and to protect the environment. Expressed differently, it is the planning and management of human activities in order to provide the minimum waste of materials and energy both in production processes and in consumption patterns. Waste should be considered as a loss of potential resources, and attempts made to reduce waste will undoubtedly produce numerous beneficial results. The development and promotion of nonwaste technology which eventually should replace conventional technology, is a long-term endeavour of the greatest importance, whose realization would contribute to positive changes in all sectors of industry which would not only promote more rational use of natural resources, but also improved environmental quality.

It is clear that research and development work to promote non-waste technology has still not reached the desirable level. There is an urgent need for further work to devise criteria for economic evaluation of non-waste proceses, especially of the transformation of wastes and for the identification and operation of non-waste production processes which would take full account of environmental factors.

Hazardous Wastes

The persistent pesticides mentioned earlier are but one of many classes of synthetic organic chemicals which are increasingly manufactured and released into the environment, where their presence has become ubiquitous. Recent UNEP reports indicate that some four million identifiable chemicals are in current use with new chemicals entering the market annually, many of which may have unintended adverse effects on man's health or well-being. Some of these effects may be delayed by transfer processes such as biological concentration as they move up food chains. Similarly, disposal of chemical wastes is in many areas proceeding without regard to future risks, for example, to ground water, which, by the time they are detected, may be prohibitively expensive or technologically impossible to correct. Man's exposure to environmental pollutants, whether in food, water or the air he breathes, is a stress which may impede his functioning or even lead to mortality, especially in cases where malnurition or other deprivations have already applied other forms of stress. Similarly, much of the biota on which man depends for his well-being, such as agricultural crops, may be put under stress by the impact of chemical (and other) pollutants. In view of the trends of increased production of synthetic chemicals and more intensive use in industry, agriculture and other development sectors, increasing attention must be paid to assessing the significance of trends in pollutant releases, pathways, loads and effects to ensure that warnings, where necessary, may be sounded in good time, and that alternative courses of action to society to reduce the threats are available.

Lifestyle and Energy

The lifestyles and development and technological patterns that have generally evolved during the past three decades have been primarily energy-intensive and are highly dependent on oil. Sharply increased oil prices and unreliability of supplies are now forcing major adjustments for both developed and developing countries. While such major changes have had significant impacts on industrialized nations, the impacts on oil-importing developing countries have been very serious indeed, limiting their access to energy and burdening them with economic costs which they find hard to bear, and sometimes devitalizing all other sectors. A major problem facing the developing countries is one of reconciling the need for increasing the energy input for productive economic activity within the context of a global situation of depleting energy supplies and rising costs. In addition there is the further problem of a highly skewed energy consumption pattern among people of different income levels, with people in the upper income brackets using disproportionate share of energy.

It is essential that possible alternative responses to this situation be urgently reviewed. Solutions could include, inter alia, an intensive drive to conserve energy in all spheres, changes in lifestyles that would use less energy, especially oil, then before, and development of alternative energy sources that are both renewable and indigenous. Further consideration should be given to coal, natural gas and other forms of energy, with careful assessment and review of environmental and other potential adverse affects associated with such systems, including the problem of deforestation due to increasing use of firewood and the transformation of good food-producing land to growing biomass for conversion to fuel. These alternatives, however, may not be the final solution fo. .nany developing countries, which after paying higher energy costs, may find themselves with insufficient resources to sustain a satisfactory rate of growth. Intensive international cooperation will be necessary to overcome this hurdle.

People's Participation

New patterns of development will require a more decentralized and participatory approach to planning. Past experiences indicate that centralized, top-down efforts fail more often than they succeed. The leaders and bureaucrats may be more educated and sophisticated than the rural populace but the 'best and brightest syndrome' often fails in development.

Accordingly, *people's participation* in shaping events that will utlimately affect their lives is an economic necessity as well as special must. The people now what is required, and are familiar with local conditions, availability of indigenous resources and the strengths and weaknesses of the community. The people must be responsible for the creation, operation and maintence of development projects. Such planning and implementation processes will ensure that their needs are properly identified and that the solutions will be viable. In addition it will make them realise that the project is theirs, and that they therefore have a responsibility to optimize the use of resources and then to maintain the development works.

Development can be sustainable if it is based on the solid foundation of equity, mobilization of indigenous resources, use of appropriate technology and full utilization of human capital. Development strategies have to be centred around people, and human resource development should be planned so as to provide the necessary conditions for the much needed change in attitudes and prepare for a more conducive atmosphere wherein new ideas and technologies can be successfully absorbed.

While some conceptual studies have been carried out in the past on the incorporation of public participation in the planning and decision-making processes, and a few individual studies are available on their implementation at the project level, much work remains to be done on how to make such practices operational, especially at higher than project levels.

Environment and Development

Much work has been done during the past decade on the question of compatibility between the environment and the socio-economic objectives of development, and on the need for and feasibility of integrating them systematically with each other. Starting from the Founex meeting before the Stockholm Conference on the Human Environment, and through the work of UNEP and other organizations, it has been established that environment and development are complementary, and represent two sides of the same coin. Throughout the decade, perceptions of the development process have been changing and greater awareness has been developing on the importance of environmental consideration in protecting and maintaining the resources base on which development depends.

Conceptually, the complementarity between environment and development was clarified during the last decade, and to a large extent was accepted by planners and decision-makers. However, there has not been much progress in translating these concepts into practical and operational terms. Whatever progress that has been made thus for has been primarily at the project level, which not surprisingly is the simplest. Integration of environmental considerations in development plans has not been a success so far. Undoubtedly this should be a priority issue for the coming decade.

A critical analysis indicates that there are at present many opportunities for promoting development processess that will sustain long-term productivity. For example, integrated water resources development can be better planned and managed to ensure better and more reliable water availability, mitigate flood damage and increase aquaculture, and at the same time reduce adverse environmental impacts on land, such as salinity or waterlogging, and prevent the spread of water-borne diseases. Agricultural systems could take advantage of integrated pest management, organic fertilizers and nitrogen-fixation, and reduce the use of persistent and destructive chemicals. Transportation systems can be planned. Land-use patterns can be controlled so that good land remains available for agricultural purposes and is not lost to urban and industrial developments. There are many other ways in which both developed and develping countries can promote environmentally sound development. However, while more than enough information is currently available which can be successfully used to promote such development, it is unfortunately still not being widely used. Measures to promote environmentally sound development should therefore be a top priority for the coming decade.

While any development activity will have some impacts on the environment, the overriding consideration in the selection and implementationm of development strategies has to be minimization of environmental costs and maximization of benefits. It is therefore essential that future strategies and projects be subjected to systematic environmental impact assessments. An important activity of the next decade has to be the development of new methodologies for environmental impact assessments that are reasonably accurate, and can be carried out within a limited budget and time-frame. The techniques should not be too complex, so that people can be trained to use them comparatively easily. Multidisciplinary and intersectoral studies and research need to be promoted in order to develop an continually refine such assessment techniques.

While there is increasing realization of the need to accept certain fundamental realities, the concepts of the essentiality of long-term ecological sustainability of any lifestyle is yet to be widely accepted. The search for appropriate lifestyles will require changes in both supply and demand of goods and services, including the choice of goods to be produced and techniques used to produce them. Furthermore, production should be responsive to the needs of the vast majority of the people, and not only of the privileged few. Lifestyles must be in harmony with nature and in equilibrium with the prevailing circumstances. In other words, wasteful consumption should be discouraged, natural resources used rationally, and the environment should be protected.

There is an urgent need for demand orientation, especially recording of consumption patterns in profligate societies, which will permit the transition from a consumer society preccupied with vast resource consumption to a conserver society engaged in mere constructive endeavours. What is needed during the next decade is more equitable development styles which would encourage the poor to productivity by granting them access to resources which they presently lack.

Exhortations about the need to alter lifestyles are unlikely to have much success in either developed or developing countries. The desirability of changing lifestyles in developed countries has been recognised by many of their citizens in recent years, and some examples of new attitudes and perceptions can be discerned; these are still very few and their overall impacts, though not negligible, have been somewhat limited. What is necessary is to find viable means which could help achieve desirable changes.

Other Considerations

In addition to the discussions under the previous three broad categories, there are a number of general comments worth making that relate to major environmental trends in the next decade. Some of these are implicit in the previous sections.

First, it should b emphasized that the various regions of the world are each quite heterogeneous in terms of types of ecosystems encompassed, extent and magnitude of different problems confronting them, and institutional infrastructures available through which solutions could be implemented. This means that programmes need to be developed in response to the specific requirements of the regions, even though it may be possible to include them within broad global solutions.

Second, while existing knowledge can be applied to ensure proper environmental management, this will prove futile if such exercises are not backed by strong environmental assessment programmes that will carefully assess the magnitude of each problem, monitor the results of its management, disseminate information on such results and identify gaps in knowledge that needs to be filled.

Third, neither environmental assessment nor environ-mental management, will progress in substantial measure without strong emphasis on the supporting measures identi-fied at Stockholm, environmental education and training, public and technical infromation and technical assistance, especially in the developing countries in the next decade.

Fourth, many of the major problems that mankind will be facing during the next decade are not new. We already know of their existence and in many cases enough information is available to solve them. Thus, what is necessary is determination and political will to implement the solutions.

Finally, recommendations, resoulutions and agreements on plan of action, while an important first step, are not enough. Much time and resources were spent in preparing the action plans that resulted from various past conferences of the United Nations. While funds were available to develop the action plans, not enough resources are available to implement them at both national and international levels. Without determined attempts to generate such resources in order to transform the plans into actions, the efforts made will be wasted and action plans will become academic exercises that would gather dust on bookshelves. This is a trend that needs to be reversed during the next decade.

Some Problems of Environemental Education

First Stage of Environemental Disruption

It is rather difficult to give proper definition to the word "environment" itself, because the concept of environment is changing alongwith the development of society, technology and politics.

In 1970s, mankind, for the first time, became aware of the menace of the serious environmental disruption caused by too rapid growth of industrial activities in industrialized countries. The innovation of technology and remarkable growth of mass production system are also thought as main causes of the problem.

This industrial development was hitherto believed unquestionably as real progress of civilisation. Now, it began to play very important role on disruption of the environment, and gave threat to human health. Through air, water and other pollutions, children, old people and weak are severely suffered. Ecosystem in nature is also severely damaged.

Citizens stood up to convict enterprises or factories which were thought responsible for the emission of polluting substances. The environmental disruption became world wide concern.

Scientists and techniciens played very important role at the stage. Their activity resulted in the fruitful UN Conference on the Human Environment, held in Stockholm in 1972.

However, in the Conference many developing countries expressed their real feeling that they did not have much concern to the pollution but to develop their own industries. They expressed their thought in the words "we want pollution".

The Second Stage

In the Stockholm Conference, many recommendations were mode on Environmental Education (E.E.) including the wide scope of education programmes to educate rather high level persons, those are, men of industrial circles and dicision makers.

But after 10 years since the Stockholm Conference, mankind was compelled to face with a new dimension of problems. They should confront with the environmental disruption originated not only from the activities of heavy industries, but also from daily life activities of common people.

The huge enterprises took necessary measures to reduce their effflements, and succeeded to some extent in reducing pollution though not yet complete. While on the other hand, the threat of environmental disruption through daily life's wastes became more an more serious, e.g., by the use of synthetic detergents and other chemicals together with the use of cars. It is needless to say, the real responsibilty comes back to makers of those substances, but users cannot be without guilt.

Thus, the importance of E.E. has become widely recognized newly, especially among common people.

Even in this stage, it is important not to forget to pay keen attention to the activities of big enterprises, national and especially of multinationals, in developing countries, which have taken insufficient measures to reduce hazards. The accident in Mexico a few months ago, and recent tragedy in Bhopal show the examples.

But at the same time it became necessary to pay more effort to educate people to behave to avoid more contamination caused by their own activities.

The Third Stage

One more problem to be considered is the relation between man and environment, especially nature. In recent years, the destruction of nature is becoming more and more serious. Deforestation in developing countries is caused both by daily life activities of natives and by big enterprises. The destructions are causing serious damage to the lives of natives in return. Moreover, this has other environmental influences on a global scale.

The reclamation of Amozonian tropical forest is now under world wide concern. The deforestation of tropical forest in South East Asia by Japanese enterprises has now become one of the most serious problems of the world. Both destructions are not only causing direct damage at a local level but also have world wide bad influences on the environment indirectly.

The disputes between citizens and some factories were limited rather in narrow spots. Nature disruption or contamination of environment in daily life are dificult to confine in narrow area. And in those cases it is difficult to take direct measures to solve problems.

It is obvious, in such cases, E.E. plays essential role, and the E.E. methodology requires important principles. Many people pointed out the importance to promote new "ethics" to match the requirement.

This new ethics should be the guideline not only for the big enterprises or decision makers but also has to be fixed in the minds of citizens.

The problem is, there is not yet common understanding of this new ethics even among ourselves. And I believe it most important and urgent to establish our common recognition on this new ethics between man and environment, and I hope this theme would be discussed on every occasion.

Summary and Conclusions

I wish to summarize my view as three main points.

First : It is necessary even now to strengthen research works, survey and training to tackle with the solution of environmental hazards caused by industries. We must keep keen watch continuously. We have many experiences in Japan, performed by scientists and teachers. They educated citizens about exact scientific knowledge of hazards originating from factories, and with confidence, people stood up to act.

Second : Many teachers in Japan have played most important roles in educating students in formal and informal education. Examples may be published in coming Conference planned by us at the end of August this year in Tokyo and other districts in Japan.

Third : International collaboration is most essential especially for the Japanese who are rather indifferent about the world wide issues of environment, because Japan is isolated from continent and less suffered from pollution from abroad. The environmental disruption caused by the Japanese enterprises in the tropical forests do not reach the conscience of common people. I hope the Japanese would learn more about the facts and feel responsibility about the global issues of environment.

Finally, we should nor forget to continue our action to the government, especially to pay more attention to E.E. I think this is the same situation in each country and to achieve our purpose, it is inevitable to work in international collaboration.

14

The Environmental Education and Other Relationships

Environmental Issues in the UK

In 1991 the government made a major commitment to children and young people throughout the UK. Just over two years after the General Assembly of the United Nations Formally adopted the *UN Convention on the Rights of the Child* it was ratified by the UK Government. In doing so it committed itself to working towards full implementation of the provisions and standards set by the Convention, and to promoting the civil, political, economic, social and cultural rights of all the UK's thirteen million children and young people. The Convention describes these rights and associated Government duties in forty separate Articles. Amongst many other responsibilities, is the duty to ensure every child and young person, up to the age of eighteen years 'such protection and care as is necessary for his or her well-being...and, to this end...take all appropriate legislative and administrative measures'. (Article 3.2) There is also the duty to ensure that all children and young people have the opportunity to 'enjoy the highest attainable standard of health'. (Articles 2 and 24.1) Physical surroundings have a major impact on the health and development of children. They are affected by housing policy, access to public facilities and services, town and country planning, transport policies and environmental pollution. Despite the fact that the UK is party to a number of international agreements and treaties relating to the environment, many children and young people still face environmental hazards.

In the UK primary responsibility for policy relating to the physical environment lies with the Department of the Environment (DoE), although the Department of Transport also has a crucial role. Current policy stems from the World Health Organisation (WHO) 'Health for All' policy and targets adopted by the thirty-two Member States of the European Region of the WHO in 1984. In 1989, twenty-nine European countries, including the UK, adopted the 'European Charter on Environment and Health' as part of their strategy to fulfil the 'Health for All' targets for environmental policy. A new framework for UK policy, related to the environment, was developed and published in 1990 in the White Paper 'This Common Inheritance'. It covered a wide range of issues and promised regular, statistical updating of the information it contained. (Brown, 1992)

In 1992 the Earth Summit took place in Brazil and resulted in commitment from the government to implement 'Algebra 21' by adopting 'national sustainability strategies', increasing the participation of children and young people in matters of environmental policy, and producing periodic national implementation reports. The UK Government is committed to producing a report covering progress towards sustainable development in the UK, the first sections of which were published in January 1994. The DoE also publishes an, annual report which describes recent and future policy development and includes its future expenditure plans. (Annual Report, 1993) The Department of Transport publishes a similar report. (Department of Transport, 1993) The UK is also party to the 'Montreal Protocol', an international agreement on the phasing out of the chemicals involved in ozone layer depletion.

The most prevalent environmental threat to the life, health and development of children and young people in the UK today is accidental injury Accidents are the largest single cause of death for children aged one to fourteen and resulted in about two million attending accident and emergency departments annually. (Department of Transport, 1992; CAPT, 1989) For children from one to four years old, accidents are most likely to occur in their homes. For older children and younger people the biggest threat is road traffic. Accidents happen amongst all groups of children and young people but are most common among those from low income families and deprived areas. (Levene, 1992; Sharples, 1990; CAPP, 1993) Twice as many boys as girls die from accidents. (Jackson, 1992; CSU, 1992)

Government strategy concentrates on educating the public to adopt safer behaviours but there is little discussion of legislation and policy to remove the causes of accidents or to ensure that parents and carers have sufficient resources to make their homes and neighbourhoods safer. (Pankhurst, 1992) Education about accident prevention can only be effective if it meets the needs and circumstances of different group of people and is supported by effective, legally enforceble, controls over the design, planning and construction of the environment in which the child is growing up.

A further major threat to children's health and development is poor housing. Local authority environmental health officers and trading standards officers are often under-resourced, hampering their ability to monitor existing laws and regulations. At the same time, housing policy over the 1980's had lead to a massive reduction in good quality, low-cost housing.

Feeling safe and secure in the local environment is crucial to health and development but is not the only important factor. Development also involves widening experiences and increasing independence. The needs of children and young people must, therefore, be an important consideration in the planning and development of the local environment and transport systems. Facilities, designed with children in mind, provide enormous potential for enhancing their physical, mental and social development. Conversely, children whose opportunities for play, social interaction and independence are restricted or denied, can suffer developmentally. At present most facilities and services in the UK, used by the general public, are designed by adults for adults, with little or no consideration given to the needs of children. Outdoor play facilities in both urban and rural areas are often badly maintained and vandalised. (BTG, 1991) In urban and rural areas, there are fewer and fewer open spaces in which children and young people can entertain themselves safely. For those with disabilities and learning difficulties the problems are even greater. Combinations of the design features, which restrict access to public places for many children, can cause particular difficulties for those with disabilities. (D.A, 1991)

Transport and the portential for independent mobility are also important in the development of children and young people. However, evidence shows that children's freedom of movement is becoming increasingly restricted, predominantly by road traffic. Transport policy is developed with very little regard for its impact on children's independence. (Hillman, 1990) Apart from the effect of restricted mobility on mental development, children do less physical activity than previously with potentially harmful effects on their long term health.

Environmental pollution is a major threat to health. In the UK today one urgent problem is the close link between increased asthma and other respiratory disease in children and air pollution from road traffic. Other problems include the continuing presence of pesticide residues and heavy metals, such as lead, in food and water, and land surface pollution. Monitoring of environmental pollution and it effects is inadequate. Most information collected is based on adult exposure and potential effects. It does not take into account the particular vulnerability of children. Despite promises by the government at the World Summit in 1992 to strictly enforce the 'precautionary principle' and the 'polluter pays', there is recent evidence that the government is failing to take these promises seriously.

Children and young people in the UK take environmental matters seriously. There is considerable interest in local neighbourhood issues, especially conservation and safety, and much distress caused by the apparent lack of long term policies to protect the wider environment. Article 12 of the *UN Convention* states the children and young people have the right inexpress their opinions on matters which affect them and have those views taken seriously. Despite widespread interest there are very few opportunities for active involvement in the planning and development of focal communities. Support for environmental education is not consistent.

The *Convention* also describes the right to education which develops respect for the natural environment [Article 29(e)]. Education and participation are interlinked and lack of environmental education is a concern for children and young people. (BCC, 1992) However, survey carried out in 1991, among a random sample of schools found that environmental education had a low priority. (RSPB, 1992)

Examples exist of where Article 12, the right to express a view, and Article 29(e), the right to environmental education, are being put into practice. In one, a 'Safe School' project in a primary school in Hillhead in Glasgow, the work lead to an understanding of why strict rules applied to dangerous places, e.g. stairways. The project involved children, parents, governors, teachers, the PTA, the LEA and local health board. (CAPT, 1993; Roberts, 1993) 'Learning Through Landscapes', a scheme for involving children and young people in the design and planning of their school environment, is another important initiative.

Greater involvement means consulting with children and young people from all sectors of community at the begining, and throughout, service planning and development. It should be implicit in all local environment statements, strategies and policies. Consultation, like equal opportunities, is everyone's responsibility.

Moral and Values Education

Educational aims are often couched in broad terms. The aims of environmental education are no exception. According to the National Curriculum Council's *Curriculum Guidance 7, Environmental Education,* 'The long-term aims of environmental education are to improve management of the environment and promote satisfactory solutions to environmental issues.' The broadness of these aims, improving the management of the environment and promoting satisfactory solutions to environmental issues, has important links with teaching about moral values.

Acid rain, the Green Belt issue, the gassing of badgers (examples from *Curriculum Guidance 7*) are all issues which raise questions about the treatment of the environment. Amongst these questions are those concerning our values:

— the responsbilities we have towards future generations;
— human interests and decisions about the environment;
— the moral significance of other forms of sentient life;
— the moral significance of non-sentient forms of life;

To help young people to address questions like these, some attention to education in moral values is required. Values in general are the criteria meaning, standards or principles, by which we judge 'things' (objects, ideas, actions, people, etc.) to be worthwhile, desirable, or otherwise. In the case of moral values the judgement would concern specific human dispositions and conduct. Dancing is a type of human conduct. Yet when we say that someone is a good dancer we are not usually passing a moral judgement. In order to make that particular judgement we might be appealing to other values, e.g. aesthetic values. Judgements of moral value would include traits of character, actions and ideals which might be termed responsible, blameworthy, despicable, honourable and so on. Judgements of moral value are related ultimately to choices. The fact that something is valued means that it is that 'thing' that is regarded as being worthwhile or desirable as opposed to some other thing, or nothing. A choice is involved. In the context of moral value judgements a person is not usually accorded praise or blame for their judgements if those judgements are the consequence of coercion, compulsion or conditioning for these remove choice. Conversely, a persons's values will inform the choices that the person makes, which is not to say that people invitably choose according to their values. Sometimes, for a variety of reasons, people fall short of their own standards.

Although a person's values will inform the choices that a parson makes, this does not mean that everyone has the right to have all of their choices respected regardless of the consequences. Not all choices are to equal worth. This would make the act of choosing pointless. In so far as a value judgement is both a judgement of the worth of a choice and an expression of choice, it is open to scrutiny. First, is the choice congruent with the values it purports to express? Second, is the value itself an expression of what is, in those circumstances, the most appropriate standard or principle?

If follows from these observations that values are not simply feelings. Certainly a value may evoke feelings and those feelings will be part of the meaning of that value. Honesty, generosity and fairness may evoke positive emotions whilst negative emotions are evoked by their opposites. However, when someone says that pollutions is wrong, that person is doing more than venting their feelings about pollution. What that person may also be doing is making a series of value judgements such as the following:

— it is in our interests to have cheap food but this requires a degree of pollution that is accumulative;
— we aren't the only moral agents involved and have a responsibility to care for future generations;
— in addition, pollution harms other forms of life which are also morally considerable and, in this context, worthy of equal regard and care.

Although it is in our immediate interests to accommodate a degree of pollution in order to enjoy cheap food, it is not our longer term interests nor is it in the interests of other forms of life. Therefore, pollution is wrong.

This is not to say that anyone would make these judgements or that these judgements are immune from criticism. However, in so far as anyone could make these judgements, and have them criticised, it becomes clear that they are more than expressions of feeling. Involved in these judgements are values to do with caring, equality and responsibility. They lead to the conclusion that pollution is wrong and they provide reasons for saying so. If someone claimed to espouse these values and yet reached the conclusion that pollution was not wrong there would be grounds to questions that conclusion. The values can be prioritised so that caring for people is important but caring for all living things, including people, is even more important because caring for all living things invokes additional values to do with responsibility and equal regard. The person making this judgement has expoused the value, or constellation of values that are, under the circumstances, an expression of the most appropriate standards or principles.

Making value judgements in the manner described invokes two other aspects of choice that should be noted. The first is that the consequences of the choice have to be considered. Thus both providing and not providing cheap food involve consequences which have to be weighed. The second aspect concerns the intentions or motives of the person making the judgement. There is clearly a difference between an intention that is purely self-regarding and one that recognises duties to all living things. There is a difference between selfish and selfless motives. In making value judgements both consequences and intentions may have to be considered.

To make the judgement it is necessary to have a concept of care equality and responsibility. In this sense too, values are more than feelings. They also have a cognitive dimension. It is also the case that our value judgements are informed by facts. In the example give it would be important to know just how much pollution, and of what kind, people can actually accommodate.

Some conclusions can be drawn about the kinds of abilities that young people need to acquire if they are to make moral judgements. Young people need to be able to :

Identify and clarify the issue—in terms of what is worthwhile or desirable concerning traits of character, actions and/or ideals. This will involve an understanding of the values involved including conceptual clarity about the meaning of those values.

Gather and use information—For the sake of clarity, one will need to know, for example, what the effects of pollution are.

Exercise choice—Given that a range range of judgements may reflect that which is worthwhile or desirable in the circumstances and in the light of the relevant information, standards of rationality will be important. The young person will also require understanding of intensions or motives and the capacity to predict the consequences of a choice.

An example of an environmental dilemma is instructive. You live in a part of the country that is the last habitat of a variety of rare plant and animal life, and that lies between a major manufacturing town and a busy port. Existing road links between the town and the port are crowded, unsafe and inefficient. The proposal is to build a new multi-lane highway through this last remaining habitat. A group of activities are plainning a compaign of civil disobedience. You sympathise with their cause but you also appreciate the safety and efficiency arguments. What should you do?

Identifying and clarifying the issue will involve weighing a number of competing demands. For example, the interests of people are morally considerable. On the one hand, building a new road will create jobs, albeit temporarily. However, the loss of a variety of plant and animal life will ultimately diminish the quality of human life. This loss might be outweighed by gains involving jobs, safety and efficiency. Jobs, safety and efficiency and even natural diversity, in the mannar expressed, are all anthropocentric concerns for they reflect human interests. However, if animals or plants have interests that makes them morally considerable in their own right. What is worthwhile or desirable should include the interests of the animals and plants involved. Conceptual clarity about the values involved is vital.

Part of the process of identifying and clarifying the issue will be the use of information. It would be important to have information about jobs, safety, efficiency, animal and plant loss, and what civil disobedience would involve.

Having identified and clarified the issue with the help of the appropriate infromation a choice of judgement may be made. One may then try to predict consequences and these will, in turn, have a bearing on what is judged to be desirable. Thus, for example, the consequences of engaging in civil disobedience would have to be weighed against the consequences of that action being successful. Intentions or motives will also have a bearing on the judgement. The intentions might be to promote a particular human interests but a variety of human interests are at stake. Morever, there are non-human interests to consider. The dilemma also asks what should be done. This indicates another ability that young people need to acquire:

> *Engage in an action appropriate to the identified values*—This final ability indicates that there is a connection between values and behaviour and that moral values education should help the young person to act.

Moral values education, that addresses environmental issues, can occur everywhere that environmental education occurs. Of more significance is the importance of this work for the school as a whole. Moral values education, if properly conducted, inevitably exposes the values of the school. As the NCC's Guidance Document argues, pupils cannot be expected to value that which is not clearly valued by the school. If the school attaches no value to its own environment then that will be a potent message. Conversely, the school that cherishes its own environment will itself be a resource for moral values education.

Politics

At a time when many schools are hard-pressed to find space for all the demands of the National Curriculum, it important to remember that Politics can contribute to a variety of cross-curricular themes, including Environmental Education. If education is about preparing well-rounded students for the realities of adult life, then we cannot afford to ignore those areas which, whilst neither Core nor Foundation, are still crucial to the development of a responsible citizen. Although dealing predominantly with the links between Politics and Environmental Education in secondary schools, many of the points made below could apply equally to those teaching in the primary sector. It could be argued that only when Politics Education begins at Key Stage I, will it be possible to fully educate students about their rights, opportunities and responsibilities as citizens.

The level of ingnorance about politics, amongst students, is often alarming. In a supposedly democratic state, where we are encouraged to believe that we have direct access to political power, many students leave school with only the vaguest notions of how local and national government works. Whilst they might be confident in describing how certain interest groups can encourage change, they are often confused about how that can then be translated into political action. This is surprising when one considers the degree of interest shown by students in environmental issues. Support for environmental groups, such as Greenpeace and Friends of the Earth, is often widespread amongst children who are not even remotely interested in the Budget deficit or the rate of inflation. This is not because, as some politicians might have it these students are idealistic. In many ways it is the reverse. Students see environmentalism as being concerned with making pratical decisions about the future. A cursory talk with most secondary school students reveals passionate support for such causes as animal rights and an end to global warming. What it will not necessarily demonstrate is any realistic understanding of how to go implementing change. At Key Stage 3, particularly within what may be called Personal and Social Education, teachers have an ideal opportunity to channel this genuine interest into a study of the political process. Students tend to be less cynical about politics and are keen to learn about how government works if their interest is stimulated by a variety of practical activities.

Learning about how an election works can, and should, be linked to some from of schools election. Students, campaigning for a place on a Year or House committee, often bring an enthusiasm for political issues which would put to shame, even the most ardent environmental activist. The political dimension of environmental issues is done most effectively by considering relevant, local matters. A candidate for a School Council election may wish to encourage voters in their form by promising to tackle the question of litter around the school or the setting up of a recyling scheme. Candidates may promise to question senior staff about the use of environmentally-friendly materials within the school or organic charity events to, raise funds for a particular environmental cause.

However, links between politics and environmental education at Key Stage 3 can be varied. Most pupils how to know that there is a local Member of Parliament but they will probably have no idea that MP's work or responsibilities. Teaching pupils how to access political power must start by encouraging them to understand the way in which elected representatives go about their business. Practical activities, such as writing mock letters to MPs about issues which concern them, can highlight the fact that they, as future voters, have a major role to play. Better still, we ought to be enccuraging the representatives themselves to talk directly to students. Naturally, not all politicians are either willing to do this or are good at it. This in itself will tell students something about the nature of politics. As is generally the case when politicians do accept such engagements, they often find themselves vigorously challenged on a host of environmental issues.

At Key Stage 4 and A level, politics tends to work on two levels with the older pupils. This first of these is an extension of Key Stage 3 within

Personal and Social Education, as well as sixth form General Studies. Politics has a vital role to play in broadening the curriculum for students. It often runs in conjunction with some basic form environmental education programme. Even so, the links to be made between the two disciplines are profound. Most of these older students are actively looking towards the outside world of either work or Further and Higher Education. An understanding of the health and safety laws governing most workplaces is an ideal starting point for a discussion about the ways in which politicians legislate for environmental factors. Those students who go on work experience are brought into daily contact with these factors, and some will even work in areas of environmental interest, such as forestry and land management, Politics, within a PSE programme, can draw out the experiences of students and relate them to the wider arena of policy-making and governmental intervention.

Many older teenagers are also involved in some sort of quasi-political activity. These activities are more often than not linked to environmental causes. They may hand out leaflets about Animal Rights at the weekend or attend anti-nuclear demonstrations. Educators frequently underestimate the amount of active involvement students have in political issues. Tutor time is an ideal opportunity for them to draw out and develop generalisations about politics and environmental issues from the specific experience of their own students.

A more intensive examination of, for example the role of the media in political life, can be undertaken in General Studies A level. Here too it is possible to select examples of environmental issues. The marketing campaigns of environmental groups often give facinating insights into their political aims and objectives. A study of the political and environmental implications of the recent Earth Summit held in Rio de Janeiro, could be the basis for a thoughtful answer in a General Studies examination. The range of possible links is vast.

The other level at which Politics works in the upper school is at GCSE and A levels. It is here that time can be spent unravelling the intricacies of politics. At examination level students can be encouraged to learn, in detail, about the decision-making processes and their effect upon environmental issues. In the teaching of American Politics, for example, environmental issues can often be brought into the discussion. President Clinton's recent NAFTA victory, and his signalling of a desire for closer links with the Pacific nations, have tremendous implications for the global environment and developing nations. Likewise, the dichotomy between the American Federal government's Clear Air Act of 1990, and the decision of some individual states, such as California, to opt for even tougher legislation, says a great deal about the growing impact of environmentalists on the American political scene. A student who understands something of the lobbying system, as it affects industrial corporations and environmental groups in Washington, has gained a valuable insight into the realities of American political life. In all of these examples, it is possible to explore fruitful connections between Politics and Environmental Education?

Equally, in British politics, it is possible to trace the history of a particular environmental issue from a political perspective. The problem of 'acid rain', which has caused disputes between Britain and such countries as Norway, dates back to the smogs of 1952 and to subsequent, inadequate clean air legislation. As a result, the failure of governments to deal with the emission of sulphur dioxide is still on the agenda. Close beside it is the growing evidence of a link between an increase in asthma sufferers and car exhaust pollution. The action taken by successive governments on this one issue can clarify, for students, a range of political processes. Further issues, such as the adoption of 'green' policies by the major political parties in an effort to secure more votes, can flesh out the student's awareness.

Ideally, students also ought to be encouraged to draw out the links between politics and environmental issues through extended course work. This could be wide-ranging enough so as to develop a theme in detail. Many Politics courses encourage such components and students frequently use them to pursue their environmental interests. The skills gained in both research and analysis will be of benefit to students in both the short and long term.

For the teacher trying to develop Environmental Education across the curriculum, the use of Politics at all stages has tremendous potential. To the students themselves, it can be seen as an immensely enjoyable activity which has a satisfying, practical relevancy. However, coordinators ought never to forget that Politics opens up channels for discussion and learning. It is not an opportunity for indoctrination. Parents in particular, see the negative potential of Politics and are often concerned. They are generally sceptical of the value of potential education, just as they remain sceptical about the value of environmental education. Clearly stated aims and objectives, as well as the parameters, of political and environmental education may ensure parental support.

Finance

Ian Duffell

Nobody likes waste. Many schools in the UK organise recycling programmes for aluminium cans, waste paper or bottles, but one should be questioning whether such schemes do more harm than good to the environment. One of the problems is that too few people ever analyse the mater objectively and, consequently, they tend to confuse the various aims :

—to save money;
—to save resources;
—to protect the environment;
—to make the participants feel better.

Debate in schools may be encouraged by considering each issue in turn, for they do not have simple answers.

To Save Money

Some readers may remember taking glass bottles back to the shop and collecting a few pennies 'deposit'. The bottles were returned to the manufacturer to be washed, refilled, relabelled and redistributed. The reason the manufacturer bottled a commodity in the first place was to make a profit and this system was cost efficient in the 1950's.

This system must now be re-evaluated. Bottle manufacturing has greatly improved so new bottles are cheaper to produce. A much greater diversity of bottles now exists. If it becomes more expedient, drinks manufacturers will change to plastic bottles, cans or carttons. Greater diversity of material available for recycling means increased handling and sorting. Such labour is probably more expensive than in the 1950's.

Health regulations are now much stricter, so ordinary washing is probably inadequate and will not cope with major contamination. The raw material for glass is silica or sand and there seems to be no shortage of that. Allowing for the following costs one must question whether recycling glass bottles, by even the most modern methods, is cost-effective :

—fuel used going to the bottlebank;
—manufacture of the skip;
—rent of space for the skip;
—lorry to collect the skip;
—energy to melt the glass;
—occasional quality-rejects.

If the figures for these costs made the process economically worthwhile then entrepreneurs would have entered the area with schemes. Add in the costs of pollution control caused by some of the above factors and one is beginning to consider the matter objectively.

A smilar calculation could be made regarding old newspapers. A local school had set up a waste paper collection centre when the paper could be sold for £24 per ton. Prices are now down to £10 per ton which makes it not worth the time and effort involved and the centre is closing.

Germany recently set up a massive waste paper salvage operation creating over-supply so that they began to export their surplus. Europe and the US now have more waste paper than they know that to do with. Again one should consider the transport costs and pollution of collection and processing, especially the environmental damage caused by bleaching the paper.

To Save Resources

It is quite possible for the human race to spoil the earth but one must have a healthy regard for Nature's ability to repair damage. Some years ago a major fire devastated a huge area of rain forest. Everyone thought it was a disaster. Now, five years or so later the following has occurred:

— the ash has fertilised the soil;
— new trees are growing from seed;
— the species mix is greater than before when only tall trees could survive;
— grass is growing and wild flowers have bloomed where it was gloomy before;
— deer and other animals have returned and most traces of the fire have disappeared.

Most paper and cardboard sent for recycling comes from new strains of very fast-growing softwood and whilst a ton of newsprint does take seventeen trees, they are trees grown for the purpose which would otherwise not be grown at all. Nearly all paper comes from farmed trees grown in response to the need for it and no trees are saved by recycling paper. Furthermore, while trees absorb carbon dioxide, they do it most at the growing stage so that harvesting ensures a constant supply of growing trees.

As previsouly indicated sand is in plentiful supply. In environmental education it is the emotional aspect of running out of resources which should be balanced by the reality that the top mile of the earth's crust is estimated to contain a million times the quantity of minerals in present known reserves, which themselves represent roughly a hundred years' supplies. Even this ignores replacement by technology, e.g., fibre optics for copper in telecomunication cables or nylon for silk in stockings. We are a long way from running out of raw materials.

Iron and steel, clothing and furniture have always been recycled for economic reasons, long before environmentalism came into vogue. Today aluminium cans are worth around 1p each and many schools and youth groups collect them. Although the recycled material uses only 10% of the energy needed to produce aluminium from bauxite ore, an individual would be hard-pressed to make a living by collecting and selling aluminium cans. Aluminium is the most abundant metal on our planet making up some 8% of the earth's crust.

People do not make uneconomic decisions. As soon as something seems to be in short supply, the price rises and demand usually falls and vice versa. A basket of $1,000 of natural resources in November 1980 was worth only $424 in November 1990. If a price continues to rise, then alternatives are sought or research yieids extra supplies, e.g. North Sea oil and gas. Natural resources are also becoming less scarce because of constantly improving technology. Rather than use less raw material, the Third World may be helped to emerge from its poverty by the West buying basic raw materials from them.

Packaging often comes in for criticism yet packaging reduces waste. The cost of packaging is less than the cost of spoilage otherwise sustained.

To Protect the Environment

Protecting the environment means different things to different people. Pupils should realise that alarmist new is more exciting than a balanced discussion. Further, it is pointless to advocate a return to past technological levels or lifestyles.

Burning trees is generally deplored yet domestic cooking acounts for 99% of all annual woodburning. Human activity, often seen as the villain of the piece, only accounts for 3.5% of the carbon dioxide produced annually. Termites are a more significant source. Carbon dioxide levels may not be so bad as suggested. The levels were 5 to 10 times higher when dinosaurs roamed the earth. It also seems that global warming might increase vegetaion growth which could self-correct carbon dioxide levels although increasing carbon dioxide might counter some of the effects of ozonedepleting CFCs.

Pollution of the air with chemicals can be up to 70 times higher inside homes than outside. Air fresheners, deodorants, hair sprays, mothballs, drycleaned clothes, chlorinated drinking water, cigarette smoke, etc. go largely unchecked while lobbyists campaign about the control of car emissions to reduce the risk of diseases caused by breathing polluted air.

The problem with protecting the environment is that human beings do pollute the planet by consuming resources, creating waste and modifying the scenery. If one carried environmental protection to its logical conclusion, one would advocate the end of the human race. More practically, one might suggest limits to population growth, bringing environmental matters into conflict with human rights. The extinction of species has been a biological fact for the last 500 million years. Were it not for the extinction of dinosaurs, the human race might never have evolved.

There is not shortage of landfill sites, in advanced economics, for domestic rubbish because of mining, quarrying and gravel and brick-clay extraction. When exhausted, these voids can be filled, sealed and returned to a usable landscape.

To save the use of fossil or nuclear fuels, wind farms might be built. However 600 windmills, taller than St Paul's Cathedral and covering an area larger than Greater Manchester, could only supply 1% of national electricity needs. The noise would require local residents to be rehoused and large numbers of birds would be killed. Windpower may not be so environmentally-friendly as first thought.

Since the trade in ivory was banned, uncarved elephant tusks rose in price from $2.50 per pound in 1969 to $34 a pound in 1978 and $90 today. In Kenya hunting is banned and poaching rife. In Botswana hunting is permitted on a limited basis, licences being sold at $25,000 per hunt. Local communities have a share of permits which they can sell and they therefore have an interest in not poaching. Economic forces can be an effective means of giving the elephant population a chance of survival.

General Motors have developed a flywheel-powered car that can accelerate to 60 mph in 6.5 seconds, producing no carbon monoxide, lead or dust particles. The engine's battery is charged in six hours from the household mains and will propel the car for up to 600 miles compared to 320 from a petrol-engined vehicle. The cost of the car would be $20,000. The benefits to the environment are clear. Using electricity generated centrally means that pollution control from burning fossil fuels is localised and more effective. British Gas suggest that, with a cost effective modification of around $1 500 per vehicle, natural gas could be used to replace petrol. A test of 300 cars indicates that the fuel is 30% cheaper, emits 30% less carbon dioxide, 70% less carbon monoxide and almost no sulphur or soot particles. These technological advances are largely by a media which seeks sensationalist environmental news.

Tribology

A useful science is that of tribology which involves the study of industrial efficiency which implies saving energy and costs.

For example if a metal part of a car engine wears out it needs to be replaced. A better quality, harder steel would have saved.

- — oil burned lubricating the wearing part;
- — manufacture of a replacement;
- — labour to replace the part;
- — fuel and labour to deliver the part;
- — manfacture of tools to make the part;

— part of factories for manufacture of the part and tools;
— a part of an iron ore mine;
— a part of a coal mine;
— a part of the mining machines used to provide raw materials—and so on, ripples constantly spreading out.

However, one must also consider the effects on employment caused by such reductions. One person's cost is another's income and the whole study can become complex and emotional. There are few simple solutions although one was found in Germany over cleaning up the Rhine. Any factory taking from the Rhine was made to take it downstream of their own discharge pipe. The effect was quite remarkable.

Green Investments

This area provides challenging material for older pupils. One needs to consider to what extent the investments of a 'Green Unit Trust' are ecologically sound. The level of wages, safety in the factory competitiveness and its effect upon the future employmnent of workers all need careful consideration. The appeal to altruistic feelings in'green investment' advertisements is also interesting. They might be used as an excuse for a 'poor' dividend. Pension funds have to decide whether they are serving their pensioners or the environment. One must be careful to gather legitimate evidence before deciding whether a company is behaving ethically or not. Again there are no simplistic answers for one person's ethical investment may be another's inefficient operation.

Conclusion

All economic activity generates by-products, some of which are unpleasant. It is difficult to measure the value of future damage when we do not know the values of future generations.

Gross National Product growth has improved longevity, diet, health, comfort, hours of work and choice for many people. Material betterment improves the prospects for civilised behaviour. Books, pictures, music, clean air and water and attractive countryside all cost money which must be generated. Pesticides and other chemical aids have meant more efficient production of food. In the past 70 years, potato production has quadruppled and many food costs have fallen. Sales of organic produce in supermarkets are poor with many considering discountinuing their sale as prices are too high.

Finance and Environmental Education should be linked but there are some deeply-held prejudices which have to be challenged. Pollution and capitalist activities have not matched the damage caused by nuclear experiments and planned economies of Eastern European totalitarian states.

The topics are complex epecially if one also takes into acount human inconsistency. Many young people believe passinately in saving whales, etc. yet play music loudly, drop litter and so on. A useful discussion could centre upon these matters considering the suggestion that if no one owns something, no one protects it.

Pupils should be taught how to see behind beguiling posters. When schools consider the financial aspects of Environmental Education, their pupils should learn how to make decisions based upon rational discussion, logical argument and reputable evidence. If that evidence conflicts with the ory, then the theory must yiedd.

Drama

Neil Kilson

Avoiding 'Motorway disasters'—a critical look at the use of contemporary drama methods in environ-mental education

For teachers of drama in education there is a standard environmental story that is both familiar and dreaded. Known as the 'motorway drama', it can also be about a canal, rain forest or attractive piece of countryside. The only common feature is that the affected community will be divided over issues.

It would appear that children have become involved in the fictions and must, as a result, be involved with the facts. There is, however, little evidence of this. More often the children experience a superficial and non-too-profound lesson. They may converse with a degree of conviction but one must question what they actually learn from environmental education through drama. In drama terms we talk about putting oneself in another's shoes and dealing with the universal issues of life. (Boulton, 1979) One may ask whether it is right to use such terms or whether these universal issues exist in the 'motorway drama'. (Hornbrook, 1993) Teachers must ensure that the issues and teaching objectives are clear. We must use drama in educatiuon as a powerful teaching strategy not just as a way of making learning appear more palatable. There is an identified value to drama or it would not appear so regularly in various approaches to environmental education. (ILEA, 1984; Boulton and Kitson, 1989) Children should be guided beyond the superficial to deeper understanding as teachers provide better opportunities than the 'motorway' format.

Taught well, Drama is an excellent way of investigating human relationships with the environment:

the environment as the common heritage of mankind;

the common duty of maintaining, protecting and improving the quality of the environment;

the need for a prudent and rational utilisation of resources;

the way in which each individual can, by his own behaviour, particularly as a consumer, contribute to the protection of the environment

Communication skills, problem-solving skills and positive attitudes towards the environment are promoted. Drama provides the pupils with opportunities for:

expressing views and ideas about the environment through different media...dramatic...,
arguing clearly and concisely about environmental issues;
identifying causes and consequences of environmental problems;
forming reasoned opinions and developing balanced judgements about environmental issues;
working co-operatively with others;
appreciation of, and care and concern for the environmental and for other living things;
independence of thought on environmental issues;
a respect for the beliefs and opinions of others;
a respect for evidence and rational argument;
tolerance and open-mindedness.

To achieve these goals one first needs to consider the drama process. We are not asking the children to act out a play nor are they living out some notion of reality. The best drama recognises the process for itself. It makes clear to the children that they are making up a story and that none of what goes on is real. It may be very tense and exciting when you confront the group, without letting them know you are making up a drama up a drama, by saying something like, 'I've just heard from the headteacher that the council are planning to build a factory on the school field.' The teacher has to know to what extent the children are involved in a drama and quite clearly they are not. What result is anger and a sense of betrayal. Drama is about playing. These children are involved in reality. We must either be other people, in another time or look at the problem from a different perspective in order to establish what Neelands (1990) calls distance through person, time or space. The quality of the interactions will not be significantly diminished by telling the class that they are making up a story about the council building on the school field. However, the quality of their reflective learning that can be drawn out from the situation is improved.

To be effective, the teacher must have a clear focus, a learning objective which the drama will consider. Without this focus one may wander in a collective fantasy, being diverted from the main point of the lesson by some minor issue. That is not to say that the children should merely act out the teacher's play. This would be unispiring. One must be aware of what Morgan and Saxton (1987) have identified as the play for the teacher and the play for the children. Both must exist simultaneously and the skill of the teacher is to integrate the two so that they (the learning focus and the excitement of the story as it unfolds) are seen as one. Drama is a collective process. It is important for the children to recognise it as such. Children and teacher must collaborate to maximise the learning potential offered by drama.

One deficiency in the 'motorway drama' is its lack of depth. When exploring environmental issues we often expect children to care passionately about something to which they are totally indifferent. Children can operate at a superficial level, satisfying the teacher's need for them to be on task using language or occupational mime. In drama we are trying to encourage the children to think and act 'as-if' they are the people in the fiction, feeling and reacting accordingly. (Weininger, 1988) We do not want them to work in a superficial, conscious mode whereby they are thinking, 'what if' I was a protester, how would I stand, speak and look? These two conditions have been explored by Singer and Singer (1989) who quite clearly see the 'what if' state as being socio-dramatic play whereas the 'as-if' state is drama. The problem for teachers using drama is how to attain the deeper state. Heathcote (1979) indicates the key is commitment and belief. It does not matter what the issue is, it is hard to feel any relationship towards it if one is not interested in it. If we want the children to respond we must help them build commitment and belief.

When exploring environmental issues using dramatic techniques we must go beyond role-play. Drama is very effective when used in the appropriate situation but the problem arises with regards to its excessive and indiscriminate use. As Boulton and Kitson (1989) point out, whilst role-play is drama, there is much more to drama than role-playt. Its inappropriate use has led to it being devalued in the euyes of the pupils. The best dramas have a beginning where we find out who we are, where we are and what's up, a series of complications to the story, a climax and a final stage where loose ends are dealt with. All too often dramas linked to an environmental theme miss out the important first two stages and begin with conventions appropriate for the climactic phase. (Neeland, 1990) As a result we end up with a 'motorway' debate that no one really cares about. Far better to start off by defining the community with each child saying something about their role in the village, a significant moment in village life or putting someone in the 'hot seat' in order to find out what it means to live in the community. The debate will then be more meaningful. Even in this simple example we can provide pupils with quality opportunities for:

arguing clearly and concisely about an environmental issue, identifying causes and consequences of invironmental problems and forming reasoned opinions and developing balanced judgements ·about environmental issues.

(NCC, 1990)

Drama is not a panacea that makes all learning easier to bear. It is a useful teaching strategy and should be given equal value along with other teaching strategies. In the context of environmental education, drama has a significant role in the teaching of skills, attitudes and understanding. To maximise drama's effectiveness in this area we need to use it with thought. We must help the pupils use drama to explore, for themselves, how the world looks to other people and what responsibilities we have. To achieve this we must consider:

— psychological distance for the children so that they feel safe;
— depth, so that they can become committed;
— belief in the work combined with a focus for the learning area covered;
— a wide range of dramatic techniques which provide the most effective way to much artistic and learning outcomes.

Without such consideration, lessons that employ drama structures run the risk of being arid with the pupils engaged in either active English or fantasy play.

15

The Social Sciences

The inclusion of Environmental Education in the cross-curricular themes of the National Curriculum is unsurprising. Concern for the environment and the relationship between human beings and nature has been a recurrent political and social issue of throughout the twentieth century. Moreover, the increasing globalisation of threats to the environment, in the shape of, for example, the depletion of the ozone layer or the widespread radiation poisoning which followed the disaster at Chernobyl, has intensified that concern. It is therefore entirely laudable that environmental education should be promoted as an aspect of the National Curriculum. However, as with the other cross-curricular themes, the relationship of the social sciences, and, in particular, sociology and psychology, to environmental education is problematic. This is partly because the social sciences stand outside the defined subject areas of the National Curriculum, but also because the definition of social sciences in the National Curriculum documentation is restricted.

Yet the aims of environmental education as detailed in *Curriculum Guidance 7* specifically encourage a social scientific contribution:

> encourage pupils to examine and interpret the environment from a variety of perspectives—physical, geographical, biological, sociological, economic, political, technological, historifcal, aesthetic, ethical and spiritual.

However, the guidance document does not go on to detail in any systematic way what that contribution might be. Rather, there is a series of issues identified throughout the document, which have a vaguely social sciences aspect. For example 'people and their communities' are referred to in the contribution of the National Curriculum subjects (NCC, 1990b) or 'home and family, school neighbourhood and peer group' when referring to activities that affect the environment which children might already be involved in. Beyond this, there are only general references to the contribution of subjects outside the National Curriculum, or snippers of social scientific concerns such as 'leisure', 'technology' or 'development' in the illustrations used (NCC, 1990).

The problem here is not just that the social sciences are apparently margnalised in *Curriculum Guidance 7,* but that the lack of any serious input from the social sciences is likely to defeat the whole point of having Environmental Education as a cross-curricular theme in the first place. Ministers of Education and commentators alike have pointed out that environmmental education is concerned with more than just knowledge about the environment. It is also understanding the complexities of the factors which might inflict environmental damage and about involving young people in taking action towards the environment's conservation and improvement. As Norman Farmer wrote:

> Being reasonably satisfied that the core and foundation subjects will provide knowledge about the environment, we must look to those activities that transform a pupil's learning into an education. For Environmental Education, these are first hand experiences (e.g., fieldwork)...
>
> (Farmer, 1990)

However, it is questionable whether fieldwork on its own can transform learning into an education. Angela Rumbold, when Minister of State for Education and Science, clearly recognised the necessity to go beyond the personal and the immediate:

> Good environmental educatio...must lead pupils and students out and on from their immediate preceptions and experiences to a wider understanding. It must develop their capacity to go beyond anecdotal and the particular. None of this happens by chance.
>
> (Rumbold, 1989)

As the traditional task of the social sciences has been to achieve such wider understanding, this statement represents a powerful, if unmeant, plea for the social sciences to be involved in Environmental Education. Indeed, it could be argued that the social sciences could be employed as the organising principle behind the delivery of Environmental Education and thus avoid the

> real danger...that Environmental Education...will be declared to be 'done' by ticking off a collection of attainment targets which sound appropriate, but which are delivered with minimal coherence across a range of traditional 'subjects'.
>
> (Hawkins, 1991)

However, one must consider what the social sciences, as broadly defined, offer in the way of an organising principle for the delivery of Environmental Education. It is the ability of the social sciences to place environmental issues in their political, economic and social contexts which is the distinctive contribution that the social sciences can make. Without such contexts, the possibility of effecting social change concerning the environment is likely to be severely curtailed and environmental education will not achieve its aim of a 'fully informed and active participation of the individual in the protection of the environment' (NCC, 1990a).

More specifically, sociology and to a lesser extent psychology have themselves been concerned with environmental issues, through their consideration of the process of developement and its impact on the human environment. While there is an argument that social scientists have usually ignored environmental issues (Redclift, 1987), the classical sociologists did explore the relationship between nature and society in considering the process of modernisation and the social and environmental effects of the transition from a rural to an industrial society. This concern with environmental issues can be traced through the Chicago School and their emphasis on 'Ecology' (Park, 1952) to new sociological developments such as 'Ecofeminism' (Mellor, 1992). Therefore, it could be argued that, while the environment has not been a central area of social scientific investigation in an explicit way, there has been an awareness of the relationship between society, the individual and the environment from the very beginnings of social scientific study.

However, during the 1980's, sociological interest in the environment has been heightened because of a series of developments both within the discipline and in global society itself. Firstly, there has been an increasing tendency for sociology to cross-fertilise with other disciplines in looking at issues with which they are all concerned. For examples, when Canter et al. define what they see as the environmental social sciences, they identify 'the domains of Behaviour and Perceptual Geography, Environmental Psychology, Urban Sociology, Social Anthropology, Urban History, Social Ecology, Behavioural Archaeology, Landscapes Architecture and various aspects of design' (Canter et al., 1988) as contributing disciplines.

Secondly, global interest in the environmental aspects of development has been aroused following the United Nations' Conference on the Environment and Development in Rio De Janeiro in June 1992, which put forward Agenda 21: 'a blueprint for a global partnership...It is a bold mandate for change, a call for a fundamental reform in our economic behaviour, based on a new understanding and awareness of the impact of human activity on the environment.' (United Nations, 1993). Central to this understanding are five types of environmental side-effects of development, including number 5 'social distribution: of which congestion and the loss of a sense of community are examples.' (United Nations, 1971).

Lastly, some sociologists have been increasingly interested in environmental issues and have responded to the call from Dunlap and Catton (1980) for a new 'ecological paradigm.' They have largely rejected the assumptions of modernism to embrace, in varying degrees, a post-modernist distrust of science and technology. For example, Giddens argues that, in contemporary society, individuals exist in a state of anxiety, because contemporary societies are societies of high 'risk'. Important amongst the risks that individuals face in the sense of impending environmental destruction, which has emerged from the activities of science and technology (Giddens, 1990 and 1991).

It is therefore an appropriate time for social scientists in schools and colleges to look again at Environmental Education and seek to provide the necessary context for their students to gain the understanding needed to develop the 'social responşibility' (NCC, 1990b) towards environmental issues which *Curriculum Guidance 7* believes is important.

Law

Don Rowe

In the real world, as opposed to the artificially constructed curriculum world, the relationship between environmental control and the law is a close one. It is by means of legislation that government implements its policies for the environment, however adequate or inadequate these happen to be. Therefore, there are many opportunities for teaching pupils about the environment and the nature of law. One significant advantage of this is that environmental issues demonstrate very clearly that the law itself may not represent the easy consensus often pictured in textbooks on citizenships. More often it is a compromise between opposing interests which remain in tension. The law may even represent a situation in which the immediate interests of industry and commerce can be seen to have prevailed over the longer term environmental ones.

Environmental education and law-related education are relative newcomers to the curriculum and are both now widely recognised as essentail elements of the entitlement curriculum. Law-related education (LRE) can be defined as the process of teaching and learning about the role of law in society as it affects ordinary citizens (NCC, 1990a; Rowe, 1992). LRE attempts to empower citizens by informing them about the extent of their legal rights and duties and how law works as an instrument of social policy. Law-related education also seeks to encourage the development of a 'criticial solidarity' stance, viz-a-viz legislation. This is to say that, in a democracy, one of the prime functions of citizens is to criticise existing legislation and directly or indirectly, to bring pressure to bear on politicians to respond to changing social and ecological needs.

To argue the link between environmental and law-related education is relatively non-problematic. But there is always a gap (sometimes amounting to a chasm) between educational rhetoric and classroom practice. Every teacher is now familiar with the rhetoric of cross-curricularity. It is frequently generalised and exhortative in style yet many of the difficulties of making such links are glossed over. Quite apart from the question of teacher skill and confidence, there is often a more fundamental problem arising from the nature of the different subjects being linked. To take an example relevant to this present discussiuon in *Curriculum Guidance 3* (NCC, 1990b) the document states that, at one end of the spectrum, the cross-curricular themes: 'can be spearately timetabled, at the other end they can be completely subsumed within the subjects of the curriculum. Environmental education, for example, could well be covered in science, geography, technology, English and mathematics.' The implication of this passage seems to be that the whole of what might reasonably be conceived of as 'environmental education' can be apportioned out amongst the mainstream national curriculum subjects. But, if such infusion is to be satisfactory and not cosmetic, it must be done in such a way that its central concerns are addressed in a sufficiently holistic manner as to do it justice in its own right. Cross-curricula delivery raises questions both of 'coverage' and of 'quality'.

It is immediately obvious that a policy of curriculum infusion would not, in fact, be able to examine environmental issues in many of their social, economic, political and legal contexts. Furthermore, reliance on infusion alone, would increase the likelihood that environmental issues are taken up only in passing, or not at all.

The infusion model of cross-curricularity has developed at least partly as a response to the historic weakness of the English curriculum so far as the social sciences and humanities are concerned and this structural weakness continues to undermine many socially important curriculum innovations including environmental and law-related education.

In *Curriculum Guidance 7* (1990c) one of the central objectives of environmental education is described as knowledge and understanding of local, national and international legislative controls to protect and manage the environment: how policies and decisions are made about the environment.' Related objectives refer to 'the conflicts which can arise about environmental issues' and 'the importance of effective action to protect and manage the environment'. This requires at least a basic understanding of the nature and role of law in society. For example, pupils should know how legislation is framed and the nature of the powers given by Parliament to ministers of the Crown. In addition, pupils should understand how and why citizens can appeal against government decisions or work to change the law. That is nothing less than their democratic right. But the infusion method of curriculum delivery (as applied to citizenship) would very probably have left pupils ignorant of such background knowledge. It is no more reasonable to ask teachers of environmental education to be responsible for delivering these core elements of law-related citizenship any more than we would expect a physics teacher to have to break off a lesson on forces to teach equations. Thus law-related education should be seen as an essential 'service' subject for the whole of the humanities curriculum, including environmental education. If all this is accepted reasonable in theory, then it is also important to acknowledge that the reality is very different. What strikes one, when reviewing many environmental resources, is how often the environment/law nexus is overlooked or, at best, left unexploited.

Teachers reading this many feel that it is quite unrealistic for them, an non-experts, to know what the law says on environmental issues in any detail. For Example one might need to know who, and under what circumstances, can pollute our rivers or emit sulphur into the atmosphere. Much of this knowledge is necessary before pupils can ask why this is allowed to happen. Most of the interest groups active in this area have education or publicity officers who are willing to provide information of this kind, and they can usually offer examples of how the law works in practice. They may quote case studies of when the law was enforced or challenged. Thus a law related perspective enables an often generalised debate about an issue to become focussed on the real world of compromise, half measures, and injustice as well as showing pupil how important the legal controls actually are.

It is not only for older pupils that a law-related perspective can be valuable. In *Curriculum Guidance 7,* for example, a case study is offered in which Key Stage 2 pupils investigated the issue of gassing badgers in the fight against bovine tuberculosis. The objectives listed include coverage of legislative controls to protect and manage the environment. Durring the course of their researcher, pupils wrote to various organistions including the Ministry of Agriculutre and conservation societies and no doubt discovered what the current legal status of the badger is, as a protected species. At such a point one may ask the children whether the law should be changed. Teachers who might have held a general class debate might instead consider the advantages of debating this kind of issue in the form of a parliamentary bill.

There are several advantages in using this format. First, the issue can be aired generally (the equivalent of the second reading). Then the subject can be taken clause by clause, allowing a much more detailed examination of the issues than the usual debate format. The reason for this is that law needs to be both clear, workable and give due consideration to a multiplicity of conflicting interests. Primary school pupils can well understand many of these detailed aspects if they are presented in the right way and at an appropriate level. For example, imagine that a class has agreed that, in principle, gassing badgers is to be allowed. In an ordinary debate that would be the end of the matter but the 'draft bill' format opens up the need to discuss a number of further issues such as who should be allowed to gas them. Children will quickly see reasons for the decision not being left entirely to the farmer. They may also see the need to prevent 'control' from becoming 'extermination'. The potential of LRE to develop critical and logical reasoning is immense. Using the law as both a resource and a vehicle, it is possible to address a wide range of environmentally crucial questions relating to the rights and responsibilities of citizens, the power of the state and the nature and values of our society (see, for example, Rowe and Thorpe, 1993). Used consistently in this way, the law itself will become less invisible to the next generation of citizens and be viewed as a powerful, omnipresent factor in the creation and re-creation of four social structures.

Communication and the Media

A vast amount of information conveyed to us, individually and collectively, is through the forms and technologies of the media. If pupils are to have an informed concern for environmental issues, they need to broaden and deepen their knowledge and experiences in order to come to a wider understanding of what this implies. It is the media that produces the representations on which much of this development is based.

Environmental issues of genuine concern to young people are often presented in the media, sometimes with very extensive coverage. To be able to judge the validity of the information they receive, students need to understand the nature of communication and the techniques that can be used to inform and influence audiences. One aim is to demonstrate that the language of very medium in not natural or netural.

National Curriculum Guidance 3: The Whole Curriculum identifies six cross-curricular skills: communication, numeracy, study skills, problem-solving, personal and social skills, and those relating to information technology. (NCC, 1990a) It gives examples of how these can be related to environmental education and it is apparent how integral is the part media education has to play in the development of these skills in this context.

For example, the study skills section includeds 'retrieving, analysing, interpreting and evaluating information about the environment from a variety of sources'. Problem-solving skills include 'forming reasoned opinions and developing balanced judgements about environmental issues'. As well as encouraging progress with skills, media education also has a key role in the development of attitudes. Indenpendence of thought, recognition of the beliefs and opinions of others, and a respect for evidence and rational argument can be encouraged through the examination and interpretation of media texts. Study of the media requires considerations of the source of ideas and information rather than the passive acceptance of what is presented.

The understanding of media agencies, languages and representations shares common ground with certain areas within communication studies. Students can become aware of how a communicator selects the message to be transmitted to the audience and how content and form of presentation are chosen. The communicator will be influenced by ideology and perceptions of the audience; the way the audience receives and makes meaning of the message will be affected by perceptions about the communicator's knowledge and trustworthiness.

> ...the key issue...is the development of an understanding about what difference it might make to the meaning, significance or authenticity of a text if it is made by say, Touchstone rather than by Zenith, or financed by British Nuclear Fuels rather than Greenpeace. (British Film Institute, 1991)

Communication and media studies provide opporutnities to examine attitudes. What we believe or know about the subject under consideration, the cognitive component, is obviously important. So too, is the affective element. Many environmental issues arouse strong emotional responses, some of which may lead to changes in behaviour. Where an individual's change in attitude is translated into positive action, there is the possibility of fulfilling one major aim of environmental education, active participation in resolving problems.

The totality of media output about environmental issues is considerable. In one issue (27 March 1994), *The Observer* included four separate features on such themes. These articles were about: a new plan to make nuclear waste safe; countering the rise in the planet's disappearing plants and animals; measures to make business cost-effective as well as environmentally friendly, and DIY chain stores' commitment to sell only 'sustainably grown' wood. On the same day, six full pages in the *Sunday Express* were given over to a feature about global warming and the Sunday and the *Sunday Telegraph* reported on plans to curtail erosion of footpaths in the Lake District.

In addition, BBC2 showed a 30 minute programme about protecting flood plains and the press contained review of film and video releases with themes based on the conservation of the earth's resources. The quality is not, however, consistent. *On Deadly Ground*, a film in which an oil-rig worker challenges his employer over pollution in Alaska was described as having dialogue which is 'truly toxic'! On the contrary, *Ferngully...The Last Rainforest* was praised for the style in which it delivers an ecological warming.

The British Film Institute suggests that media education must address the totality of children's cultural experience. There is a tendency to focus on informational and persuasive forms, less heed being paid to fictional and entertainment ones. These, too, contribute to knowledge of the world, different areas, groups, attitudes, economics and environments. Children need to understand how ideas and meanings are constructed in different media and in different genres.

There are case studies of projects in which learning objectives for both environment education and study of the media have been successfully met. Two are described in *Media Education: and introduction*. (Alvarado and Boyd. Barrett, 1992)

The first was completed by a class of Year 3 pupils in an inner city Leeds school. The focus was on visual representations and extended the children's experience of decoding photographic images. Pupils then took their own photographs in the local park. Some of them were designated to show it as a pleasant place, some unpleasant. Awareness was raised of issues relating to the local environment and there was an increased level of understanding of the media element.

The second project was based on the care of tees, a subject relevant to the school involved and also an issue of wider concern. The 19 pupil primary school produced a video programme. The technology gave them the means to communicate their views and the unit of work illustrated how media empowers, making it possible to influence others.

Secondary Media Education : A Curriculum Statement contains a summary of a Year 10 project, ' The World Food Problem'. Students were shown how to recognise media devices, such as the narrative behind images, and discussed how preconceptions can be exploited by media agencies. By examining material from numerous sources, they learned how to deconstruct and decode media output.

Environmental education raises issues and creates opportunities to extend experience. It provides meaningful and important contexts for activities in which attitudes can be refined and skills enhanced. In whatever subject area the environment is being studied, there will be the need to refer to a range of secondary sources, such as television programmes, photographs, films, maps, documents and books. Media education and communication studies enable students to understand and appreciate the knowledge, attitudes and values within each of these texts.

However, the place of the study of the media within the National Curriculum is under threat. The Dearing Review has undertaken to reduce statutory requirements and media study has lost ground in previous processes of rationalisation within statutory orders.

English for Ages 5-11 (the first Cox Report, 1988) saw benefits for pupils through the application of their critical faculities and the focus on 'language, interpretation and meaning'. It was recognised that in the secondary school media studies may exist discretely, as well as being embedded elswhere in the curriculum. The orders for English were considered the most appropriate ones in which to include media education, given common aims about exploring language, interpretation and meaning.

The statutory orders were published in March 1990 with *Attainment Target 2. Reading,* containing the elements of media education. *Non-Statutory Guidance* (June 1990) included a media education section (D16-20), which contains suggested appraoches. It also gives exemplar units of work, one of which is the *Local Area*, a module with an environmental education focus. Proposals for revised orders for English were published in April 1993. These were intended to reduce English to its essential core and media education was virtually omitted. This fact was commented upon as a particular concern by 14% of the respondents during the consultation period (NCC *Consultation Report: English,* September 1993). Reports suggest specific guidance will be produced for teachers by the subject advisory team designing the revised orders.

The future status of media education in the prescribed curriculum may be as a peripheral element. Thus far, its value has not been fully recognised in the National Curriculum, with a piecemeal rather than coherent approach. It has been left to such bodies as the British Film Institute to sugest structures and frameworks which can ensure progression in the development of skills and understanding. Committed schools and teachers will obviously continue with successful practice, however little reference is made in statutory orders.

The aims of environmental education are fundamental to the quality of life now and in the future. They include the acquisition of knowledge and values, the development of skills of examination and analysis and a growing awareness and commitment that leads to active participation. The marginalisation of media education in statutory curriculum orders is occurring at a time when more information is being transmitted in ways which demand through intepretation. It is and will remain, an essential part of effective environmental education.

Records of Achievement

Ian Curts

Young people have a rare enthusiasm for environmental causes. Such issues stimulate their imaginations and challenges their sense of justice and fairness. They speak knowledgeably about the damage to the ozone layer often long before they understand what ozone is; or of the destructive potential of the motor car before they know what a gas is, harmful or otherwise. Environmental damage is seen as instinctively wrong just as killing animals for throwing down litter is wrong. Understanding why it may be wrong usually comes later. They have little patience with the 'ifs' and 'buts' arguments which seek to justify particular forms of action. They are not easily swayed by viewpoints which appear to support the polluter or the environmental exploiter. It is sometimes argued that these concerns are transient and fashionable, the result of manipulation by the media, and that consequently their impact is shallow and short-lived. However, to dismiss all issues as such is to fail to recognise the extent of threats to the future of the planet which affront children's sense of fairness and may cause foreboding about their own futures.

Hearing seven year olds talk with passion about the need to protect woodlands is a refreshing experience. In a very real way those children are saying something about their future. It is not native idealism that guides their thinking but a picture of the future that they want. For that reason, pupils' voices are some of the most important in any debate on the environment.

Educators have been effective in helping young people to learn from, and about, the environment. (NCC, 1990a) This learning may not always be particularly coherent or structured but at least it has left many young people with a clearer understanding about the world that they inhabit. Where there has perhaps been less success is in educating for the environment. Educating for the environment involves the consideration of moral and social issues which are themselves complex and controversial. They also present the educator with specific dilemmas in the way in which they are to be presented and offered for discussion. Talking deploringly about the loss of the rain forest is one thing: helping young people to appreciate the social and economic conditions which impel the farmers and loggers to exploit the forests is a challenge of a different order. If pupils are to form a balanced view of the process of forest depletion it is important that these factors are considered.

In a school curriculum which is increasingly restricted to a pragmatic definition of appropriate skills and knowledge, opportunities to educate for the environment are limited. As one of the cross-curricular themes in the National Curriculum, environmental education inevitably enjoys a lower profile for many teachers than the curriculum subjects. This is in spite of the foreword to the National Curriculum Council's guidance document endorsing it as 'an essential part of every pupil's curriculum'. (NCC, 1990b) Being a cross-curricular theme there are no specific subject statements which identify by which a pupil's progress may be assessed. True, there are statements in science and geography which refer directly to an understanding of environmental phenomena as in 'know that human activity may produce changes in the environment that can affect plants and animals' (HMOS, 1991) but there is no coherent framework against which a pupil's developing knowledge of the environment can be measured.

This is not a weakness. If the study of environmental issues is, as has been argued, such a complex one involving the consideration of social and ethical issues, one may question whether any system of assessment and record keeping is possible. But it is instructive to consider what might happen if no such system existed in a school. In the absence of a means of assessing and recording the learner's progress in the acquistion of environmental concepts there is the danger that new learning will be presented in an incoherent and random manner. There is less likelihood that knowledge and skills will be built up progressively and, as a result, the learner's environmental awareness could become a ragbag of confused and contradictory concepts and ideas. However, a formal assessment programme which depends sloley on a series of discrete statements, whether drawn from the National Curriculum or not, may also miss vital pieces of information about a learner's understanding. This may be because what is assessed is unrelated to those areas of knowledge which are of greatest significance to that learner. Any system which reduces the complexity of the environment to a number of digestible but weakly related concepts and pieces of information is unlikely to capture the fullness of the learner's understanding.

What is required, therefore, is a system which is sufficiently regorous to provide a framework for the recording of achievement in a number of skills and areas of knowledge yet flexible enough to allow for learners to demonstrate the fullness of their own achievements in the manner most appropriate to them. A Record of Achievement can provide such a model. Put simply a Record of Achievement is a folder or file in which various assessments of a learner's work, skills, abilities and personal qualities are collated acumulatively. If fulfils four principle purposes:

— the recognition of achievement, by providing teachers and pupils with an opportunity to give recognition to achievements in a broad range of experiences,
— the enhancement of motivation and personal development by

encouraging perseverance and the development of pupils' talents and interests through that recognition;

— the organisation of the curriculum and learning;

— the Record of Achievement process provides comprehensive and detailed information from which the school and pupil can plan the next learning experience; it is a document in which these attainments and achievements are recorded and which can be regularly updated and reviewed.

The record does not confine itself, therefore, to the work and experiences that the learner has in the school. It provides a much fuller picture of their interests and achievements so that anyone reading it has a more complete view of the learner's competencies. Through the Record of Achievement recognition is given to those many areas of involvement which may otherwise have been missed or ignored. For example, many children becomes involved in environmental projects in the outside community. If this activity is unknown to the teacher, then the opportunity to take the experiences gained into account in planning future work may be missed.

Frequently it is the learners who retain editorial control over that goes into the Record. This provides a mechanism for them to indicate what they feel to be the more relevant and significant aspects of their work. It also provides the teacher with an insight into the pattern of reasoning being adopted by the learner, an understanding which can be further explored in the idalogue and negotiation which forms an important part of the process. There is no one standard method of completing a Record of Achievement and this lack of a prespective format also encourages flexibility in what is recorded. By having access to wide variety of types of recording device the learner may demonstrate, through the Record of Achievement, levels of understanding which are difficult to record by other more rigid means.

The compilation of the record also allows the learner and the teacher to discuss progress together and, through this discussion, the teacher is able to investigate the learner's level of understanding or commitment to that aspect of their learning. Records of Achievement also often lead to learners engaging more fully in their own assessment. By asking questions of themselves they confront those areas of their knowledge which are less secure.

The Record of Achievement is built up comulatively and shows the progression of a developing interest or skill. By referring to it the teacher or parent is able to form a picture of how that development has proceeded. Some pupils leave school to pursue careers where a knowledge of environmental issues and causes is of considerable benefit. The employer, seeking evidence of such knowledge, will find it in a thoughtfully developed Record of Achievement. The evidence may be in a variety of forms. Examples could include diaries of work on conservation projects or certificates showing involvement in litter-picking activities. Entries of this nature provide the prospective employer with an indication of the true level of a pupil's commitment.

However, Records of Achievement in practice have their problems. Whilst they can be potent source of motivation they can, if not developed sympathetically, also become an unremitting chore. The young person required to go through the ritual of completing entries for the Record of Achievement when there is little of significance to record can quickly become disenchanted and, instead of being further stimulated and motivated by the process, react with antipathy towards the subject being studied. Similarly for some the record can become one, not of achievement but of non-achievement and failure to succeed which can further erode self-confidence and esteem.

Whilst these potential hazards must be borne in mind the value of a Record of Achievement to the environmental educator is considerable. It provides a process by which the totality of the learner's knowledge and understanding can be judged and information from a number of areas of the learner's experience synthesised. Perhaps most importantly, it offers a means by which an interest and enthusiasm for the environmental can be nourished. For the future well-being of the planet it is crucial that the passion for the environmental felt by young people is not dissipated by sterile teaching and learning. Any method that depends on the active participation of the learner in the acquisition and retention of an understanding of environmental issues merits consideration, particularly at a time when there are so many other areas of study competing in an otherwise greatly overloaded curriculum.

Community Education

The links between community education on the one hand and an understanding of the nature of environmental education on the other are both complex and poweful. Environmental education is, in a very real sense, an integral part of that demanding and exciting pedagogical orientation commonly called community education.

The issues raised by this claim are useful ones to consider and argument about them might helps readers to clarify their understanding of these two themes which must be kept to the forefront of educational discourse and action.

There are four principal ways in which community education maintains its supremacy:

- by keeping environmental considerations keyed into such educational issues as equality of opportunity, empowerment and relevance in the curriculum;
- it keeps environmental approaches realistic by encouraging development outwards from the problems and needs of individuals, groups and communities to the wider global issues;
- it strives to enlist all social classes and ethnic groups to the view that constructive discontent with the way we handle one another and the globe is a vital powerhouse for local and world wide survival;
- it maintains a kind of quality control by ensuring that aspects on each curriculum are relevant, appropriate and sensitive to the lives and needs of the target groups concerned.

There is a simple framework associated with each of the two areas in question which can, perhaps, be used to demonstrate the nature of the relationship. One may suggest four headings which summarize the aims of community orientated activity in schools. Then there are three frequently used summarizing categories for environmental education.

Community Education

- Promotion of the ideas of community and community spirit and the regeneration of aspects of behaviour associated with them.
- Promotion of the idea of education as a lifelong process.
- Achievement of equality of opportunity.
- Development of inter-cultural sensitivity, empathy and harmony.

Environmental Education

- Education about the environment.
- Education for the environment.

Education through the environment.

In their approaches to education about the environment community educators seek to maximize the immediate relevance to the children of the activities. The intention is to give them the information and skills which will help them to gain control over their own lives and destinies, and enable them to become sensitive, participating and influential members of their immediate, and wider, community. They also seek to adjust the content and approach to the nature of the community served by the school. In a disadvantaged catchment area methods would be used which took pains to validate the life experiences and language of local families. In this way cultural barriers between the school and its curriculum, on the one hand and the cultures served by the school, on the other hand are lowered. The resulting 'user friendly' structure loses some of the arrogance inherent in the middle class imposition of environmental topics far removed from some parents' very real worries about maintaining a reasonable life for their children in a relatively hostile environment. The involvement of parents in the process, which would certainly be promoted by community educators, would bring a reality and continuing education aspect to the work.

For example a project on 'Birds in our Neighbourhood' becomes part of a wider topic called. 'Migration', In an inner city school such a topic might cover such aspects as:

(1) When families arrived in the neighbourhood and where they came from. Contributions here from parents, orally and, perhaps, in print if the school has resources to produce booklets written by parents.
(2) Similar studies of the wildlife of the area, including a comparison with a completely different catchment area.
(3) Why living things migrate, the history of migration, etc.
(4) Hostile and non-hostile environments.
(5) How different environments affect the skills and information necessary for survival.

Clearly, such an approach does the purely environmental job, in that it should raise awareness of the importance of maintaining species through preservation of their habitats. The community education orientation keeps it relevant to the lives of the children concerned and therefore, perhaps, increase a commitment to learning. The fact that parents would be learning alongside the children and teachers enhances this aspect and provides opportunities for continuing education for all the adults involved. Urban life skills would be discussed, migration of humans better understood and information about, and sensitivity to, other human cultures in the neighbourhood developed in closely linking human migration with that of other species we are making a very inportant point concerning general survival.

Education for the environment appears to be, basically, about survival. Many would see it as the central theme of environmental education, some appear to see it as the only theme. It is in this area in which environmental considerations can most fall into the trap of being too far removed from the concerns of the target group. Classes of eleven years olds may work hard on a 'Save the Whale' project in an area where parents are deeply concerned about saving their children from racist attacks, gang violence and substance abuse. In a leafy suburb pupils of similar age may know all about the swan being a protected species but do not know anything about the Children Act. Even the most aware may suddenly realize that they are teaching children in Notting Hill about tea plantations and the wheatfields of Canada, whilst totally ignoring in the curriculum, their rather perilous lives in that part of London. It was the time of very bad race riots and it was the age of Rachmanism which was rife in that neighbourhood. These are lessons hard-learned but crucial!

A more effective approach might be to follow a topic called 'Survival' which would follow on quite neatly from the one on 'Migration'. As an illustration of how community education approaches guide environmental education, some aspects which might be covered are:

(1) The basic elements of survival—safe habitat, balance with other species, gaining knowledge, acquiring skills, etc.
(2) Endangered species, linking our own survival of other species. Most children and many education students answer 'No' when asked, 'Are we an endangered species?' The point to get across is that if one species is threatened then to some degree, they all are.
(3) Surviving in the neighbourhood. An inter-agency approach to the dangers of life in the catchment area and to the development of the skills, information and attitudes necessary for survival. Parents and other members of the community would also make an input.
(4) Beyond mere survival. Improving the environment, widening personal choice, helping other species and helping other members of our own speices. Political implications and machinery, promotion of constructive discontent and empowerment. Compare local with other habitats.
(5) Survival of heritage. Customs, language, dialect, regional and ethnic differences in dress, food, etc., as an enrichment of the general culture and worthy of protection. Historical heritage and its survival in buildings, local memories, institutions, etc.

These suggestions are not considered to be exhaustive or to be the necessary components of such an approach. They are intended to illustrate how community education approach typified by the four headings above, guides and coordinates environment education, linking it with the central concerns of the target group and extending it to the wider global issues.

Education through the environment may be considered of less importance environmental terms. From a community education stance it is seen as using the community as a resource for the curriculum, opportunities to use the people, places and institutions of the locality to enrich, enliven and bering relevance and realism to the curriculum are numerous and are still. relatively. unrecognized in many of our schools. Reflecting the community in the school is an important aspect of a community approach and the suggestions given above demonstrate how this can be done. Equality of opportunity provides a familiar content which validates rather than dismisses local experience. This heading also services work which may not be specifically environmental in essence.

A topic on 'Bridges' might start with a visit to one or two local bridges and end with a consideration of the effects of all the bridges within a few miles of the school failling down at the same time. A topic on 'Sources of Energy' might include a visit to the local filling station and visits from mothers or fathers employed in appropriate businesses. The local environment should continue to be used in this way so that its people, places, institutions, problems and benefits can be used to enrich and bring reality to the delivery of the everyday curriculum. This is a very important way in which the school can lower the barriers between itself and its community and lead children towards some mastery of their environment, empowerment within it, sensitivity to the different groups that make up the local community and also help develop the self-esteem and motivation needed for them to maximise their opportunities.

The approach being suggested accepts environment education as an inherent part of community education and, seen in this way, environmental issues gain in relevance to the children, gain the support of other adults in the community served by the school, gain linkage with major movements such as equality of opportunity and multicultural education and lose some of the do-gooder, middle-class image from which they often suffer. The ultimate result of these expressions of the complex relationships discussed would be the enlistment of large numgers of previously uninvolved people in support of vital environmental causes.

16

Key Issues of Human Settlements in Indian Perspective

Modification of nature by man is a pre-requisite for creating human settlements. Unlike the abode of other animals, human habitat is the product of an intellecutual precess, which through history created civilizations. Nature and the constraints posed by it were interpreted according to the genius of people living in different climatic and geologic regions and locations. Depending on the ability to control the options, settlement morphology varied between places.

Modification of nature by man for building habitation, however, created no serious concern until the industrial revolution, because the process of production and consumption maintained a symbiotic relationship with nature. The process of recyling continued. Irretrievable consumption was of a low order compared to the earth's resources. The process of industrial production, the growing population and the disparity in development standards between various settlements have put the whole range of human beings and their settlements under threat.

Pollution of air, water and earth due to the unimaginative control over production process, and callous attitude towards safety has resulted in serious situation drawing world attention. The location of petrochemical refineries; fertiliser, pesticides, chemical and steel manufacturing units; power generation works in or around human settlements without due cognisance to their effect on life of human beings have created situations of serious hazard. The example of Bhopal tragedy readily comes to mind. But there are number of settlements in India which are highly polluted, such as Ahemdabad, Baroda, Calcutta, Bombay, etc. These large urban centres have attracted a disproportionate share of environmentally hazardous uses, which is turn attracted millions of job-seekers into their death trap.

The United Nations forecasts suggest that the urban population in the developing countries is likely to treble between 1970 and 2001. Out of the total urban population of the developing world, the share of India is likely to be between 20-25, which alone is likely to be larger than the total population of most countries including USA and USSR. The rapidly diminishing landman ratio demands employment generation in sectors other than agriculture. In order to catch up with the demands of employment generation in other sectors, development of urban settlements is imperative. The historic lag in development created by the colonial exploitation needs to be made up in a few decades. Industrialisation in west took place over a span of centuries. Thus the effects of the ills of industrial process was ironed out to some extent. However, the rapid pace of development enjoined by India within a short span of time has resulted in untold misery. Slums have come up around employment centres, some of which produce toxic and poisonous wastes, endangering lives. The housing construction has not been able to keep pace with population influx, resulting in slums, squatter settlements and shanty towns. Although no conclusive study has been undertaken, it may be reasonably assumed that unplanned slums and squatter seettlements outnumber planned housing. The evolving pattern of settlements and the structure of its distribution needs to respond to the national demand.

The growth of population by another 300 million and the need to develop employment in areas other than agriculture would demand a changed outlook in settlement planning. The traditional classification of town and country would no longer appear to be valid. If the present trends are any indication, the larger urban settlements are growing at a faster rate resulting in few pockets of human concentration. Cities like Bombay and Calcutta no longer stand for human excellence in its ability to shape nature but are pictures of abject misery. The misery inflicted by the ever increasing pull generated by such large centres at the expense of all other settlements in its influence region prevents growth of all other centres and creates a regional imbalance. Of 3265 urban centres in India only 12 are metropolises and of these only 2 are over 10 million population. But in another 15 years we may have 20 or more metropolises and 5 or 6 super metropolises. What kind of settlement pattern will it give? Will it provide for a vast country like India? Can we afford to distinguish between settlements only on the criterion of size class? Or do we have to look beyond the rather arbitrary classification into a more dynamic order of settlement pattern.

First of all, human settlements need to be treated as an asset, brought about by human reason and endeavour, and as such needs to be respected. Economic class, occupational pattern are products of various factors, and they need not be used as determinants. Interdependency of settlements should be accepted irrespective of size. This pattern of interdependency over a spatial frame should be the concern. To sustain the population judicious and innovative exploitation of the resources is imperative. The spread of resources vary from area to area, region to region. A set of settlements need to be treated as part of a resource region, and ecosystem. Population and activities need to be distributed in a way that it allows, exploitation of resources within the sustenance capacity of the ecosystem.

The key-word is sustainable development. Development can only be sustained when it keeps pace with the rising expectation of the population. Rise in expectation is synonymous to growth. Efficient public transport, and perhaps efficient personal transport cannot any more be denied by provision of more mundane options. Similarly the technological options available for enriching the quality of life are likely to be in greater preference. Rural population who constitute the majority are likely to demand same level of amenities and facilities as an urbanite. The distinction between rural and urban in terms of the standard of living must get blurred with time. Perhaps a fair distribution in the order of settlements is called for. While ordering the pattern of human settlements one should bear in mind that a compatibility between ecological balance and the technological options is ensured.

The doubling of urban population between the decades of 60's and 80's and the forecasted doubling of the urban population of 1980's by 2001 is likely to put a severe strain on the settlements. The NBO estimated in 1980 that there were a shortage of 4.6 million housing units in urban areas and 16.1 million in rural areas. The same study also estimated that 17.9% of the urban population lived in slums. The available housing stock is also of poor quality. 41.72% of the urban households live in one-room accomodation and 28.08% of them lived in two-room accomodation. The situation is worse in large urban centres.

In order to accommodate the rising population in urban centres a massive programme of housing needs to be undertaken. But if we adopt 'standard housing' as a technique the cost figure would be between 1000 billion, which is well beyond the resource of the country. The availability of materials for construction of 'standard housing' would require rise in steel output by 3 to 7 times, bricks by 4 to 8 times, and would require consumption of 4.2 million acres of additional land for habitation purposes. Under the overwhelming circumstances can we continue to take traditional approach to solve the gigantic problem facing us.

The practice of planning for human settlements has been based on the British model of controlling development. But the essential difference between India and Britain is that the development in Britain is generated by pressure for development, and therefore. plan is needed to control over-or injurious development.

Whereas in India there is need to promote development to eradicate the imbalance in spatial distribution of population and settlements and also to ensure equity in the standard of development and living. In India the pressure for development is high where development is costly and socially injurious. The high level of private sector investment in large cities like Bombay, Calcutta, Delhi, etc. and investment in posh housing manifest the trend and attitude. Private capital is scarce in areas which need development to uplift them from the morass of poverty and backwardness.

Unfortunately the national planning objectives have poor spatial bias, and have not provided adequate guidance for spatial distribution of opportunities and facilities. There is urgent need to arrive at the spatial pattern in the distribution of settlements, order their hierarchy, assess their need and demand, and allocate resource on a programmed and co-ordinated basis.

While the spatial organisation of settlements have a low priority in national planning, the settlements are growing in an unplanned manner, consuming fertile land, destroying forests, creating problems of erosion of land, sitlation of lakes and river beds in an unchecked orgy towards destruction. More vulnerable settlements are reaching a state where the existence of the settlement itself is threatened. Spatial planning concerns itself with the task of identifying on ground the area to be developed for various purposes. The characteristics of the land and its resources achieve their full dimension and the implications of investment decisions become apparent at the time of translation of a decision to reality. Decisions, however well intentioned, arrived at without considering the realities of space, land and its physical attributes, population and its societal structure, the interelationship between various settlements over land, create inefficiency. One of the main reasons of partial success of the Fiscal Planning has been its dissociation with spatial planning. To elaborate, a pesticides factory is necessary for increased food production. But merely the finance or know how of pesticides manufacture is not enough. The location, the microclimate, geology, hydrology, landuse pattern of the area are also serious concerns to be taken note of. When these are ignored, you end up with a tragedy like that of Bhopal. One could go on citing examples of non-spatial planning in this country, the consequences of which has been rather serious.

India is a country of historic cities. No other country can match India in historic rich heritage of settlement pattern. Yet it is an area which has received very little attention. All our ancient cities, some of which date back to more than thousand years, are today subject to destruction by the process of relentless unplanned development. Ancient cities like Hardwar,

Pushkar, Jaisalmer, are wonders of architectural genious of people. Any other country would have taken great care to conserve them. Fortunately, the late Prime Minister Mrs. Indira Gandhi was and our present Prime Minister is alive to the issues of conserving the cultural and historic heritage. However, these settlements can be saved only by a totality of conservation approach, rather than by piecemeal efforts of preservation.

The School of Planning and Architecture, New Delhi, concerns itself with the task of training professionals in the field of spatial planning and physical development. Through courses in various disciplines, the students are trained to understand and appreciate the various facets of environmental issues. Case studies are undertaken of areas serious environmental concern and approapriate solutions are sought. The School has endeavoured to put up a small exhibition by drawing upon samples of work carried on in the school to provide some ideas of the nature of studies undertaken.

The exhibition tries to project the environmental problems faced by settlements such as Nainital, Pushkar and Bangalore, all of which are dependent on natural ecological balance for sustenance. The denudation of the resources by human activities such as defoerestation, building on unstable stopes, filling up of existing waterbodies for making more land available for settlements is resulting in danger of landslides, siltation of lake, drying up of water resources. Similarly the natural and man made environment suitable for settlement by other species of animal and plant life are being invaded by the human beings, thereby destroying the habitat and its environment. Man made built environments of historic cities like Hardwar and Jaisalmer are threatened by unsystematic development, thus slowly obliterating the heritage of thousands of years. These and many issues are projected in the exhibition.

The complex pattern of interaction between man and his settlement, needs of sustenance and the environment requires careful analysis and understanding. Unfortunately the education on the environmental issues is considered to be appropriate for the mature trained mind. From the very ancient times however, the societal behaviour pattern was in harmony with the environment and every man knew his relsationship with nature and respected it. It is necessary that the same kind of tatent understanding is brough about from a tender age. While the techniques of control and prevention require mature technologist, the environmental deterioration is not entirely the products of unplanned development alone. Our cities look dismal because of the attitude of the inhabitants who care very little. Garbage is littered all over the place, buildings are not painted, public transports are not cleaned regularly. Simple sense of hygiene could provide us with a cleaner environment. Whereas average Indian has a sense of personal cleanliness, he is generally careless about environmental hygience which affects the community. There is need to bring about greater awareness of community hygiene and incalculate this sense from the early childhood. The education system has a role to play in this regard.

Similarly the sense of aesthetics is a product of environmental concern. Sense of aesthetics is a cultivated art. Villages in some parts of India are rich in aesthetic quality which is a product of the live concern of the people living there. But the city, is an anonymous agglomeration of people who do not share the same concern for the aesthetic environment. Therefore, the educational process has a definate role to play in developing the aesthetic sense in people living in urban area.

In the end I would like to conclude by identifying a few major areas of concern which are as the following:

1. There is need to recognise settlements within a spatial frame of ecology, resource, manpower and opportunities and order their growth through planned intervention and financial assistance to encourage and achieve a rational distribution of population, facilities and amenities and employment. The national planning must seriously concern itself with spatial allocation of resources.
2. In doing so the sustenance capacity of the environment of every settlement for supporting optimal population and activities, level of maintenance and conservation of resources need to be taken special note of. It is also very important to give due weightage to the rising expectations for a higher standard of living. No planning in a developing country can succeed without matching the expectations with achievement.
3. Environmental education need to be given priority from a tender age i.e. at the level of elementary schools. The present educational system has some bias towards environmental education, but this needs to be enlarged. Professional courses, however, has to be re-oriented to provide a far greater bias towards the understanding of environmental issues, impart training to adequately deel with environmental problem. Institutions which are in a position to impart such training needs encouragement and support.

Bibliography

Baczala, K. (1992) : *Towards a School Policy for Environmental Education: Environmental Audit*. London: National Association for Environmental Education.

Baines, J. (1990): *finding Out... About Conservation and Development.* London: Hobsons Publishing.

Castri, J. (1990) *Paradigms Lost.* New York: Scribners (pp.32-33).

Cleaton, D. (1987) : *Survye of Careers Work.* London:/Newpoint.

Cleaton, D. (1993) : *Careers Education and Guidance in British Schools.* London: NACGT/ICG.

Dearing, R. (1994) : *Review of the National Curriculum,* London: School Curriculum and Assessment Authority.

Goodball, S.C. (1993a) Environmental Education' Edwards, I and Fogelman, K. (eds.) *Developing Citizenship in the Curriculum*. London: David Fulton Publishers (p. 40; (b) pp. 39-42).

Harrison, J. (1993) : *Cross-curricular Theme Pack 3: Health Education*. Cambridge: Pearson Publishing.

Harrison, J. and Edwards, J. (1994) : *Developing Health Education in the Curriculum.* London David Fulton Puonshers.

HMI (1988) : *Careers Education from 5 to 16*. London, HMSO.

Kennedy, P. (1993) : *Preparing for the Twenty First Century.* London: Harper Colins, Law, B. (1992) *Understanding Careers Work.* London: NACGT.

King, A. and Schneider, B. (1991a) *The First Global revolution: A Report by the Council of The Club of Rome—the World twenty years after 'The Limits of Growth'.* London: Simon and Schuster (pp. 33-53; (b) p. 34).

Lean, J. (1990) : *Atlas of the Environment*. London: Arrow Books.

Learning Through Landscapes Newsletter (Summar. 1992) *Gounds for Examination. The Challenge of the Secondary School Site*. Winchester: Learning Through Landscapes Trust.

NCC (1990a): *Curriculum Guidance Document 5: Health Eduction.* York: National Curriculum Council (p. 4; (b) p. 20).

NCC (1990) : *Careers Education and Guidance, Curriculum Guidance 6.* York: National Curriculum Council.

NCC (199a) *Curriculam Guidance 7. 'Environmental Education* York National Curriculum Council (p. 1; (b) p. 3; (c) p. 4; (d) p. 24).

Banarjee, A. N. 1982. Environmental Management in Coal Resource Development, Proc. National Seminar on Minerals and Ecology, Indian School of Mines, Dhanbad.

Mahendru, R. G. 1985, Coal—the The Technology Drive. MGMI Presidential address, Calcutta.

Banerjee, S. P. and G. G. Marwaha, 1984. Environmental considerations in exploitation of mineral resources with special reference to the conditions in LDCs. Paper to XII World Mining Congress, New Delhi.

Barrow, C.J. (1991) : *Land Degradation.* Cambridge: Cambridge University Press.

Buckley, R. (ed.) (1992) : *Amazonia. An Ecological Crisis. Understanding Global Issues.* Cheltenham: European School Books Publishing Limited.

Hargreaves, D.H. (1991) : 'Coherence and Manageability: Reflections on the National Curriculum and cross curricular provision' *The Curriculum Journal,* Vol. 2, No. 1.

NCC (1991) : *Curriculum Guidance 7 : Environmental Education.* York: National Curriculum Council.

Palmer, J. (1989) : The National Curriculum- Framework for Opportunity. The Location of an Environmental Education as a Cross Curricular Issue. NAEE Occasional Paper 13.

Peace, D., Markandya, A. and Barbier, E. (1989) *Blueprint for a Green Economy.* London: Earthscan Publications.

United Nations Conference on Environment and Development (UNCED) (1992) : *Good Earth-Keeping: Education, Training and Awareness for a Sustainable Future.* New York: United Nations Environment Programme UNEP-UK..

World Commission on Environment and Development (1987), *Our Common Future. Report of the World Commission on Environment and Development (The Brundtland Report).* Oxford: Oxford University Press.

WWF UK (1980) *World Conservation Strategy: Living Resources Conservation for Sustainable Development.* London: IUCN, UNEP. WWF, UK.

WWF UK (1991). *Carrying for the Earth: A strategy for Sustanable Living.* London: IUCN, UNEP. WWF. UK.

Young. I. and Williams. T. (1989) : *The Healthy School.* Edinburgh: Scottish Health Education Group/World Health Organisation (p. 32)

Index

A

Academic Disciplines 35
Access to Resources 136
Ahinsa Parmodharma 42
Almora Hills 24
American Federal Government's Clear Air Act 172
Approach Paper 11
Appropriate Technology 153
Areas of Exprience of Modern Froeign Lanugages Programmes of study 118
Art 121
Aryan Civilization 42

B

Background to Environmental Concern 25
Baczala, K. 207
Balancing People's different Needs 108
Barrow, C.J. 208
Bat Conservation Trust 88
Belgrade Charter 10
Bengal Smoke Nuisances Commission 38
Biogas 18
Biomass Research Centres 22
Gasifier 23
British Trust of Conservation Volunteers 94

C

Careers Education 60
Central and State Boards for Prevention and Control of Water pollution 15
Ganga Authority 21
Children Act 198
City of Palaces 38
Club of Rome 7
Communication and the media 189
Conventional Energy Sources and Environmental Degradation 16
Council for the protection of Rural England 88

Council of Europe
  Community 111
Curriculum
  Guidance 112, 184

D

Deforestation 146
Department of Non-Conventional Energy Sources (ONES) 17, 22
Desertification 145
Drama 179
Duke of Edinburgh 95

E

Education Physical 125
  about the environment 127, 160
  in the environment 128
  religious 133, 135
  Community 196
  through envrionment 197
EIU Enivironmental Educational 53
Emperor Asoka 42
Energy 148
Energy From Urban
  Wastes 20
  Plantation 21
English Nature 90
Environment and Human ·Development 13
Environmental Curriculum 1
  Ideologies 33
  Aspects of Health Education 59
  Conditions 46
  through demonstration project 47
  Education in the University in Karnataka 72
  Engineering Education for Mining Engineers in Developing countries 74
  Studies 117
European Community 31
Europeans in
  Calcutta 38
Evaluating the Quality of Environments and Suggesting Improvement 106
Evelyn, John 27

F

Five Year Plan 50
Food and
  Agriculture 144
Forests as an Important Facts
  on Environment 43
  Crisis 43

G

Gandhi, Shri Rajiv 21
Gandhi, Indira 44, 205
Garhwal Himalyas 74
George Perkins Marsh 27
Georaphical Skills 115
Green Investments 178

H

Harrrison, J. 207
Hazards to General Public and Environmental Damage 74
Hazardous Wastes 155
Health Education 56
Hedgeroue Planning Day 93
Himalayas in India 24
Hindu Philosophy 42
History 109
Human Environments in Stocholm 30

I

Ian Curts 193
Impact of Environmental Education 48
Importance of Including Design of Environments with in National Curriculum Technology 106
Incidence and Charater of Smoke 39
Indian Standards Institution (ISI) 15-16
Industries of Greater Bombay 9
Information Technology in Environmental Education 83
Integrated Environmental Approach 69
Inter-Governmental Conference on Environ-mental Education Tbilisi 10
International Union of Conservation of Nature 10
Interelationships 141
Investigation
and Communications 122

J

James, Lovelock 31
Janeiro, Rio de 31

K

Key Stage 80
Kilson, Neil 179
Knowledge and Institutings 35

L

Law 186
Leys School in Leicester 99
Lodhi Hotelin Delhi 19
Lord Curzon 39

M

Mahandra, R.G. 208
Marine Environment 150
Marx, Karl 27
Mathematics 99
Mc. Cormick, John 35
Modern Foreign Lanugages 117
Munhsi, K.M. 43
Music 129

N

National Curriculum 1, 52
National Curriculum Council (NCC) 194
National Forest Act 9
National Environmetnal Engineering Research Insitute (NEERT) Nagpur 9
National Council for Education Research and Training (NCERT) 11-12, 13, 24
National Sciecne Centre at New Delhi 12
National Air (Preventation and Control of Pollution) Act 15
National Fuelwood Study Committee 15
National Solar Photovaltaic Energy Demonstration Programme 20
New Environment Age 37
Patterns of Development and Lifestyles 150
Nicolas Houeksmoor Pocket Park Assciation 95
Night Shelter Project 81
Northampthanshire Country Council 93

O

Ok-Tedi 74
Ok-Ma 74
Opportunities to Create Positive Change 107
Ordnance Survey 114
Our Hoary Conservation Tradition 42

P

People and Environment 32
People-Resources-Environment-Development 140
People's Participation 156
Parmanent Needs the Forests Fulfill 44
Pest Maragement 148
Playground Project 80
Plenary Session of the Conference 10
Pocket Parks Officer 90, 93
Politics 170
Population 141
Pratical Management 37
Present Sceniaro 14
Principles of E.G. 61

Q

Queen 95
Queen Anniversary Trust Awards 95

R

Rational Use of Natural Resources 143
Reading to Learn 12
Records of Achievement 193
Relevance of Gandhian Approach 71

Report of the Education Commission 11
River Water Pollution in India 14
Role of Environmental Education 24
Planning 67
Rowe, Don 186
Rural Development 151

S

Second City of the Empire 38
Secondary School Activity 80
Seventh Five Year Plan 22
Silent Valley Project 24
Silver Jubilee Celebrations 12
Smoke Inspector for Leeds 38
Solar Energy 18
  Photo-Valtaic Systems 19
Sources of Energy 23
Soviet Union 139
Speaker's Commission on Citizenship 79
Studies in Aspects of Physical Geography 116
Supreme Court of India 74
Sussex Wildlife Trust 90

T

Theme one-Communicating and Handling Information 84
Thompson 79
Torrey Canyon 30
Tribology 177

U

Union of Soviet Socialist Republics (USSR) 31, 202
United Kingdom (UK)
  Government 31, 164
  Political Colours 34
  Green Party 35
  Education Policy 36
  Department of the
    Environment 37
Environment issues 163
United Nation 138, 160
United Nations the Confer-ence on the Human Envri-ronment in Stockhalm 10, 44
  united Nation 138, 160
  World Conference 140
  Conference on the Human Envriornment 160
  Convention on the Right of the Child 163
  Conference on the Environemnt and Devel-opment in Rio De Jareio 185
United National Conference on Environment and Development 7, 31
United States (U.S.) 116, 138, 159
United States of America (U.S.A.) 2, 16, 202
  Environmental Protection Agency 37
University of Karnataka 73
Urban Sociolcgy 185

V

Vedas and Upnishads 42

W

Water Resources 146
Wildlife Trusts 88
Wind Energy 20
  Conversion System
    (WECS) 20
World Envrionment Day 24
World Commission on Environment and Development 53
World Bank 144

Y

Yamuna River 14
Young, Mr. 57, 208
Yound Ornithologists Club 88
Young Bat Worker 88
Young People's Trust for the Environment and Nature Conservation 88

Z

Zachriah 98
Zimmer 122

●●●